CONTEMPORARY SOCIAL RESEARCH SERIES
General Editor: MARTIN BULMER

6

The Survey Method

CONTEMPORARY SOCIAL RESEARCH SERIES

The Survey Method

The Contribution of Surveys
to Sociological Explanation

CATHERINE MARSH

London
GEORGE ALLEN & UNWIN
Boston   Sydney

George Allen & Unwin (Publishers) Ltd,
40 Museum Street, London WC1A 1LU, UK

George Allen & Unwin (Publishers) Ltd,
Park Lane, Hemel Hempstead, Herts HP2 4TE, UK

Allen & Unwin, Inc.,
9 Winchester Terrace, Winchester, Mass. 01890, USA

George Allen & Unwin Australia Pty Ltd,
8 Napier Street, North Sydney, NSW 2060, Australia

First published in 1982
Second impression 1983

British Library Cataloguing in Publication Data

Marsh, Catherine
    The survey method. – (Contemporary social research series; no. 6)
1. Social surveys   2. Surveys
I. Title   II. Series
001.4′33   HN29
ISBN 0-04-310014-7
ISBN 0-04-310015-5 Pbk

Library of Congress Cataloging in Publication Data

Marsh, Catherine.
    The survey method.
(Contemporary social research series; 6)
Bibliography: p.
Includes index
1. Social surveys. 2. Sociology – Methodology.
3. Social sciences – Methodology. I. Title. II. Series.
HN29.M36   300′.723   82-6705
ISBN 0-04-310014-7   AACR2
ISBN 0-04-310015-5 (pbk.)

Set in 10 on 11 point Times by Fotographics (Bedford) Ltd
and printed in Great Britain by Biddles Ltd, Guildford, Surrey

Contents

Editor's Preface

The structure of the social sciences combines two separate elements, theory and empirical evidence. Both are necessary for successful social understanding; one without the other is barren. The Contemporary Social Research series is concerned with the means by which this structure is maintained and kept standing solid and upright, a job performed by the methodology of social research.

The series is intended to provide concise introductions to significant methodological topics. Broadly conceived, research methodology deals with the general grounds for the validity of social science propositions. How do we know what we do know about the social world? More narrowly, it deals with the questions, how do we actually acquire new knowledge about the world in which we live? What are the strategies and techniques by means of which social science data are collected and analysed? The series will seek to answer such questions through the examination of specific areas of methodology.

Why is such a series necessary? There exist many solid, indeed massive, methodology textbooks, which most undergraduates in sociology, psychology and other social sciences acquire familiarity with in the course of their studies. The purpose of this series is different. Its aim is to focus upon specific topics, procedures, methods of analysis and methodological problems to provide a readable introduction to its subject. Each book contains annotated suggestions for further reading. The intended audience includes the advanced undergraduate, the graduate student, the working social researcher seeking to familiarise himself with new areas, and the non-specialist who wishes to enlarge his knowledge of social research. Research methodology need not be remote and inaccessible. Some prior knowledge of statistics will be useful, but only certain titles in the series will make strong statistical demands upon the reader. The series is concerned above all to demonstrate the general importance and centrality of research methodology to social science.

The Survey Method is a particularly welcome contribution to methodological debate at the present time. The survey is probably the most widely used method of social research, but in recent years it has been the object of much damaging criticism, particularly by sociologists. Some critics have maintained, and not a few cohorts of sociology students have been taught, that surveys are so vitiated by potential error that their value in social science research is limited. Catherine Marsh examines such claims, to show that much of this criticism is ignorant and ill-founded. Maintaining an important distinction between the scientific survey and public opinion polling, she shows that the former has great potential for addressing major theoretical questions in social science. *The Survey Method* will help to re-establish the credentials of survey research among social scientists.

MARTIN BULMER
The London School of
Economics and Political Science

Author's Preface

Many people have given me support and encouragement while I have been writing this book. There are two overwhelming debts that I must recognise at the outset: first to Martin Bulmer for getting this book started and secondly to Dave Marsh for getting it finished. I am aware how time-consuming it is to get consistency between tables in even the cleanest data; George Brown went to a great deal of trouble to help me get the figures in Chapter 5 right. Both Gill Sutherland and Jane Caplan tried to dissuade me from 'first chapter history', I know, but their thoughts on the second chapter were extremely valuable. Indeed, contact with them and another Newnham colleague, Pat Altham, who tries to keep me on the straight and narrow in statistics, seems to provide the perfect vindication of the college system. Others who have been especially helpful are: John Barnes, Nick Bateson, Bob Blackburn, Colin Brown, Tim Bryson, Jim Davis, Jeff Evans, Tirril Harris, Martin Harrop, Michael MacKuen, James Marsh, Louis Moss, Jennifer Platt, Alan Stuart and Charles Turner. Prefaces are a good place to record long-term debts that might otherwise be inadequately recognised. I should like to take this opportunity to record my thanks to John Utting, who taught me so much while I was at the Survey Unit. Most importantly, I must acknowledge the help and encouragement I have received from Geoffrey Hawthorn, from my undergraduate days when he was my supervisor, through to the present day when we work in the same department. He is a great teacher, a tireless colleague and a good friend.

CATHIE MARSH
Social and Political Sciences Committee
University of Cambridge

1

Introduction

Perhaps the best way to begin a book which aims to convince you, the reader, that survey research has an important and valuable contribution to make to sociology, is with a bit of autobiography. My aim in telling you something of my own background does not stem from the Weberian injunction to forewarn you of my likely prejudices and values – I make no attempt to hide these in what follows – but to explain briefly how it came to pass that someone should end up with political and epistemological convictions seemingly so at odds with one another, by today's standards.

I did my undergraduate degree at Cambridge University, doing the Social and Political Sciences Tripos as a Part II subject. There was not then, nor is there now, a full three-year course in the social sciences (see Bulmer 1981). This is partly due to the fact that Cambridge University has a history of resisting all innovations until they become unavoidable. It is partly due to the predominance of social anthropology, the social science of empire, in this ancient seat of learning. And it is partly to do with the association of the outburst of social scientific activity in the 1960s with political subversion.

If it couldn't resist the advances of sociology, the university would have to pass it off as a brand of philosophy. The compulsory 'research methods' paper that everyone took in their finals could be answered using only material from the philosophy of the social sciences. I was lucky enough to have received encouragement to battle on with statistics, but by the time I graduated, I had absorbed a sufficient amount of the prevailing *Zeitgeist* to be convinced that survey research was hopelessly empiricist, the product of vulgar American sociology, atheoretical and generally a waste of time.

I floundered for one year trying to organise a Ph.D., but it was very hard, given that I had only two year's social sciences behind me, and given my strange views on methods. A fellow graduate student suggested attending a summer school, organised by the Social Science Research Council's Survey Unit, on survey research methods, and I decided, grudgingly, but in truth desperately, to go. It was an eye-opener, and the principal ocular surgeon was Professor Jim Davis, then director of the National Opinion Research Centre at Chicago. He gave a course of lectures on survey analysis, on the Lazarsfeldian ideas of elaborating variables in a survey, which seemed to relate in a much more direct way than anything I had heard before then to *sociology*. I retained my rather arch views on other aspects of survey research, but I was hooked on this method of handling data analysis.

Shortly after this course, a job was advertised for a research assistant in the Survey Unit, which offered the prospect of a thorough training. The drive of intellectual curiosity which might have propelled me through my Ph.D. proved no match for the desire to work as part of a team, to be trained in a particular set of skills and, in honesty, to receive a wage! I worked, mainly in the apprentice mode, in that Unit for two years, painfully unlearning my easily held prejudices on a variety of matters empirical. I became more aware of the depth of the ideological battle over methods in the social sciences. One had, on the one hand, to listen to the point of view of the professional survey practitioners, who thought that survey research was a discipline in its own right, standing outside any of the social sciences, in a direct relationship to the policy-maker. One was subject, on the other hand, to harangues by sociologists on the utter worthlessness of surveys for any purpose. Neither 'side' seemed to acknowledge a place for the sociologist survey researcher, nor, indeed, did there seem to be many role models around among British sociologists to aspire to.

The Survey Unit had been set up in 1970 and modelled fairly explicitly on analogies with the National Opinion Research Center at Chicago (Sheatsley 1978) or the Survey Research Center at Michigan; its aim was to become a repository for survey skills which could be made available through the unit's advisory service, through the involvement of members of the unit with other projects and through providing teaching. It was in an uneasy position, caught in the crossfire between the commercial market research world which feared it might interfere in its direct relationship with clients, academic and governmental, and the sociological community who resented the funds required to run such an institution. Such repositories do not spring into existence overnight, and when the director, Mark Abrams, retired in 1976, the SSRC decided that they did not want to commit such a large sum to the development of one particular method, and closed the Unit. Instead they set aside a sum of £200,000 to fund applications to do methodological research, which has never been spent.

I returned to the academic fold, convinced that there were no inherent contradictions between good sociology and good survey research, and exasperated by the pseudo-battle that was raging. In arguing with various people since then, and in engaging in some polemics on paper, I have come to the conclusion that there is a need for a lengthier defence of good survey research to be made to sociologists. That is the aim of this book. The majority of complaints that come from sociologists which parade as fundamental criticisms of survey research are, I believe, usually reactions to poorly designed, inadequately conceptualised and theorised, unpiloted or just ill-managed surveys, and the good survey practitioners are more aware of the problems and the solutions to those problems than most sociologists. It is true that there are a lot of such surveys around, of little or no sociological or even social value; the point I am making is that they do not have to be like that.

The most common characterisation of the survey's fundamental epistemological flaw is that it is inherently positivist. Many people recently have questioned the utility of this term as applied to current sociological practice (Cohen 1980; Tropp 1980; Platt 1981). It seems to have become little more than a term of abuse. Its application to survey research has been rather ill thought out. Not only do the critics believe that survey research is positivist, but they also imply that the current orthodoxy in funding bodies is also positivist in the same way, and that it gives special pride of place to survey research as a method, out of a misguided or even malevolent desire to turn sociology into some kind of technocratic science. It is questionable whether this has ever been the orthodoxy in British sociology, but it is certainly not the orthodoxy today. In fact, current orthodoxy among sociologists as a whole is a rather asinine mirror-image of this position; the survey is rejected out of hand as being incapable of producing any information worth having. Some go further, and argue that in fact science is ideology, measurement a fiction and rigour a joke. The stereotype of the survey researcher is of a senescent, plodding servant of the establishment who hasn't yet quite caught up with the new and devastating revolutions that have taken place in the philosophy of science.

This disdain for surveys seems to be confined to sociologists. In other disciplines, the use of survey research in the 1960s and 1970s underwent a dramatic period of growth. It is not as though survey research had not penetrated universities – geographers and planners have taken it up eagerly. The only systematic evidence available for the organisation of social research in Britain comes from a survey of funded social science research carried out by the SSRC Survey Unit in 1972 (Perry 1975). Sixty per cent of projects reported (that is, of the last five completed projects from each contacted institution) were surveys; the exact proportion should be treated with caution since the definition of 'funded research' predisposed the subject matter towards surveys. Surveys were more popular in non-university organisations, even excluding market research where they constituted virtually 100 per cent, than in university teaching departments and in university-based research units; the differences were not striking, however – 60 per cent as opposed to 55 per cent. Unfortunately these results are not broken down by subject so we cannot tell if this holds as true for sociology as any of the other social sciences.

It has been estimated that the value of survey research commissioned in Britain in 1979 was £85 million (Simmons and Gordon 1980). The Market Research Society has grown into an organisation twice the size of the British Sociological Association and two-thirds the size of the Royal Statistical Society, as you see in Table 1.1; do not make hasty comparisons between rates of growth of different organisations in Table 1.1, as they were established at different dates.

Table 1.1   Membership of Organisations Connected with Social Research

	MRS	RSS	BSA
1949	66	2,064	n.y.f.*
1963	1,300	3,457	625
1970	2,300	4,183	1,184
1980	3,450	4,829	1,525

*n.y.f.= not yet formed.

In 1979 a new organisation was formed, the Social Research Association, to 'provide a forum for discussion and communication about research development and methodology, to promote a cohesive professional identity among social researchers, and to advance the development and use of social research as an aid for social and community planning'. Within one year this organisation had 634 members, the majority of whom are not university based. It had shown itself prepared to take up professional and representational functions on behalf of researchers that the BSA has never been prepared to do.[1]

In short, there is a vast new industry of survey research. It goes on in universities, but a large part of it goes on outside, in market research companies and social research organisations like Social and Community Planning Research, Policy Studies Institute (the result of the merger between Political and Economic Planning and the Centre for Studies in Social Policy), in the Government Social Survey Department of the Office of Population Censuses and Surveys which does contract work for government departments, and in research organisations based within different government departments, such as the Home Office Research Unit and (until recently) the Centre for Environmental Studies. It is almost totally metropolitan in character, servicing policy-makers in one way or another.

But this growth in survey activity seems to have passed sociology by. Despite the existence of increased funding for social research of a more basic, theoretical nature, and despite access to the improved technology of survey research which the growth of this industry has made available, the type of study that one might have expected to ensue from the changed situation failed to materialise (see Platt 1976).

The survey activity that does go on in sociology departments is of low average quality. When survey results are reported in British sociology journals, the authors of the articles are usually North Americans (Harrop 1980). Some have felt that the only way to pull standards up is by putting more effort into training; indeed, this was what the Clapham Committee of 1946 recommended that money should be spent on. There are constant complaints from supervisors and employers of social researchers that an undergraduate sociology methods training leaves them completely green about how to conduct research. The SSRC conducted two conferences on this problem in postgraduate training in 1979 alone. Yet, where training is laid on outside undergraduate or postgraduate departments, sociologists rarely take advantage of it, as we discovered in the SSRC Survey Unit summer schools, as the European Consortium for Political Research summer schools at Essex continue to find, and as centres like the Strathclyde Area Survey find when sociologists do not utilise the teaching resources they make available.

In later chapters of this book I shall try to meet the critics among the sociologists who argue that the reason for this relative neglect stems from a quite correct appreciation on the part of sociologists of the value of surveys. But the fact that the critics have been so popular and that the doubts they raise have gained such wide currency should give pause for thought. There are several puzzles about this attitude. Britain has a tradition of some fine survey research – it is no American import. Moreover, in the postwar years there have been some good examples of major contributions to sociology based on survey findings. And when one casts one's attention elsewhere in the globe, one discovers that sociologists in other countries have not eschewed the survey. In many ways this problem seems particularly British, and requires some knowledge of the development of social research in Britain before it can be fully understood.

The strategy for this book, then, is to look at the history of survey research in Britain, to see if we can glean from it clues which might explain the current separation between sociology and survey research. After a variety of institutional, political and intellectual reasons for some of the developments have been noted, the criticisms of survey research will be rehearsed and addressed. In the following two chapters it will be argued that surveys *can* provide causal explanations and that they *can* provide meaningful explanations.

Finally, in the last chapter I shall argue that there is a profound difference between a sociological survey and an opinion poll; I suspect that much of the opprobium that attaches to surveys comes from their association with polling.

Definition of a Survey

But before proceeding further, I must give some definition of what I mean by this word 'survey'. The word has a long tradition in the English language, and developed from being the fact of viewing or inspecting something in detail (as in a land survey) to the act of doing so rigorously and comprehensively, and finally to the written results. The idea of the social survey started with this connotation of the collection of social facts, but has undergone an evolution such that nowadays the survey method is not just a way of collecting data but also of analysing the results.

For the purposes of this book, a survey refers to an investigation where:

(a) systematic measurements are made over a series of cases yielding a rectangle of data;
(b) the variables in the matrix are analysed to see if they show any patterns;
(c) the subject matter is social.

In other words, the surveys we shall be looking at have a particular method of data collection, a particular method of data analysis and a particular substance.

The only restriction made on the survey as a method of collecting data is to insist that it be systematic, looking at more than one *case,* be it individuals, hospitals, countries, or whatever, and measuring the same variables on each case, so that you end up with each case having one and only one code for each variable. The data could come from observation, from fixed-choice responses to a postal questionnaire, from content analysis of newspapers, or from postcoding tape-recorded depth interviews. The important thing is that there is more than one case and that variation between cases is considered systematically. 'Survey analysis' involves making casual inferences from some kind of passive observation programme. The word 'survey' *is* sometimes used to refer to such investigations as a split-ballot question-wording trial, where there has been an experimental manipulation, but I think it is clearer if we use the word 'experiment' to describe such investigations.

Surveys and experiments are the only two methods known to me to test a hypothesis about how the world works. The experimenter intervenes in the social world, does something to a set of subjects (and usually also refrains from doing that thing to a set of controls) and looks to see what effect *manipulating* variance in the independent variable has on the dependent variable. If the subjects have been assigned in some fashion to control and experimental groups, the experimenter can be sure that it is what she did to the independent variable that has produced any differences between the groups.

The survey researcher has only made a series of observations; to be sure, as we shall come on to argue, these cannot be seen as passive reflections of unproblematic reality, but they must be logically distinguished from the manipulation that the experimenter engages in. The only element of randomness in the survey design comes in random selection of cases; *random sampling does not achieve the same result as random allocation into control and experimental groups*. The survey researcher may have a theory which leads her to suspect that X is having a causal effect on Y. If she wants to test this, she has to measure X and Y on a variety of different subjects, and infer from the fact that X and Y covary that the original hypothesis was true. But unlike the experimenter, she cannot rule out the possibility *in principle* of there being a third variable prior to X and Y and causing the variance in both; the experimenter knows that the relationship is not spurious because she knows exactly what produced the variance in X – *she* did.

In other words, in survey research the process of testing causal hypotheses, central to any theory-building endeavour, is a very indirect process of drawing inferences from already existing variance in populations by a rigorous process of comparison. In practice, one of the major strategies of the survey researcher is to control for other variables that she thinks might realistically be held also to produce an effect, but she never gets round the purist's objection that she has not definitively established a causal relationship. Furthermore, although having panel data across time certainly helps with the practical resolution of the problem of how to decide which of one's variables are prior to which others, it does not solve the logical difficulty that, in principle, any relationship which one finds may be explained by the operation of another unmeasured factor.

Finally, the subject matter of the surveys that sociologists are interested in is always social. Many different disciplines collect systematic observational data and make inferences from it. Biologists looking at correlations between plant growth and different types of environment, psychologists coding films of mother–child inter-actions, or astronomers drawing inferences about the origins of the universe from measurements of light intensity taken now, are all performing activities whose logic is similar to that of the social survey analyst, but they would not describe their studies as 'surveys'. I once analysed the product of one week's cuttings from all references in the national and local newspapers and magazines to the word survey. This produced a list of very different activities descibed as 'surveys' – a building society investigating house values, a local authority checking up that hospitals were instituting adequate safety precutions, commercial surveys of different markets, and so on.

We are only talking about *social* surveys. But that still means that the subject matter is very broadly defined; human social activity occurs and is supported in a wide variety of ways and settings. We shall see in the next chapter, however, how some particular subject matters for social surveys have been so popular that various writers have defined a survey more narrowly.

It may seem a bit pedantic to have spent so much time worrying about definitions – after all, it might be argued, we all have a rough idea of what a survey is. But when we are dealing with critics, it will be useful to have some idea which of the criticisms surveys could not avoid, and which they share with other methods in the social sciences. It would be ironic if people were deciding against survey methods because of a dislike of structured questionnaires, or because they thought that the only thing that surveys could be used for was town planning inquiries or opinion polls.

Note: Chapter 1

1   It also shows signs of being prepared to take up the question of the employment problems of research workers which the Association of University Teachers has been slow to do. It will grow rapidly.

2

History of the Use of Surveys in Sociological Research

Methodologists are traditionally uninterested in the history of their subject (for example, Jones and Kronus 1976). This lack of interest is usually presumed to result from a belief in the cumulative and progressive changes in knowledge. The assumption is 'we know how to do surveys today so much better than they did 50 years ago that it cannot possibly be of more than antiquarian interest to know how people used to do them'. This view would be contested by those who believe that there is no way that the social sciences can claim to build their knowledge up to converge on methodological excellence or substantive truth. But even those who, like myself, believe that sociology can, and in some spheres does, acquire knowledge that can be cumulated, could still find reason to fault such a position. Unless we are convinced that the path taken to present understanding is the best possible, and that the practices of today are the best possible, we shall want to know something of the development of those practices. Apart from being intrinsically interesting, we have a specific question to try to answer, namely, how it came to pass that sociologists failed to take advantage of the enormous growth in social survey research.

The survey was defined in the introduction as an inquiry which involves the collection of systematic data across a sample of cases, and the statistical analysis of the results. But is the history of surveys to be taken to be the history of the word, documenting the activities of those who did what they themselves described as a 'survey'? If it is, very little methodological continuity will be found in the activities to be described, for the word has been used to cover most types of empirical research at some point in time. It would be found to be mainly a history of data collection, for the self-styled 'survey tradition' has never been very analytic, as we shall see. In order to document the development of the causal logic now applied to survey data, it will be necessary to trace a rather different path.

A rather arbitrary ordering would occur if I were to try to trace the development of the survey tradition and multivariate analysis simultaneously, so I have chosen to deal with them separately. This is unsatisfactory, because it gives the impression that the development of data collection and data analysis are unrelated, which is often not the case. There can be spin-offs in both directions, and we shall see examples of this. But it is a fact that for a long time the two developed along rather separate lines, and so must be given separate treatment.

(1) The 'Survey Tradition' of Fact-Finding

Origins

A society with a bureaucracy of any complexity needs occasional data-gathering exercises in order to administer efficiently, to assess manpower available for war and to levy taxes. The ancient Egyptians, the Romans, the Chinese from the Ming dynasty onwards and our own Normans all conducted inquiries of this kind. But a new type of data-gathering became necessary with the birth of capitalism. As Zeisel points out in his afterthought to *Marienthal,* 'Almost the very day on which the European feudal order suffered its first political defeat became the birthday of the first sociographic study' (Jahoda *et al.* 1972: 100).

The tradition of systematic social investigation in Britain originated in the desire to know something of population trends. In the seventeenth and eighteenth centuries the prevailing mercantilist ideas taught that population growth was a major cause of increased wealth. The incidence of disease and war in various parts of Europe had alarmed some into fearing that a decline in population had occurred, and provided the stimulus to the first modern attempts at census and civil record-keeping.

The desire to assess the effects of the plague in London and to assuage people's fears about depopulation led to schemes to aggregate the parish 'bills of mortality' so that the numbers and causes of deaths could be assessed. This provided the raw material not just for a new industry of insurance, but also for the earliest attempt at systematic social science in Britain. The name given to it was 'political arithmetic', and it is associated with the names of Graunt and Petty.[1] They used these bills of mortality prepared by the parish clerks to draw *Natural and Political Observations with reference to the Government, Religion, Trade, Growth, Ayre, Diseases and the several Changes of the said City of London* (Graunt, 1939; 1662) in a work of statistical complexity quite before its time. The first crude age-specific life expectancy table was presented in this work. Noting regularities in a series of statistical information was often to act as a spur for the development of social theories to account for these patterns, and is an early example of the fact that methodological changes can themselves lead to theoretical advances.

Petty, who coined the term 'political arithmetic', worked energetically for the Commonwealth, and undertook the Down Survey, the 'first sociographic study' that Zeisel referred to earlier, a detailed description of life and property in the newly conquered Ireland. He was a reformer who passionately believed that population studies would improve rational government, an early example of a would-be social physician.[2] After him, or perhaps after the rapid social change under the Commonwealth, it is a century and a half before any comparable work emerges.

Fears that the home population had declined since the Glorious Revolution persisted throughout the eighteenth century, and on two occasions crystallised into open polemic between the 'optimists' and 'pessimists'. The factual dispute was based on very thin evidence (which partly explains why it persisted so long); the method used to calculate the population was to estimate the number of houses from the numbers paying window tax and to multiply the estimate by the presumed average family size. The results, not unnaturally, varied widely, and there were occasional calls for a census to settle the matter, but Parliament was not convinced it was necessary (Glass 1973).

But at the beginning of the nineteenth century the rate of capitalist development increased sharply, and the debate about population was turned on its head by the publication in 1798 of Malthus's *Essay on Population*. The population of Britain was growing at a phenomenally rapid rate, and the overcrowding in slum dwellings was bringing with it hitherto unimaginable problems of disease. The high-handed response of the church and aristocracy was utterly inadequate. There was a growing fear, especially among the early industrialists, that the poor, discontented with the promise of heavenly rewards, might become so morally depraved that they would ignore the teachings of the Bible and demand their just deserts in this life. Squalid prisons were teeming with a new and frightening 'criminal class' of offenders against a whole barrage of new property laws, and a fair sprinkling of innocent people as well; John Howard had been campaigning in the eighteenth century, collecting facts and figures of the numbers involved, to secure reform in these vile institutions.

While pre-industrial Britain of the seventeenth and eighteenth centuries had developed a long way beyond the golden age of Norman feudalism, it was still essentially a village society, where social conditions and relations were available for all to see. As capitalist relations spread socially and geographically, they broke up the face-to-face relations that existed between people, often effectively hiding one class from another; it became increasingly necessary to make a determined effort if one wanted to discover what was happening to the social structure. The new method of extracting a surplus, the factory system, hid the increased exploitation it brought about behind closed doors. There was a careful zoning of people with similar life-styles in the new towns and cities, so that there was increased contact within groups, but the middle class never had to come into contact with the wretched migrant labourers uprooted from the countryside (Foster 1974). The misery and indignity of the life of the poor in the first decades of the nineteenth century, both in countryside and town, was often concealed, but many feared, with good reason, that they were not forming an allegiance to the new ruling order.

These new conditions provided the spur to social investigations in many areas. The fact that a new era had begun in the nineteenth century is symbolised by the fact that the pro-census lobby finally won. The publication of Sir John Sinclair's *Statistical Account of Scotland,* an inquiry into the climate, industry, agriculture and church in Scotland, and an enumeration of the population and its age, health and fertility, was widely applauded. Parliament finally agreed to a census, and the first one was conducted in 1801.

Investigative Journalism

Social surveys were not, however, the immediate reaction to the new conditions. The first response of the ruling class was to avert its eyes from this newly created hell, and to reassure the poor that at least in the long run they would suffer none of the agonies of the rich as they tried to wriggle their way through the needle-eye entry to the kingdom of God. But there were some who believed, for reformist or agitational reasons, that this situation should be known to a wider audience, and who undertook a kind of investigative journalism. They would travel to the parts of the country or city that they wanted to know about, immerse themselves in it and write of what they discovered for the consumption of those better insulated from the realities they described. This type of research was often referred to at the time as a 'survey', although in fact systematic inquiries in the modern sense were often a reaction to these accounts. It will therefore be worth looking briefly at this tradition of research before returning to our account of what we now call surveys.

The method was regularly used by political radicals to expose the miseries of early industrialism. The results of Cobbett's *Rural Rides* were all grist to the mill of those agitating against the miserable conditions of early nineteenth-century Britain (Cobbett 1975; 1830). One of the first literary efforts of Engels was to write a description of the English working people as he came into contact with them as a young man of 24, although it is something of an insult to call this a journalistic work, for it strives throughout for the analytic framework that Marx was to supply, to *explain* how it should happen that the explosion of industrial wealth should bring in its train such utter misery (Engels 1969; 1892).

Henry Mayhew was perhaps the best exemplar of this type of

qualitative research. He wrote a series of articles for the *Morning Chronicle* in which he described the life situation of a wide variety of trades operating in London; these were later collected together in *London Labour and the London Poor* (1861). Recently it has become fashionable to argue that Mayhew was much more than a journalist – that he was a forerunner of Booth and as a social scientist in his methods (Yeo 1973). This is overdoing it; he certainly was concerned to be systematic, but his main method was still to collect qualitative information by sampling individual 'representative' cases. He did try to collect data that could be aggregated by calling meetings of particular tradespeople and distributing questionnaires to them, but this was such an inadequate way of collecting systematic data that he must still rank as a journalist.

There were, however, pressures on this form of investigation to become more systematic. Social exploration into the black continents in the centre of Britain's cities continued and developed, but its results were always open to contestation. James Greenwood could horrify the readership of the *Pall Mall Gazette* with his accounts of a night spent disguised as a pauper in a workhouse in Lambeth, for which, incidentally, it was suggested that he be awarded the Victoria Cross! (Keating 1976: 15). A multitude of penny pamphlets could document the conditions of the poor of the cities. One pamphlet, *Bitter Cry of Outcast London* (Keating 1976: 91–111), written by Andrew Mearns, a clergyman convinced that there was no point in expecting people in the depth of misery and poverty to be religious until something was done about their physical needs, provoked a widespread controversy in the 1880s. Despite the assurances given by the author that what is described 'is simply . . . a state of things which is found in house after house, court after court, street after street', the evidence of these inquiries was inconclusive and unsatisfactory; lone investigators of this kind could always be countered by other single examples which proved the opposite.

Nevertheless, this style of 'survey research' continued into the twentieth century, and some examples still make fine reading. Lady Florence Bell, wife of a Middlesbrough steel-owner, wrote of her encounters with the workers who lived in her town; although this book is permeated with the patronising self-confidence of the owner's wife, horrified, for example, at how the ignorant workers were feeding their children, it is still ultimately a sympathetic account (Bell 1907).

The Early Victorian Period
The liberal and utilitarian ideology of the new industrialists, which had replaced the hand of God with the hand of the market as the providential regulator, did not prescribe how to deal with the immediate social problems that the capitalist market brought with it.

In the 1830s and 1840s, times of great social unrest which gave birth to the first expression of a working class political movement in Chartism, some sectors of the new industrial bourgeoisie decided that they must group together to campaign for concerted action to improve the moral and sanitary conditions of the labouring poor. Fear of cholera acted as a spur, both real, in as much as disease was no respecter of class in the crowded cities, and symbolic, as a reflection of the fear felt by the middle classes of the political threat from the mob, much in the same way as fear of rabies holds symbolic power in Britain today in expressing a covert xenophobia.

Statistical societies were founded in most major cities. By and large their members were opponents of the old poor law, advocating relief only where it would 'encourage industry and virtue' (Cullen 1975: 109); Chadwick of the London Statistical Society was a key figure in the Poor Law Report of 1834 (Finer 1952). But they were not content just with the poor law reforms of the 1830s which created the penal institutions of the workhouses. They wished to deal with the physical and spiritual diseases that they diagnosed, and were fervent campaigners for sanitation to remove the evil effects of 'miasma' which they believed exuded from drains, and religion and education to remove the dangers of political subversion. Kay, of the Manchester Statistical Society, who was to become chief educational policy-maker within the government, wrote many tracts proselytising his views on the need for close supervision of working class children in schools to make up for the neglect of their parents who now worked in the factories (Johnson 1970). They tackled the task of lobbying the authorities with vigour, collecting 'statistics' on the health and conditions of whole trades and neighbourhoods, on the 'moral equipment' the labourers had in terms of literacy, choice of reading, religious belief and attendance, and even ability to whistle a cheerful tune, the physical equipment they had, the sanitary arrangements, the degree of overcrowding and that illuminating moral statistic – the number of people of each sex per bed. They steered carefully away from inquiring too closely into wages; the blame for these conditions was to be laid at the door of urbanism, not the factory system as such, and government regulation was only sought in public health and education.

By 'statistics' was not meant necessarily numerical information, but merely facts about the state and its activities – the early years of the *Journal of the Royal Statistical Society* show what the earliest statisticians thought their subject was about. The collection of facts was seen as sternly opposed to any expression of mere opinion, and the foundation of the London Statistical Society was conducted on the basis that members would agree that 'the first and most essential rule of its conduct is to exclude all opinions'. The motto of the

London Statistical Society was *aliis exterendum* – we collect the facts, others work out what they mean and what conclusions can be drawn from them. In fact, however, while publicly mouthing this catechism of objectivity, the sponsors of these surveys were committed to political positions; they rarely allowed inconvenient facts that did not fit in with their overall view to prevent them from campaigning for the reforms that they thought necessary to prevent upheaval.

Many of these inquiries were quite sophisticated and demonstrate knowledge of the use of precodes and percentages, and used carefully trained interviewers following a schedule (Elesh 1972). Some historians have wondered why these activities and methodological achievements were not continued into the mid-Victorian period. The explanation sometimes given is that they were not consolidated into research organisations capable of codifying their procedures, disseminating and cumulating their experience (Elesh 1972; Cole 1972; Ben-David 1960).

This explanation does not go far enough, for it does not ask why they were not. A more complete explanation is given by remembering that these expensive investigations were conducted by individuals who, while wealthy, did not have limitless resources. And, although the 'movement' may have failed in as much as most of the statistical societies petered out, it succeeded in persuading the government to take up these problems, to start routine data collection and *ad hoc* investigations of its own, and to regulate some of the worst excesses of industrialism through legislation (Cullen 1975).

In 1837 the General Register Office was established, and civil registration of deaths was forced on an unwilling Parliament. During the 1840s regular statistical series were started on the number of births, deaths and crimes. Committees of inquiry were established into education and poverty; the first was the famous Royal Commission on the Poor Law, but by 1849 more than a hundred had been established, and a precedent had been set for the principle of always conducting an inquiry before major legislative changes were made. The modern census with household schedules was established in 1841 and the census of 1851 was a very wide-ranging and sophisticated affair. The reformers were co-opted into government, sat on the various committees and staffed the General Register Office.

One might imagine, from the current experience of our Social Survey Division at the Office of Population Censuses and Surveys, and from the experience of countries such as Sweden and India, that government might provide a very suitable location for organised social research, for codifying research procedures, for providing the possibility of such an organisation reaching a critical mass in terms of size, and for stimulating broader sociological questioning. But it would appear that an additional ingredient is necessary, and that is that the government itself needs to be an active, if not directly inter-ventionist, one.

The government of mid-Victorian Britain was not. The mid-Victorian period was not conducive to the kind of widespread social research undertaken by the statistical societies, and it is only when the economy slumped, social unrest was once more forcefully on the political agenda and a revived socialist movement was appealing to the working class that we see the resurgence in the 1880s of fact-gathering activities by private individuals.

The Classical 'Founding Fathers' of Surveys

It is to the activities of the philanthropic investigators, the 'chocolate sociologists' of the end of the nineteenth and early twentieth centuries, that many historians have traced the origins of survey research (Abrams 1951; Easthope 1974). As we have seen, this is to deny the achievements of the early Victorian statistical societies. But it is not a 'mistake' in one sense, for it is in this period that a close link was forged between survey research and policy research which continued as an unbroken tradition through to the establishment of the welfare state and the regular intervention of government into the life- chances of its citizens. Abrams (1951: 2) insists that an intrinsic feature of social surveys is that they have a utilitarian character:

> Occasionally surveys originate in an abstract desire for more knowledge about the structure and workings of a society; more frequently, however, they are carried out as an indispensable first step in measuring the dimensions of a social problem, ascertaining its causes, and then deciding upon remedial action ... Most surveys have been concerned with curing obviously pathological social conditions.

The early Victorians agreed that the social conditions were patho-logical, but not that they were curable. Once the foundations of a welfare state were laid, the stage was set for a partnership between the state and the social researcher which is still the predominant feature of British survey research. In order to understand the political milieu of social research, then, it is important to have an understanding of the forces shaping these foundations and their subsequent develop-ment. The history of the welfare state is sometimes written as a development of the sensitivity and humanity of a benevolent government. This is as wrong as the counter-view which has been more popular recently that it is a series of attempts at social control by a wicked bureaucracy. It must be understood as the result of a dialectic between popular demands for forms of social insurance and the state's adaptation to these pressures to suit its own needs as well as possible. The decisive factor was the formation of an organised labour movement capable of formulating demands, and eventually capable of sustaining a powerful enough struggle to achieve them.

Beatrice Webb, however, would not have agreed. 'A new consciousness of sin amongst men of intellect and property', commitment to the values of a science of man, captivation by the positivist doctrines of Comte and his English disciples and 'scientific curiosity ... the desire to apply the method of observation, reasoning and verification to the problem of poverty in the midst of riches' were, in her estimation, what impelled the Liverpool shipping magnate Charles Booth to devote seventeen years of his life to seventeen volumes of *The Life and Labour of the People of London* (Webb 1971; 1926: 187, 226). When, however, we inquire into the circumstances of Booth's decision to embark on the project, we come to different conclusions. The traditional story that Booth was needled into it by the Social Democrat Hyndman's claim that 25 per cent of the people of London were in abject poverty has recently been questioned (Hennock 1976); nevertheless, whether there ever was such a Social Democratic Federation inquiry or whether the claim was made in the *Pall Mall Gazette*, there is no doubt that Booth wanted to disprove the claims of this agitational literature, and, supported by a group of helpers (one of whom was Beatrice Webb, and from whose autobiography we get important insights into his methodology), he undertook a piece of research which, in the end, covered 80 per cent of the population of London.

One reason for the size of the project was the untheoretical nature of the inquiry; since there were no conclusions drawn from each volume as it rolled in, describing in quantitative and qualitative terms the life of the inhabitants, there seemed to be nothing to do next but to commence another inquiry (Glass 1955); Selvin (1976) endorses this view, and reckons that Booth's greatest contribution to social science was £30,000. The mythology about Booth is that he discovered that an even higher percentage, 30 per cent, were in poverty, and so turned to campaigning for welfare reforms. In fact, his classification system was so crude and impressionistic that it allowed him to interpret his own figures as a refutation of the 'sensationalists' (Hennock 1976).

The 'success' of the enterprise was not really in taking further an understanding of the causes of poverty. Apart from the blindingly obvious association between casual labour and low earnings, there is nothing of analytic bite that emerges from this marathon. Indeed, Beatrice Webb was convinced that static surveys could never hope to do this, but merely yield 'clues' (1971: 256). Nor was it a methodological advance; even the famous eight-fold classification of social classes was hopelessly subjective. Nor can we accept the evaluation of the Fabian commentators (Webb 1971; Abrams 1951) that these revelations of poverty were the major factor behind the massive state intervention into insurance, wage and factory regulation and other educational and welfare provisions. Hobsbawm (1964: 250) has drawn attention to the remarkable ability of the Fabians to blow their own trumpets and to exaggerate their own importance. Booth's own words are more revealing. Where these Fabian intellectuals were enormously influential was in convincing that

> the Individualist system breaks down as things are, and is invaded on every side by Socialistic innovations, but its hardy doctrines would have stood a far better chance in a society purged of those who cannot stand alone. Thorough interference on the part of the state with the lives of a small fraction of the population would tend to make it possible, ultimately, to dispense with any Socialistic interference in the lives of all the rest. (Booth 1892: 167)

There were wide divergencies in the way these early investigators collected their data. One of the most important variations was whether or not they trusted the objects of their inquiry to speak for themselves. Many government officials equated the move towards collecting more systematic, reliable information with collecting it from more stout and reliable informants than from the poor themselves. Royal Commissions and parliamentary committees adopted the method of interrogating people who might be presumed to be experts, rather than taking their information directly from the horse's mouth.

Booth did not rely on the statements of the poor themselves, and instead resorted to what Beatrice Webb called 'wholesale interviewing', getting some qualitative impressions from visiting and observing their subjects, but relying on a variety of school board visitors, police, rate-collectors, sanitary inspectors and almoners for the information that they later quantified. Part of the rationale behind this was also the impossibility of doing anything else in a survey which aimed to cover the whole of London's working class; one of the reasons that these were expert witnesses was that they could produce data already aggregated, thus providing, *en route*, one solution to the problem of excess information that sampling advances were later to meet.

Those who did interview the poor directly were frankly disbelieved. Mayhew's claims that a vast majority of London's needlewomen and journeymen tailors subsisted on twopence-halfpenny per day was rejected by *The Economist* as 'entirely false and irreconcilable with known, recorded and public facts', being based on the statements of the poor themselves whose 'utter untrustworthiness' was well known (Thompson 1973: 43). In another attempt to collect information about wages and rents from 25,451 men of 'Certain Selected Districts of London' by means of a question-naire which they filled in themselves, William Oglethorpe, then Superintendent of Statistics at the General Register office, virtually dismissed them in his introduction to the report: 'after devoting much time and labour to a careful examination of the returns, and after informing myself fully as to the conditions under which the data were collected, I have come to the conclusions that these returns are of small statistical value' (Board of Trade 1888: lxxi).

The idea of interviewing a *respondent*, who was at the same time the subject of the inquiry and the informant, was very slow to develop; one result of this was an almost total disregard for the problems of question-wording. The investigators who chose this method were often the radical sympathisers with the working class. Karl Marx, in his *Enquête Ouvrière*, recruited a volunteer sample from the *Revue Socialiste*, and asked them to fill in a hundred open-ended questions about their conditions of work (Weiss 1936). The intention of this questionnaire was to raise important questions in the minds of those who answered them, as well as to provide information for the investigator, so the questions are not at all neutral. One question, for example, asked workers to consider whether those who worked in the so-called profit-sharing industries could go on strike 'or are they only permitted to be the humble servants of their masters?' Marx had in mind that the results could be presented as *cahiers du travail* like the *cahiers de doléances* of the French Revolution, and would form an agitational basis for 'preparing a reconstruction of society'. In point of fact, there were so few returns to the 25,000 questionnaires sent out that they were not worth analysing – the methods of postal questionnaires have improved markedly since then! But the idea that surveys could have an active political component for the respondents continued into the idea of a 'community self-survey' before and after the First World War, and is being rediscovered today (Carr-Hill 1973; Institute for Workers' Control 1977).

We have mentioned that some inquiries of the early Victorian movement made important methodological advances in question-naire design and the use of precodes. This aspect of the history of survey research has been almost entirely neglected, and is an area where the discontinuity and failure to consolidate and build on earlier achievements is most marked. To get a flavour of what I mean, try comparing the two questionnaires on pp. 20-4, one from the 1845 inquiry into the parish of St George's in London's east end (Committee Investigating the Poorer Classes 1848), and one from an inquiry in 1919 in the city of Sheffield (St Phillips Settlement). The systematic and careful way the evidence is collected in the 1845

Questionnaire 1   Inquiry into the Parish of St George's in London's East End, 1845*

Name and Condition of Street or Place	Number of house	Number of families in the house	Number in family	Male Children under 16		Female Children under 16		Able-bodied Males above 16		Able-bodied Females above 16		Aged and Infirm Males		Aged and Infirm Females	
1 Height of houses, in stories 2 Length and width of place 3 Open or not at each end 4 Paving and lighting 5 Cleansing 6 Sewerage 7 Supply of water				Well	Ill	Well	Ill	Well	Ill	Well	Ill	Well	Ill	Well	Ill

Age of father when first child born	Age of mother when first child born	Present age of mother	Number of children she has had	Number now living	Occupation and weekly earnings of head of family	Occupation and weekly earnings of others than the head of the family	Weekly earnings of the whole	Number of times that the family has animal food in the week

Questionnaire 1 (cont.)

Clothing

| 1 Sufficient, and clean |
| 2 Insufficient, but clean |
| 3 Sufficient, but dirty |
| 4 Insufficient, and dirty |

Rooms

Number	Rent per week	Number of beds	Furnished			Cleansed		
			Well	Scantily	III	Well	Tolerably	III

Books

Serious	Theatrical	Miscellaneous

Pictures

Serious	Theatrical	Miscellaneous

Number of Children Attending School

Infant and dame schools		Day schools		Sunday schools only		Payments made for the schooling of children in day schools
Males	Females	Males	Females	Males	Females	

Religion

Church of England	Roman Catholics	Methodists	Jews	Other religious denominations	No religious profession

Questionnaire 1 (cont.)

| Newspapers generally read | Country of Birth | | | | | Length of Time in Present Residence | | Receiving what gratuitous medical aid, if any | Numbers of persons in benefit societies |
	London	England and Wales	Ireland	Scotland	Foreign parts	Years	Months		

* Survey by the Committee Investigating the Poorer Classes, reporting in 1848.

inquiry compares very favourably with the vague and woolly instructions in the 1919 one; the former asks for details about clothing and reading material, where the latter just asks for 'aesthetic feelings'. (On the reply printed as an example at the back of this latter inquiry the answer to this question was: 'Nil. Rarely you see him with a collar on. Scarf twisted round his neck'!) It is only really since the widespread application of automatic data-processing technology, Hollerith cards, counter-sorters and computers to the analysis of survey results that major and sustained advances have been made in layout and precoding.

Questionnaire 2   *Inquiry in the city of Sheffield, St Phillip's Settlement, 1919*

STRICTLY PRIVATE

Name of helper
Address
X's full name
Exact address
Sex   Age
Married, widower or widowed, single
Exact occupation
Size of tenement occupied by family
Precise mode of helper's approach to X

I   Educational Ideas

1   What does X think of the WEA?
2   Does X attend any classes, lectures, etc?
3   What does X think about the education of his children?
4   How does X regard the university?
5   What is X's opinion of education in general?
6   Other information under I.

II   Leisure

1   How does X spend evenings?
2   How does X spend free afternoons?
3   How does X spend Sundays?
4   How does X spend annual holidays?
5   What are X's hobbies?
6   What are X's chief amusements and pleasures?
7   Is X keen on garden or allotment?
8   Other data under II.

Questionnaire 2 *(cont.)*

III   Musical Tastes

IV   Aesthetic Feelings

V   Religious and Social Activities

1   Is X a member of a trade union?
2   Is X a keen member?
3   Is X a member of a co-operative society?
4   Is X a true co-operator?
5   Is X a member of a provident or friendly society?
6   Is X a member of any other club or society?
7   Is X a member of a religious or similar organisation?
8   What is the value of X's membership?
9   What is the nature of X's relations with other members of the family?
10   Note any points that would serve to indicate X's goodness or badness
11   What is your personal impression of X?
12   Other data under V.

VI   Reading

VII   Home

VIII   Political Ideas

(With a view to indicating X's fitness for local and national citizenship.)

IX   Root Desires

1   What is X's ambition?
2   What would X do if a millionaire?
3   What would X like to do in old age?

X   Other Data

Beatrice Webb never came round to the idea that there was anything to be gained from administering a questionnaire to *respondents*. In *Methods of Social Study* the Webbs report that they tried sending a postal questionnaire to trade union officials, with little success (Webb and Webb 1975; 1932). Their response rate was low, and they had asked questions that they thought would make sense – 'Do your members work at piece rate or at time rate?' – but discovered that this question was unanswerable to the majority of officials who got their questionnaire. They were perhaps the first in a long line of people who decided that questionnaires had nothing interesting to offer, instead of concluding that if you intend to ask people structured questions of this kind you must do some very careful piloting.

But another of Booth's successors, Seebohm Rowntree, was more enthusiastic. Rowntree was, like Booth, a wealthy industrialist who decided to spend his money conducting an inquiry into poverty in a 'typical' English town. He was a Quaker who had made his money in the cocoa and confectionery trade, and it was not surprising that he should select York as the town to be investigated, since it was a major centre of the chocolate industry. His work was much more sophisticated than Booth's; he covered every wage-earning family where Booth had excluded those without schoolchildren, obtained the information directly from families by using interviewers and structured schedules, and refined the definition of poverty (Moser and Kalton 1971: 8).

Once the tradition of direct interviewing was established, other important methodological breakthroughs were made possible and necessary. The use of standard question-wording and standard definitions became vital. Rowntree had tried to give a physiologically based definition of poverty by attempting to define in terms of calories what a subsistence diet was, and then to calculate the sum necessary to buy it. Being a major employer in the town, he had a harsh definition of subsistence; he defined 'primary poverty' as a situation where the family did not have enough income to meet this standard, and 'secondary poverty' as the situation where money was being diverted to strictly inessential items like furniture or drink. He was probably the first to combine LePlay's method of collecting detailed family budgets with systematic interviewing of a cross-section of people. His findings agreed strikingly with Booth's, but where Booth had suggested vaguely that casual labour was associated with poverty, Rowntree pinpointed strong life-cycle effects bringing people out of and pushing them into poverty as their family circumstances changed.

But it was Bowley who made the decisive methodological breakthroughs for the social survey as we know it today. He was responsible for a much more rigorous attitude towards the precise questions to be asked and the precise definitions of the unit under investigation and the qualities sought of these units. *The Measurement of Social Phenomena* (1915) was ahead of its time in an effort to standardise definitions of such things as income, poverty, household and other commonly used terms. The need for such standardisation still plagues survey research, and several international organisations have tried to lay down standards in the way that Bowley did in order to ensure compatibility across time and across nations. Unfortunately, there is a great deal of conservatism inevitable with designing classification schemes; once you have committed yourself to a particular scheme for classifying occupations, you will want to continue it just to see if things change over time. Only recently has much effort been put into making new classification systems compatible with old ones.

But Bowley is more commonly remembered for his exposition of a practical sampling scheme to solve the problems of sheer magnitude of the tasks like Booth's. The early social researchers, imbued with Enlightenment philosophy, often saw their job as filling in the cracks, the unknown parts of the world, in a general division of labour. This meant that when they did an investigation, the idea of sampling only one part of the area was unthinkable. Something of this encyclopaedic drive was continued into the local surveys of the interwar years that we shall come on to. It would have been as unthinkable for these investigators to do a one in ten sample of households as it would have been for a cartographer to map only one square in ten on his grid.

So the need for some information about *everybody* was accepted fairly early. The idea of a sample survey took much longer to develop. Of course, the sheer impossibility of doing empirical research in this comprehensive fashion meant that some intuitive sampling was necessary, but this usually took the form of claiming typicality for an area studied.

The statistical ideas underlying random sampling had been known for a long time (Stephen 1948). Classical error theory had been formulated by the astronomer Gauss in the first half of the nineteenth century, and the chi-squared distribution had been discovered independently in different places. But the implication of many of the discoveries for practical sampling procedures and the development of small sample statistics did not proceed apace. An important spur to this came from the need for quality control techniques in industry. A researcher who worked for Guinness, whose real name was Gossett but who wrote under the pseudonym of Student in order to keep his professional identity secret, was the pioneer of small sample statistics. You cannot test entire batches for the quality in industry, as almost all types of test involve using and therefore destroying the product. Presumably testing Guinness involves drinking it and seeing how nice it tastes. Instead of consuming the entire output of the factory, Gossett worked out the *t*-distribution for the differences of means in small samples with unknown standard deviations as early as 1908, and he and Fisher discovered the theoretical distributions of large numbers of sample statistics before the First World War.

For the application of these ideas to sampling procedures for surveys and to the estimation of likely errors, Bowley's name is again supreme. He quickly understood the significance of discoveries of the properties of random samples, and in the studies of five English towns that he organised with the support of the Ratan Tata foundation in 1913, he carefully drew up complete lists of houses and drew a random sample from this (Bowley and Burnett-Hurst 1915). In the last chapter of the report, he estimated the reliability of his findings and presented confidence intervals for the findings. Moreover, he had some intuitive understanding of the advantages of stratified random sampling, for he points out that in this estimation no allowance is being made for the fact that, because the addresses were originally ordered by street, one aspect of variance has been held constant and is not causing error.

Thus before the First World War began, major advances had been made in the technology of surveying. The results of the surveys that were done at that time were published in the *Journal of the Royal Statistical Society*, however, and not in the newly founded *Sociological Review*. Neither Booth nor Rowntree would join the new Sociological Society, dominated as it was by two individuals, Patrick Geddes and Victor Branford, whose conception of sociology was pervaded by their passionate interest in LePlay's theories and the strange concept of 'civics', and whose idea of survey research was, as we shall see, different from the traditional poverty study.

They would not even have been happy describing themselves as 'sociologists', for this word connoted the attempt to erect grand social theories and explanatory schemes at variance with the dominant philosophy of social engineering which motivated the early poverty researchers. British sociology before the First World War utterly failed to agree on aims and objectives and to come together as an academic discipline (see Abrams 1968 for a masterly portrait of the intellectual and ideological battles). Bowley's activities would today come under the purview of economics. He and many of his successors were grappling with the problems of definition of national income, and the effect upon wages of various social insurance schemes.

The Interwar Period

It is hard to generalise about social and political conditions in the interwar years. The First World War had clinched the foundations of the welfare state; a safety net level of existence had been provided through national insurance. The *laissez-faire* economic system had irretrievably collapsed and the British ruling class was involved in managing an increasingly highly centralised financial empire. The imminent threat of Bolshevism worried political leaders after the war; welfare reforms were continued and new ones granted. But in the later 1920s this threat seemed to have subsided, and, after a period of intense unrest and industrial conflict, the morale of the labour movement was effectively sapped in the defeat of the General Strike. Unemployment and recession deepened throughout the period, and yet some industries and areas were undergoing expansion – the motor industry and the south-east, for example, grew throughout the period. While the majority of workers were unemployed in some of the traditional areas of heavy industry, in other areas their wages were buying a new range of mass-produced goods – processed foods, radios, make-up, motorbicycles, and so on.

A thorough assessment of the social research of the interwar years has not yet been made. A recent historian of the period opens his book with the ringing words, 'The inter-war period in Britain was one of the great achievements in the field of social inquiry and investigation' (Stevenson 1977: 7). There were, it is true, a great many more surveys being done than ever before, and they have yielded unique data for the social historian, but they were very pedestrian, and failed to connect with the pressing social problems of the day.

In this period the state increased its support by funding large-scale social research in universities, and even beginning some inquiries of its own. The Ministry of Labour established the post of Director of Statistics to co-ordinate the documentation of its increased activity since various pieces of welfare legislation had been enacted in the first two decades of the century. As the Second World War approached, the Ministry decided that it needed more detailed information on the kinds of things that people bought; it instituted an expenditure survey to aid the planning of supplies and provide a reasonably objective basis for an index to measure the cost of living.

The only social remedy for unemployment seemed to be to provide a minimum of relief for those affected while waiting for the economy to pick up. The ideas of John Maynard Keynes about sustaining the economy through deliberately creating full employment were not yet widely known, let alone accepted. The major stimulus to other aspects of the welfare state, comprehensive health and education programmes, were to be given by the war; there were no major advances on this front in this period.

Despite the growing problem of unemployment, these surveys did not concern themselves centrally with it (see Wells 1935 for a comprehensive bibliography of the surveys of the period, as well as for a flavour of the way surveys were viewed at the time). There were a few studies of unemployment, and one or two of them are very good; one in particular, organised and financed by the Pilgrim Trust, and with the co-operation of a sociologist, a Dr Wagner who had worked with Lazarsfeld and his associates in Marienthal, was particularly sensitive (Pilgrim Trust 1938). The investigations performed by the state attempted to estimate how many people were being supported by various forms of insurance, but they were mainly concerned to provide demographic information. John Hilton, first Director of Statistics at the Ministry of Labour, argued that the picture of unemployment which was obtainable from the official returns was inadequate. He organised a 1 per cent sample survey, administered by Labour Exchange officials, to get an age and industry profile of the unemployed. But, given the scale of the problem, the research is depressingly meagre.

The only major area recognised as a 'social problem' was housing. As in the 1830s, attention was focused not on industry, but on the existence of terrible slums in all Britain's major cities, many without water or drainage. The interwar period witnessed the rapid growth of sprawling and unplanned housing estates, and people were being forced to travel further and further to work. Philanthropists and active municipal authorities threw their energies into injecting a greater element of planning to control this urban sprawl. The town planning movement was gaining sway under such pioneers as Abercrombie. Quaker philanthropists and other 'model employers' became very enthusiastic about providing adequate housing. The number of housing surveys grew rapidly.

George Cadbury established the Bournville Village on the outskirts of Birmingham at the turn of the century, to be managed by a Trust which had more general philanthropic aims. This Trust conducted a comprehensive survey of housing conditions in Birmingham at the end of the 1930s, and many similar surveys were conducted elsewhere, in Becontree and Dagenham by Terence Young, and in Watling by a young woman then known as Ruth Durant but who was to become the best of the postwar urban sociologists under the name of Ruth Glass. Where the state involved itself in these research activities, it can be criticised for using research to whitewash and contain social problems. A marathon attempt to survey the housing of all working class homes was undertaken by local authorities in the winter of 1935–6, charged under the 1935 Housing Act to deal with overcrowding (White 1977). Because the standards set under this act were so inadequate, it concluded that only 4 per cent of working class families lived in overcrowded conditions.

Very few further methodological developments took place in the interwar years. The mood of the day was a kind of institutional sobriety. The task of social surveys was to act as a tool in a rational bureaucracy, filling in the cracks of administrative ignorance, encouraging the compilation of books like *A Survey of the Social*

Structure of England and Wales by Carr-Saunders and Jones (1st edn 1927, 2nd edn 1937). This is an early prototype of *Social Trends*, a statistical abstract of contemporary social data 'from the morphological point of view', covering a range of topics from vital statistics, housing and industrial composition to crime and intelligence.

David Caradog Jones of the University of Liverpool, and chief investigator in the Social Survey of Merseyside at the end of the 1920s, summed up the prevailing view of social surveys in a textbook he wrote after the Second World War (Jones 1948). The primary aim of a social survey, he tells us, 'is to make an accurate and impartial collection and presentation of the facts', because 'the administration of government, the development of new ideas to be translated into action, the reform of evils, all depend upon accurate knowledge of existing conditions' (Jones 1948: 11). In order to achieve such an impartial collection, investigators had to stick to objectively ascertainable conditions; they were very careful to distinguish this activity from opinion surveys and from the community or regional surveys associated with Branford and Geddes which we shall discuss shortly (Carr-Saunders 1934; Jones 1948). The idea that surveys should be factual had been accepted in principle by all those in the 'survey tradition', but in this period the range of the factual domain became severely curtailed.

The major interwar surveys were repeats of earlier prewar surveys. Bowley repeated his five towns study. Rowntree revisited York. Llewellyn Smith at the LSE replicated Booth's study and similar investigations were carried out on Merseyside and Tyneside, in Bristol, Southampton, Brynmawr and Sheffield. Sir John Orr, an early pioneer of the science of nutrition, did a survey in 1935 which showed that one-half of the nation was not eating sufficient food to maintain itself in a healthy state. These surveys still relied on the beneficence of a philanthropist or a trust, more often than not American.

It is not just me who finds the major surveys of this period dull. In the discussion that ensued after Jones read his final paper on the Merseyside Social Survey to the Royal Statistical Society (Jones 1931), it was pointed out (admittedly by the Registrar-General) that neither this survey nor the New London Survey seemed to generate any information not to be obtained from the census, and suggested that since their main virtue seemed to be that they were done in the period between censuses, a better solution would be to encourage adoption of a quinquennial census.[3]

And finally we must mention that strange phenomenon of early sociology both in Britain and the USA known as the 'community self-survey'. In the USA, where social insurance of various kinds was even less developed than in England, it grew into a huge movement, into which early Christian-reformer-sociologists threw themselves with great zeal (see Burgess 1916 for a programmatic statement). The movement is well described in early editions of Pauline Young's methods textbook (1939). She looks enviously at Britain and wishes that the US survey movement could be equally 'successful' (she had read Webb's erroneous account of the effect of Booth's study); this is ironic, for the externality of the American movement from government allowed it to maintain its vitality much longer.

The community survey movement had its intellectual origins in the thinking of Patrick Geddes, a remarkable blending of the survey methods of the French sociologist LePlay who was concerned above all else with family budgets, and the theories of organic social integration of Spencer and Comte. His aim was to show by survey methods how the family and the community were the twin pillars of social integration in their ecological setting. The survey was done to arouse community feeling as much as for scientific purposes. It was to be organised not from within universities but from the communities themselves, conducted not by paid officials but by volunteers, and often culminated in an exhibition in the local town hall. The kind of patchy urban anthropology that resulted from this movement has been roundly criticised by Ruth Glass, who is scathing of the laborious obviousness of its findings, typical among which was the 'discovery' that women who do not work have more acquaintances in their neighbourhood than do women who work (Glass 1955).

The charter for the use of the social survey for a new sociology known as 'civics' is an article by Branford, Geddes's most devoted disciple, in the *Sociological Review* of 1912. The task of the survey is to provide a social map, gathering the social and cultural fragments omitted by cartographers and surveys like Booth's. The aim is to 'make us see Eutopia, and, seeing it, to create it', and Branford called for the 'socialisation of the Ordnance Survey and emancipation of the scientist for human service'.

It was all this talk of Eutopia that probably put the more sober social statisticians off. The close link between the ideas of mapping and the idea of doing a survey was not the product of the community survey; the aim of many investigators had been to describe the social landscape (and, indeed, the original meaning of the word 'survey' has this connotation). Booth had presented his main findings in the form of beautiful maps, symbolically coloured to represent the residential areas of the different social classes. Jones (1931: 566) had also suggested a regular social mapping of the different regions of Britain by specially appointed registrars. The main regional surveys of the interwar years were infused with this kind of thinking.

The Geddes/Branford tradition proper died with its founders. With its strange views on the essence of sociology, its rejection of a university base and its weak methodology, it must carry a large burden of responsibility for convincing a generation of British sociologists that surveys were not for them. Its traces may be discovered in the development of more systematic town planning surveys which even today account for a large proportion of the survey industry, and the 'community study' tradition which received its postwar embodiment in the Institute of Community Studies. Neither makes analytic use of surveys for answering sociological questions. In the latter case, the explanatory component is supplied by depth interviews with respondents in parallel with the more demographic survey material (Platt 1971).

By the beginning of the Second World War, then, no major methodological advances in survey research had been made for two decades. There had been a numerical increase in census-like inquiries in various localities, in planning surveys and in a plethora of rather worthless community studies. The predominant policy interest of this period in housing was reflected in the subject matter. Great stress had been placed on collecting objective data only, and when, in some surveys, leisure, crime, or religious activities were considered, they were inquired into by rather barren questions. (The other major interwar interest in mental deficiency will be examined in the next section.) The questionnaire had become the standard measuring instrument and the skills of social observation were not demanded. (To get a flavour of the change since the early Victorian era, look back at the schedule for the St George's inquiry on pp. 20–2, fifteen of the forty-two items could have been discovered by observation.)

One reaction to this was the formation, in 1937, of a fascinating organisation known as Mass-Observation, a 'several-pronged reaction to the disturbed condition of western Europe under the growing threat of fascism'. It sought to 'supply accurate observations of everyday life and *real* (not just published) public moods, an anthropology and a mass documentation for a vast sector of normal life which did not, at that time, seem to be adequately considered by the media, the arts, the social scientists, even by the political leaders' (Harrisson 1978: 13). An army of volunteers were inspired by this programme, and busied themselves either in writing diaries, poems, or even making films, or in observing by more or less unobtrusive (that is, covert!) methods the behaviour and speech of others (Mass-Observation 1938).

At its worst, its publications were like bird-watcher's notebooks; the resulting descriptions of bird-calls (long lists of informants' statements) and nesting activities (see *Britain and her Birth Rate*, Mass-Observation 1945, for example), could be dreary in the extreme. At its best, as, for example, when it documents the effects on morale of the Blitz (Harrisson 1978), it produced one of the finest pieces of social research of the period. Its antagonists have criticised, rightly, its tendency to be unsystematic and magpie-like in its collection of facts. But it did make attempts to generalise these observations, and must be treated as an important precursor of that survey method pioneered in the USA by Reiss known as systematic social observation (Reiss 1968 and 1971). It could not in the end compete after the war with the many new polling companies that came into existence to document public opinion in much drier (and more questionable) fashion.

The Second World War and Beyond

War has stimulated the need for social research on many occasions. Empires needed to be able to count those available for military service. Britain's earliest imperial ventures in the West Indies and later in the Boer War were the occasions for some very careful studies of the health of the troops. The First World War demanded research into the physical conditions of those who were expected to fight and to work in the crucial munitions industry. But the Second World War involved the civilian population in a hitherto unknown manner. Food and clothing had to be rationed, and there was widespread fear that civilian morale would collapse under the pressure of aerial bombardment. For these reasons, government survey activity increased markedly during the war.

In 1940 the Wartime Social Survey was founded by the Home Intelligence Division of the Ministry of Information, with the active encouragement of the navy, whose chiefs were very anxious about the effect of the Blitz on sailors and their families and on dock-workers (Harrison 1978: 297). To start with it was based on a pre-existing institution in the Department of Employment, run by academics. When the war began to look desperate in the summer of 1940, and the early morale surveys had run into a reaction against 'Cooper-snoopers' (Cooper was the then Minister of Information), a young researcher from Gallup Poll, Louis Moss, was brought in to re-organise it. Thereafter it restricted itself to a variety of surveys on diet, efficacy of rationing, knowledge of venereal disease, the effect of Ministry of Information publicity campaigns and other more directly factual topics (Box and Thomas 1944).

A comparison between the actual work of the British Wartime Social Survey and the activities of the Research Branch of the US Army is instructive. The active involvement of academics was much more marked in the USA, because there was a much larger and more flourishing sociological community. Respected figures like Stouffer, Merton, Lazarsfeld, Likert and Guttman were all associated with the US project. The reaction to morale surveys in the USA was not so touchy either; they were mainly confined to surveys within the armed forces, since the civilian population was not being bombed. But the major differences come in the use that was made of the material. In Britain, the data was not only not offered to academics to analyse independently, but it was actually covered by the Official Secrets Act and not released to anyone. The reflective perusal of the wealth of wartime material that was such a tremendous spur to American sociology and which led to the publication of *The American Soldier* (Stouffer 1949, Merton and Lazarsfeld 1950) and a spate of scholarly works thereafter, had no counterpart in Britain.

Some description of the postwar growth of the survey industry has been given in the Introduction. At the end of the war, sociology had a very productive period, flourishing at the LSE and Liverpool, as we shall see in the next section. But the two major developments in the fact-gathering aspect of survey research came in the rapid expansion of research done by central and local government, and the growth of the market research and opinion polling industry.

The Wartime Social Survey had proved its worth to government and was continued after the war as the Social Survey and attached to the Central Office of Information. Its work increased rapidly in the first years of the Labour Administration (see Gray and Corlett 1950, and Moss 1953), doing work for many different government departments. It survived an early threat from the 1950 Conservative administration to close it down completely on financial grounds; after the Heyworth Committee on social science research reported in 1965, it had a brief period under the direct control of the Treasury, but eventually it was merged with the Registrar-General's office when the Office of Population Censuses and Surveys was formed in 1970, under the influence of Claus Moser at the Government Statistical Service.[4]

The Social Survey has been responsible for innovations in two major methodological areas. Its main contributions have been in the field of sampling, pioneering the details of multistage sampling in earlier years, and more recently investigating the use of the rating lists and GPO postal codes as sampling frames. It has also from the early days paid very careful attention to questionnaire design, coding and interviewing, and has pulled standards up in a difficult area (Fothergill and Willcock 1953). Jean Atkinson's *Handbook for Interviewers* (Atkinson 1971) is the best guide to interviewing that there is, and she, as head of the fieldwork branch, has improved quality enormously by insisting that interviewers are trained to recognise the differences between questions of fact, opinion and knowledge, and to probe each in different ways. The Social Survey has not been so innovative on analysis, however. It is still firmly within the tradition of fact-finding surveys, and this has not encouraged the development of analytical procedures to explain these facts.

The amount and quality of data turned out by the Social Survey is quite extraordinary. As well as doing a wide variety of *ad hoc* surveys for almost every government department, it has done major pieces of work for Royal Commissions and special inquiries, and it has also a programme of regular data collection. The Family Expenditure Survey was started on a regular basis in 1957 and has continued ever since, providing detailed income and expenditure information from which the weights for the Retail Price Index are derived, but with other spin-offs too. It has put efforts like Orr's on to a regular basis, and an annual Food Survey is carried out for the Ministry of Agriculture and Fisheries. And in 1970 it started a more general survey of housing and social conditions which has provided a wealth of high quality data for current and future social researchers. The General Household Survey is the nearest thing in the United Kingdom to the American National Opinion Research Center's General Social Survey; the questions in the GSS, however, are somewhat more attitudinal and are rather more closely researched. But the big difference comes in the two organisations' attitudes to other users. NORC market this rich data source actively, whereas the Social Survey has not prioritised making the data easily available for academics.

For many of the survey historians, this is the natural end point of the story: active governments, committed to welfare and social intervention, linking with those who have the technical expertise to provide them with the data they need for their compassionate social programmes. There are, of course, other ways of recounting the history of the welfare state (Gough 1979) and previous complacency is getting a rude shock with the advent of a stridently anti-egalitarian and anti-welfare government, which may be expected to bring with it an attack on social research.

The other tremendous growth point in the last thirty years has been in what might be loosely termed consumer research. Welfare capitalism, unwilling or unable to plan production very successfully, has taken great strides forward in planning consumption, not only of its goods and services, through market research of various kinds, but also of its cultural products, through readership surveys and audience research, and of its political products, through both public and private political opinion polls. This has opened up the domain of the subjective to much wider, rigorous inquiry than ever before. Publications such as *Social Trends* include more subjective items, and have carried a couple of articles on 'subjective social indicators' (Abrams 1973) which aim to give a kind of consumer's verdict on the satisfaction derived from various social goods. The main vehicle for such inquiries has been the survey, and a large number of commercial research organisations, some tied to specific companies (like Unilever) or specific newspapers (like the Daily Mail's ownership of National Opinion Polls), and some independent ventures have grown up over the years. It remains to be seen whether the growth will continue into a period of industrial and commercial decline.

Several methodological innovations have accompanied this growth. The commercial companies have pioneered the use of quota sampling, which is spurned by statisticians because its error margins are not calculable, but which the market researchers have found much better value for money when performed with adequate controls. These companies have also exploited to very great advantage recent advances in telecommunications and automatic data-processing. But research into the key problem of question-wording has lagged behind. There were some investigations into the effects that changing seemingly similar minor words in a question could have on responses in the 1940s, mainly in the USA. Despite some interesting and provocative findings, after the late 1940s virtually no more work was done on this topic until the late 1970s, when the Institute for Social Research and National Opinion Research Centre in the USA and Social and Community Planning Research in the UK began to give the matter some attention.

The reasons for this are hard to fathom. They undoubtedly stem partly from the sheer embarrassment that the findings caused to the new companies eager to establish their scientific credentials and to sell their wares. But they also stem from the hold, in this country at any rate, that the statistical profession has had over surveys. Science, as Peter Medawar (1968) has argued, is the art of the soluble; statisticians have concentrated their attention on sampling because it is the big success story. No adequate theory of 'response error' (the well-known syndrome of blaming the victim when things go wrong) has yet been put forward. Still this does not completely explain why the detailed studies that are beginning to take place now in documenting at least the size and scope of the problem have taken so long to be performed.

Opinion polls have brought with them methodological changes, one of which is a further development of thinking about the subjects of study. We saw how at the beginning of the twentieth century a transition was made from informant to respondent. A further shift has occurred from respondent to citizen, albeit not a particularly free citizen. The polling conception of a survey has become so dominant, and has penetrated so fundamentally into our very idea of sociology, that I shall concentrate on it, and on the fundamental differences there are between it and a sociological survey, in the final chapter.

(2) The Causal Logic of Survey Analysis

The self-styled 'survey tradition' is usually the only history of the survey method that is recounted. Histories concentrate on the development of the social survey as a way to collect together social facts to settle debates about population growth, to expose terrible urban conditions, or help administrators make plans of various kinds. The task now is to try to give an account of the much less well-understood development of some kind of inferential reasoning on the basis of the information gathered about the causes behind the patterns discovered. This is in part the history of the development of a social science, rather than the development of complex processes for social administration. We must trace the development of an understanding, in whatever crude form, that one can infer from the way things are something of the cause of their being in that state and that one can on that basis begin to erect explanations over and above descriptions.

Now, clearly the line between description and explanation is hard to draw for several reasons, and it is especially dangerous to start equating explanation with science and description with non-science. As biologists will tell you, many years of careful biological activity went into the pre-Darwinian classification of species into different groups; perhaps, some may argue, sociology has been forced to have an extended period in its Linnaean phase. Explanation and description interact. The major conclusion from much of the recent activity in the philosophy of social science is that there can be no theory-free observation language for recording facts in an entirely neutral way. The very certain categories we use for collecting the original data predispose us to answering particular types of questions.

There are three things that are required for the development of causal thinking in surveys: (1) The theories the scientist is working with must themselves be expressed in valid causal terms. (2) The original data collection and measurement must be adequate to produce worthwhile data; the categorisation must be sensitive enough to pick up important variation, and it must try to avoid circularity in setting categories up which prove only one point of view and do not even allow the test of alternatives. (3) Some technical apparatus has to be to hand to measure association between variables and to allow controls to be placed on some intercorrelated variables.

Epidemiological Intuitions about Cause
When one reads the early surveys and statistical investigations of the pioneers, it is very hard to appreciate how little they had worked out their views of causality on a systematic basis. Indeed, in the first volume of the *Journal of the Statistical Society of London* in 1838, it is carefully explained that 'The Science of Statistics differs from Political

Economy, because, although it has the same end in view, it does not discuss causes, nor reason upon probable effects; it seeks only to collect, arrange and compare ... facts' (Editorial 1838). One can often find intuitive causal logic being applied, but it is never made explicit, so the insights of a few geniuses get lost. The early construction of life tables with age-specific mortality rates could represent the germ of an idea of imposing logical controls in order to make valid conclusions about causes of death, but it is very easy to overinterpret the gains of the seventeenth-century demographers in this area.

However, by the nineteenth century, in the inquiries into the health and sanitary arrangements of the working class and the army, we can see an implicit but quite sophisticated view of causality. A study of morbidity and mortality rates of troops stationed in the West Indies in the 1830s by a young Scottish Lieutenant Tulloch is a good example (Lever 1839). He was able to show that the current belief that mortality decreased with age was wrong. By constructing age-specific mortality rates, he showed that other factors, such as diet, were much more important; mortality was much lower among the officers who got fresh rations of meat. He also showed that temperature and moisture were not causal factors because they did not vary systematically with sickness and mortality. Similarly, Edwin Chadwick tried to use correlational evidence of this kind to show that there must be a causal factor called 'miasma' which was responsible for the very high rates of illness and death in early industrial towns. Although his miasma theory was of course incorrect, none the less it acted as useful propaganda for sanitation, because 'miasma' (that is, a terrible smell) was most marked in poor living conditions where disease microbes concentrate.

But the most impressive of all is the tireless work of the head of the statistical branch of the General Register Office, William Farr. He was not hampered by Chadwick's notion that there must be one underlying cause of death and disease, and this allowed him to attempt to assess multiple influences. He also elaborated a sophisticated 'nosology', a classification of diseases, so that he was explaining variance in a measure that had some substantive importance. The combination of these two intellectual building blocks meant that he could use the data collected by the Registrar-General's office and published in the Annual Reports to make statements about the causal influence of region, weather, overcrowding, epidemics, and so on, on death rates; the early Annual Reports all have a letter from Farr as an appendix.

Theories of Cause

One of the earliest people to systematise some of this causal logic was a Belgian mathematician called Quetelet, who took an interest in 'social physics' and who helped organise the census in Belgium in 1826. He started collecting and publishing averages and rates of things like crime, and he noticed that the empirical distribution looked rather like the error distributions that French astronomers were discovering, and began to see if normal and binomial distributions could be fitted to these empirical distributions. Although we would not nowadays accept that the regularities in these distributions have the status of 'laws', nor that there was any quintessential 'homme moyen' or social average type, this was a significant advance. Moreover, Quetelet was quite happy to contemplate multiple causality, and constructed multivariate tables, breaking down crime rates by age and sex. Many see his contribution as pivotal to the development of quantitative social science. Indeed, Lazarsfeld reckons he really grasped that observations across a cross-section of people could replace observations over time (Lazarsfeld 1961).

But although many people were working with *de facto* theories of causation, no one had tried to make explicit the method of recognising a cause. The problem is still with us and continues to stimulate hot philosophical debate. John Stuart Mill, in his *System of Logic*, had put forward hypostatised conditions under which one might recognise a cause, but had no suggestions about how to achieve them. His canon of concomitant variation only gave guidance in the case of perfect relationships and simple causality. This and other mistaken notions about causality held many early sociologists back. Durkheim in particular was very influential in authoritatively documenting his confusions in a set of Rules which others then attempted to follow (Selvin 1965). Durkheim was not alone in believing that each outcome, event, or effect could have only one cause. The notion that there might be several inputs into an outcome, or that variables might be related to one another in a probabilistic rather than in a deterministic fashion, was very slow to develop. Indeed, in a classic methodology text of the late 1960s, the authors still find it necessary, in a chapter entitled 'Some Mistakes about Causality', to spell these misconceptions out and show how they have misled a wide number of different criminological researchers (Hirschi and Selvin 1973).

The other two requirements for the development of causal survey analysis were a good classification system and the techniques for measuring association and partial association. Durkheim is responsible for another confusion in the requirements of a classification system, in his demand for 'aetiological' rather than 'morphological' classification systems. He insisted that you should classify suicides into different types according to different causes, rather than according to different superficial appearances. He suggested there were three (or four) basic causes of suicide – egoism, altruism, anomie (and sometimes fatalism). But if you make such sweeping assumptions in your very classification system, how are you ever going to show independently that your causal hypothesis is valid? You constantly run the risk of circular reasoning. The only independent evidence that Durkheim could try to adduce for his scheme was that he had ruled everything else out – a rather dangerous line of argument, for you can never be sure that the things you did rule out constitute the universe of possible rival explanations.

None the less, and despite Durkheim's best efforts to subvert the enterprise, the ideas of independent classification systems which could be justified on outside criteria, and the apparatus of measuring association and the logic of multiple causality did develop. And at this point of the story, the three prerequisites come together for a powerful period in the eugenics movement, where a concern with measuring one particular thing, namely IQ, was being developed alongside a particular theory of causation and control, namely regression theory.

Eugenics, Regression Theory and Mental Testing

Fear of the lowest strata of society, the mob, criminals, lunatics all barely distinguished, was, as we have seen, a characteristic of much nineteenth-century research. Booth had shaded this element in with black on his maps of London, and considered a policy of forcibly removing this sector to labour camps (Jones 1971: 306-7). The link between poverty and other forms of distress and low intelligence or 'feeble-mindedness' was a tenet of faith for many of the middle class investigators long before they had any means of measuring IQ. This lumpen element was poisoning the 'respectable' working class. The eugenicists carried this belief through to a political programme of Social Darwinism, which aimed to restrict the breeding of those whose stock of mental attributes was inferior.

It is under something of a cloud today. Disgusted by the racial doctrines of Nazism, of Aryan supremacy and purity of stock, many have searched for the intellectual antecedents of such a repugnant philosophy and, finding the nearest thing in Britain being the eugenics movement, have in turn been repulsed by that. But it is a mistake to call the eugenicists early fascists (Searle 1979). They were not; they were a particular brand of middle class intellectuals, many of whom considered themselves socialist, at least in an anti-*laissez-faire* sense of the word. Eugenics happened to provide a very convenient ideology for the newly mobile; the idea that innate mental qualities are unevenly distributed and are found predominantly among the children of those who were successful in the previous generation was undoubtedly appealing to them (Mackenzie 1979).

Galton and Pearson, the two pioneers of both the eugenics movement and the early apparatus of correlation and regression, both passionately believed that social qualities were largely inherited, and they wanted measures of inheritability and coefficients of correlation between parents and children. Galton, himself one of a most distinguished family, was driven by no abstract interest in mathematics, but by a desire more concretely to apply his cousin, Darwin's, ideas of natural selection to humans; building on ideas of the positive effect of mutation and random selection, he was keen to see how the two distributions of characteristics of fathers and sons might be related, and thus worked out the fundamentals of the theory of regression, which hypothesised a process generating human characteristics in this fashion. Pearson, a founder member of the Eugenics Society, elaborated this into a mathematical system and derived formulae where Galton had only managed to express his ideas graphically. Thus he equipped the eugenics movement with the technical apparatus for fulfilling its proclaimed socialistic intentions of a complete meritocracy where only the able would be allowed to reproduce.

The techniques for measuring intelligence directly had not been invented at this time. The work of Binet in France was under way, but the great spur came when Spearman introduced factor analysis to the statistical community. He was a disciple of Galton's, and was also convinced of the inherited qualities of intelligence. He thought that this assumption was corroborated by the fact that there was always one general factor which resulted from the reduction of items in an intelligence test by a method of extracting principal components (Sharpe 1978). He must also get credit for elaborating an important set of ideas about the kinds of errors one could expect in measurement and how to assess them, ideas which have been part of the psychologist's stock in trade for years, but which have still not adequately penetrated sociological thinking.

These advances in regression theory received a very powerful boost in the hands of the brilliant statistician R. A. Fisher. Working at the Rothamsted experimental plant station in the 1920s and 1930s, he generalised ideas of analysis of variance, and began to argue for improved techniques of experimental design based on the principle of random allocation. His books, *Statistical Methods*, published in 1925, and *The Design of Experiments*, first published in 1935, gave his supporters the texts they needed as a basis for a distinctive new discipline of mathematical statistics, which was very remote from the activities of the social surveyors. We find it very hard to remember nowadays quite how new and revolutionary these ideas were (see Box 1978, Ch. 6 for an account of the impact of *The Design of Experiments*). The practical outcome was that experiments could now be designed which genuinely fulfilled Mill's canons and held everything constant but for one factor; the way this was achieved was through the simple device of creating a control and experimental group through random allocation. The excitement about this innovation was so great that interest in 'natural experiments' suffered an eclipse, certainly among statisticians of the Pearson ilk.

The dominant interests of Galton, Pearson and Fisher were in attributes which could be measured on an interval scale, and since they assumed that the process generating these attributes was inheritance with random mutation, posited that the error distributions for all these qualities must be normal. Interest in counted data was temporarily suspended. This delayed the development of the apparatus of association in survey data which was more often than not collected in a form which permitted numbers in a category to be counted and little more. The prevailing measure of association was Pearson's, based on the assumption of underlying multivariate normality. The only tabular information that this can be applied to is a 2×2 table, where again you have to make the assumption that the cutting points are arbitrary divisions made on top of an underlying normal distribution. One must assume, for example, that the division of cases into those where a drug worked and those where it did not, is an arbitrary line drawn down the middle of an underlying spectrum of successfulness. This denies some very important 'natural' divisions, such as the difference between none and some, or between natural integers like number of children. But it fitted in well with a theory of regression.

There was no shortage of other ideas, but these simply did not gain ground. Retracing our steps a bit, we find George Udny Yule, in many ways the real founding father of survey analysis, battling with Pearson at the beginning of the century about how to measure association in a contingency table; he rejected the assumptions on which Pearson's measure for 2×2 tables was based, and proposed a measure of his own that did not rely on underlying multivariate normality (MacKenzie 1979). Moreover, he understood the logic of controlling variables in non-experimental situations where the variation had occurred naturally, without randomisation and manipulation. In the *Introduction to the Theory of Statistics*, first published in 1911, he insisted that multiple causality was a reality, and that controls must be introduced. He introduced his own measure of association for contingency tables, Q. By the fifth edition in 1919 the chi-squared distribution was included. By the seventh edition in 1924 the simple notion of crosstabulating, of laying the aggregated numbers out in rows and columns, was introduced.

But these quite simple ideas were neglected in other statistics textbooks which dealt solely with Pearsonian ideas, and in social survey texts which never mention anything other than sampling theory, and occasionally percentages as a descriptive tool. Once again, we are faced with a problem of understanding why these ideas, once elaborated, did not spread. Selvin has even shown that ignorance cannot be the explanation, because Yule engaged in debate with Booth about the presentation and interpretation of his data, and it is also likely that Durkheim had read periodicals in which Yule was writing (Selvin 1976). Once again, the unsatisfactory explanation that there was a failure to institutionalise is put forward. More plausible is the view that enthusiasm for methods based on the analysis of variance were more exciting from a mathematical point of view, and provided grist to a political mill of eugenics. Moreover, as we saw in the last section, the kinds of surveys done in the crucial interwar years were not very exciting and did not attract the attention of the best statisticians to them.

So the apparatus for tables with more than two rows or columns was not developed; analogous measures to partial correlations and interactions in analysis of variance were not elaborated. Yule's discovery of the importance of the cross-product ratio in many different measures in contingency tables was not discussed again until 1935 when a paper appeared in the *Journal of the Royal Statistical Society* on interactions in tables (Bartlett 1935), and then nothing further developed until well after the war. Great excitement about experiments dominated the field, and led to a concentration on measures of significance rather than on measures of association; the reason for this is that when you have manipulated the variance, the marginals do not contain any new information, and so significance tests and the analysis of variance are much more important. All the technical developments for elaborating statistical models for contingency data were there for the asking by 1919, but it took until after the Second World War for Lazarsfeld to elaborate the logic and for Goodman to develop the concepts and models for handling contingency data.

The social and political climate of eugenics did not just give rise to this technical apparatus, however. It also stimulated research that certainly asked causal questions, attempting to give a sound empirical basis to its central tenets. Previous studies had failed to separate social class and intelligence in their basic classification schemes; take, for example, the study in Sheffield in 1919, which attempted to classify people as follows: 'Class 1 includes those who are more or less free from the prison of the flesh . . . the educated. Class 3 are positive failures . . . these are the rotters, the wastrels, the Yahoos. From their loins come the intellectually feeble' (St Phillips Settlement 1919). It is not hard to see why the proponents of IQ testing were so convinced of the class independence of their measures when they replaced these sorts of classification systems!

The other group that had an interest in IQ and influences on mental attainment were educationalists, propounders of meritocratic philosophy and local authorities providing education. They felt it was important for them to know what the stock of mental capacities was, and how open to environmental influence (that is, education) it was. The London County Council took the unprecedented step of appointing a psychologist, Cyril Burt, to look into some of these questions (Sutherland and Sharp 1980). (He is in disgrace today, since it has been discovered that he faked some of his data; see Beloff 1980.) He conducted many investigations into the determinants of IQ, the correlation between IQ and social class, the inheritability of IQ, its influence on income, the causes of 'feeble-mindedness', and so on. His are the most famous studies, but the concern of administrators in this period of population decline also showed in other studies. Godfrey Thompson in Edinburgh was doing very similar work and the Merseyside survey did a special sample of those who were socially inadequate in a variety of ways, for example.

The Logic of Survey Analysis

By far the biggest contribution to thinking about the use of survey data to answer sociological questions, which are of their essence causal, was given by the quite extraordinarily original and prolific writings of one man, Paul Lazarsfeld. An Austrian social democrat, trained as a mathematician but, because of his political interests, soon concerned by the problems produced by the collapse of Austrian society in the 1930s, he worked with the Buhlers in Vienna at their new Psychological Institute, and led the team of investigators who documented the social disintegration of a village, Marienthal, where virtually everyone had been made unemployed. Before he left Austria, he had become convinced of the urgent need to bring together the insights of sociography with the rigour of more systematic investigations. In an autobiographical reflection (Lazarsfeld 1969) he says that the desire to weld the qualitative and the quantitative, introspectionism and behaviourism, intensive and extensive methods, subjective and objective stemmed from him alone – they were his 'personal equations' with which he could not interest anyone else.

When he first went to the USA on a Rockefeller fellowship he gained a quick reputation by pointing out that the disturbing negative correlation between unemployment and education would disappear if you controlled for age; the older you are the less education you are likely to have had and the more likely you are to be unemployed (1969: 294). Being Jewish, he decided not to return to Austria after the Dolfuss coup, and became one of the intellectual émigrés who so enriched postwar American academic life. He threw himself into establishing a research organisation and became director of a large

Rockefeller project on radio research. He found that the new market research industry could provide funds for many projects which had potentially important spin-offs in advancing basic understanding of the cultural determinants of choice; when the US psychological profession proved unprepared to dirty its hands with this, he moved more into the orbit of US sociology, and during the war his Office of Radio Research changed into the Bureau of Applied Social Research at Columbia.

A whole literature on the importance of the 'managerial scholar' in social research has grown up wishing to treat Lazarsfeld as the paradigm to be copied (or to be bemoaned – C. W. Mills's (1959) attack on abstracted empiricism and his arrogant remarks about intellectual administrators directing research technicians was a direct parry against his fellow sociologist at Columbia and his Bureau). His combination of ferocious intellect, mathematical ability, political sensitivity and organisational drive turned the Bureau into one of the most successful research institutes ever. But the literature wrongly regarded this success as the norm, and wondered repeatedly why there was such a 'failure' to consolidate and institutionalise in this way elsewhere whereas in fact the Bureau is the exception requiring explanation. Indeed, since Lazarsfeld's death in 1976 the Bureau has virtually collapsed, and the verdict of its biographer is that, in the end, not even Lazarsfeld could institutionalise social research in a way that was not dependent on the person involved (Barton 1979).

Intellectually, Lazarsfeld's contributions have ranged far and wide, but his most significant one was in developing the approach known as 'survey analysis'. The early papers on this new approach to elaborating complex paths of causality in contingency data (Kendall and Lazarsfeld 1950; Lazarsfeld 1955) are not worth reading as introductory texts; other writers since have elucidated them and taken the basic ideas further (Hyman 1955; Rosenberg 1968; Hirschi and Selvin 1973; Davis 1971). But they represent an entirely original approach to the problem of elucidating cause from the evidence of association.

Other statisticians also became interested in contingency tables as the results analysis began to pepper the intellectual scene, and Leo Goodman formalised ways of fitting models to such causal structures. It is always an advance when it is possible to hypothesise models for how distributions were generated and then to measure how well the model fits the data. The application of this development to sociology is too early to assess, however; there are still arguments about the interpretation of these models. Many sociologists still feel happier with the research *style* of elaboration, starting with an interesting correlation and then unplugging it in different ways (Oldman 1973).

American sociologists, especially those connected with the

Bureau, soon took advantage of the explanatory power of these techniques and many postwar classics of American sociology depend on it. It has never really caught on in British sociology. Perhaps it is seen as a foreign cultural product; the differences between US and UK sociology must not be underemphasised. In the 1950s and early 1960s there was a burst of activity arising from the programme of research at the London School of Economics, headed by David Glass, around issues of social stratification, education and social mobility. Researchers attached to Glass's team included Floud, Kelsall and Tropp, all of whom went on to do important surveys, Floud collaborating with Halsey and Martin at the LSE to produce *Social Class and Educational Opportunity*, Kelsall studying the recruitment, status and organisation of higher civil servants, and Tropp developing theories of professionalism by studying schoolteachers.

Another important institutional locus of good survey work in the late 1950s and early 1960s was Simey's department at the University of Liverpool, where interest was more directed to occupational rather than class theory. Scott, the Bankses, Gittus, Woodward and Mumford were all associated with the department and some very rich studies emanated from this group – *The Dock Worker, Coal and Conflict, The Computer and the Clerk*, to name but a few. What gave rise to this burst of activity after the war is quite complex. Liverpool and the LSE had both become firmly established before the war, and so were in a position to respond to the postwar interest in social stratification. And the personality of David Glass was probably very important in encouraging this work, although the position of Simey in this respect is less important. But this generation of sociologists failed to create inheritors. There are departments of that level of both theoretical and empirical activity today. Goldthorpe and Halsey continued with some impressive work based on Nuffield College. Blackburn and his colleagues at the Department of Applied Economics at Cambridge can perhaps be seen as continuing the Liverpool tradition in Cambridge. They both demonstrate that there are British sociologists who are capable of linking the quantitative sophistication of recent developments in survey analysis with clear sociological thinking. Yet neither group is located in a teaching department which might allow them to have a central impact on training. We are forced to conclude that this fifteen years of activity was not a permanent move away from the traditions of survey research and British sociology well established in the rest of the twentieth century.

Conclusion

There is always a danger of presenting a history as a 'how we got from there to here' account. It is wrong to view the present as an end-point, for there are some extremely exciting and important developments taking place in statistics. The technological base of survey research is being revolutionised by advances in computing, both in the rapid extension of hardware which, when linked to telephone interviewing, reduces costs dramatically, and in the development of more sophisticated software which can handle complex data structures. John Tukey and Frederick Mosteller are giving classical hypothesis-testing and the theory of probability a good shake, and the results (Tukey 1977; Mosteller and Tukey 1977) will be very important for survey analysis. There is a resurgence of interest in the problems of question-wording, and the measurement of the subjective. There is no question of developments stopping.

Survey researchers should take a keener interest in the history of their method than they have done in the past. They should appreciate that the 'survey tradition' of fact-finding is not their only intellectual heritage. They should realise that the fixed-format questionnaire survey does not and has not in the past exhausted the range of possibilities for data collection. The survey method can be, and has been, put to a wide variety of different ends; perhaps the most important thing we have to gain from scrutinising our past is an understanding that a particular method does not restrict you to a particular object of research or institutional or political position.

Notes: Chapter 2

1 There is a dispute about which should be given prime credit for the intellectual developments; they worked closely together, and it is suspected that things supposedly written by Petty were in fact penned by Graunt.
2 This is not a chance metaphor; his later work was entitled *The Political Anatomy of Ireland.*
3 The commitment in principle to a quinquennial survey had been on the statute-book since the beginning of the century. It was finally activated in 1966, but the 1976 census did not take place for absurd financial reasons. It has been estimated that local authorities had spent the sum that the census would have cost within two years doing surveys like the ones described in the 1930s for their own purposes.
4 The personal influence of Harold Wilson, Premier at the time but also a statistician who had worked with Beveridge, is reputed to have been important.

3

The Critics of Surveys

In Search of a Science of Society
In the background all the way through the last chapter there lurked the spectre of a social science. It was, perhaps, much easier to see how various efforts were *not* scientific than to understand what it would involve if they were. The aim of this chapter is to briefly review the major critics of surveys. The most influential of the critics have argued that the mistake made by survey researchers is in their very attempt to be scientific, and at the end of this chapter I shall try to shed some light on the reasons for the popularity of the anti-scientific position. But others have argued that they are insufficiently scientific, and of course at the heart of this dispute there is a disagreement about what any science should be. Sociologists who criticise surveys have often lumped very disparate criticisms together under the eclectic banner of anti-positivism.

Anti-positivism
The criticism that surveys are positivist seems to have grown in popularity as the funds for surveys have declined. While it would take a bold, if not foolhardy, person to argue any too direct a connection between these two trends, none the less the coincidence is too convenient to pass without comment. Surveys are indeed very costly things. And a good quality survey may cost two to three times as much as an inferior version of the same thing, as anyone who has had experience tendering jobs to commercial companies will know (Marsh 1976). Companies offering good fieldwork services have a precarious existence, and badly need the protection of assured funding from some non-profit-making body. If it could be shown that something as costly as this was fundamentally flawed in its conception, how much money could be saved!

The idea of surveys being inherently tarnished through their inevitable positivism has gained sway. This section will examine this claim. But first it will be necessary to examine the nature of the claim, and to consider the growth in popularity of the use of this term 'positivist', whose meteoric rise to fame is even more startling. To fully document how this has happened would take an intellectual historian of unusual acumen, for I do not believe that the story would contain much reference to the printed word. It seems to be part of the *conscience collective* of sociologists which only rarely surfaces to print. It seems particularly prevalent among our students who constantly amaze me by their mouthing of the incantation of the positivist nature of survey research within two days of the start of their sociology course, before they have read any Durkheim or even heard of Auguste Comte. It has become a term of abuse first and foremost, a synonym for crassness in sociological parlance.

It is very hard to define what exactly is meant by the term, for it is, with the exception of Comte's writings, almost never a self-applied label. Kolakowski (1972) defines positivism as a philosophy which says nothing about the origin of knowledge, but which aims to provide a demarcation between the knowledge that deserves the name science and that which does not. He extracts from the wide range of philosophical schools to which the term might apply four main elements which sum up its essence:

   (i) the rule of phenomenalism, which asserts that there is only experience and which rules out all abstractions be they of matter or spirit;
  (ii) the rule of nominalism, which asserts that words, generalisations, or abstractions are linguistic phenomena, and do not give us new insight into the world;
 (iii) the separation of fact and value;
  (iv) the unity of the scientific method.

Much of the scorn against positivism is in fact an attack on the idea of a social science, but it is important that we be clear that these rules are inadequate as a basis for any science. The first two amount to saying that all knowledge is limited to experience, and that it is impossible to go beyond this to some deeper reality; they amount to the rules of empiricism. While historically the development of these postulates about knowledge served a useful purpose in refuting forms of theological idealism, they deny the possibility of cognitive knowledge. Their adoption would deny the search for underlying personality or social structures with dynamics which affect the world of observables but which themselves are not *directly* open to perception. I stress this; positivism is correct in asserting that evidential criteria have to be sought in our sense perceptions of the world, but is incorrect in asserting that theories flow directly from these perceptions. Yet recent developments in the philosophy of science have demonstrated that pre-theoretical observation, and a pre-theoretical observation language, has never existed, and indeed strong arguments have been adduced to show that it never could.

The third postulate would make sociology a purely technical endeavour, collecting the facts *aliis exterendum*, to use the motto of the London Statistical Society; let others use the facts to inform their value positions while we get on with the job. If this postulate is accepted, the only thing that can go wrong with research is that the facts might be wrongly perceived or wrongly reported. The notions that categories used are inevitably based on theoretical positions is denied by the positivist. One can laud attempts to avoid the *personal* faults of bias to be found in social scientists, without hoping to achieve a theory-free *method* of research.

The final postulate asserts the unity of the scientific method. There is no objection to this if we define the scientific method broadly enough. Any scientific endeavour presupposes the existence of regularities in the world which could be uncovered. It strives to build theories which model these regularities. It tries to express the theoretical terms precisely and unambiguously, and to show how they can be operationalised. It leads to formal propositions and rules about what counts as proof and disproof. And it conducts tests of those theories in as open and systematic a manner as possible, checking that the results are generalisable and not specific to a particular investigator, particular place or time, or a particular measuring instrument.

But it is also true that no one has yet managed to specify precisely one method for achieving these laudable goals. It has been tempting to take the common methods of the most 'successful' sciences, like physics, and declare these to be *the* methods of science. This has, quite naturally, come under attack from social scientists who do not find the methods of physics the most useful way to approach their data. The methods of research are bound to be different for conscious and non-conscious subject matters, especially when it comes to that highest form of conscious activity, namely choice, or 'free will'. The 'law of price' is clearly of a very different nature from the 'law of gravity', because it is a result of a social structure that is itself open to manipulation. For this reason, we must minimally expect the laws of the social world to change much more rapidly than the laws of physics. As social scientists, however, we shall often question the freedom of that will. Pierre Bourdieu was able to show how choice of marriage partner in a tiny French village led to inevitability in marriage partners, and yet was still accompanied by the couples falling in love – that emotion that feels the free-est of all. He called this *'amor fati*, that love of one's own social destiny, which, by the apparently hazardous and arbitrary paths of free choice, unites partners already socially predestined for each other' (cited in Le Roy Ladurie 1980: 186). But this is not to rob the human subject of the ability to imagine and intend, of the dignity of refusing to divulge the name of a comrade under torture, of the excitement of falling in love.

Nor does calling the endeavour 'science' say anything about the form of organisation or social location the research should take. We have seen in the historical overview how often research was just needed as a kind of intelligence service for a ruling class which had become separated from the urban poor, conducted by many whose desire for research was motivated by high-handed, manipulative and otherwise offensive doctrines; their ignorance was the product of the social distance between themselves and the objects of their research, which, had their subjects been the researchers, would have obviated the need for almost all the questions. But can the post-Robbins sociologists really see themselves cast in that mould? Do they begin to suspect themselves of inculcating bourgeois ideology? Is it a collective self-doubt that leads to the current spectacle in Britain of the hunt for the positivist 'other'?

Much sociology still acts to show people to one another, but it could be much more profound if conducted by 'insiders'. There is another survey tradition to turn to, that of a social science as a collective effort of a group to become conscious of itself and understand its own dynamics more fully. The earliest manifestations, especially in the 'community self-survey', restricted the group to architects and planners, but Mass-Observation showed that it was possible to involve a wider group. The words 'social science' had none of the same manipulative reverberations in China in the Cultural Revolution when it was used to describe a collective activity. If sociologists are worried that social research is an adjunct of a centralised and manipulative government which they do not sympathise with, perhaps they should criticise the government rather than the research methods.

Positivism is, in fact, like sin: everyone is against it. The question is whether surveys are inherently sinful. Are they good or bad *in themselves*? Do you have to buy this unsatisfactory epistemological package to get the free gift of survey methods? To make this argument, critics would have to show that either the systematic data collection required to produce a case by variable matrix, or the process of analysing the relationships in such a matrix, was bound to be tarnished by the postulates outlined above. The rest of this chapter will consider the most influential criticisms that have been made, first of methods of data collection and measurement in surveys, secondly of the levels of analysis they use and thirdly of the kinds of explanation the analysis leads to. It will quickly become apparent that the criticisms fail to add up to a coherent assault.

Positivist Data Collection and Measurement
The first line of criticism has come from phenomenologists, ethnomethodologists and symbolic interactionists, all of whom see language and meaning as the central reality of social life, and who

make use of a set of arguments in philosophy that hold that social life is not the appropriate subject matter for science; it is created by subjective beliefs, intentions and desires which cannot *a priori* be considered as causes. It cannot be 'explained' but merely 'understood'.

Some, influenced by the philosophical writings of Wittgenstein, see the reason for the distinctiveness of human activity as arising through the use of language. It is through this linguistic capacity that people create the societies they live in and give their actions meaning. Human action is not governed by laws, but is, rather, constituted through the rules of language, and any regularities which we find in human behaviour reflect these common rules rather than any constraining laws (Winch 1958). Rules of course can be broken, whereas it is assumed that laws cannot. Intentions cannot properly be considered as causes because they are an integral, logical part of the outcome, not separate events.

The argument is that all human action is the result of this conscious activity, that people are choosing to follow these linguistic rules and that there is a one-to-one relationship between intentions and outcomes. These are all questionable propositions when one probes them. The idea of a rule, and the equivalence between rule-governed and meaningful, are rather muddled. Taking a stroll can be meaningful without there being a correct way of doing it, as opposed to an incorrect way (MacIntyre 1967). There have been some very powerful demonstrations in social psychology that there are determinants of individual behaviour which are utterly unknown to the actor. Moreover, even where there is a large component of 'intention', it is impossible to show that intentions always lead to the intended outcome (Davidson 1963). The minute you acknowledge the obvious truth that one intention can lead to more than one outcome, or that one outcome can be the result of more than one intention, then the relationship between the two is no longer simply logical – it is up for empirical investigation. In any given piece of behaviour, we are justified in asking whether or not the intention imputed to the actor in it was indeed the cause of the behaviour. A particular intention is not *entailed* by a particular action.

It is very important that we retain our perspective on other languages and other cultures, and continue to ask causal questions about social activities. We must not confuse moral and logical relativism (Lukes 1977), and argue that because it is wrong to view one culture as morally superior to another, it is equally wrong to say that all explanations of the world, from science to magic, have equal status (Gellner 1974). The importance of language in human activity is not denied, but it does not make causal explanation impossible. We can and must go on to probe the extent to which stated intentions or unconscious desires did or did not produce certain outcomes.

But, a second argument runs, the trouble is that identifying causes and identifying desires requires two very different types of evidence; the former type will be external and behavioural, whereas the latter type is bound to be internal and subjective. The only way we can get at the subjective is trying to shed as many of our own preconceptions as possible and to emphasise with the actor's inner life; this type of data collection exercise is radically different from the collection of extensive, behavioural data. The trouble with this argument is that it quickly become solipsistic: how is the subjective experience of another to be known? If there is no other way to explain the activities of bread roundsmen than by becoming one, why not just leave the sociology to the bread roundsmen? One could try to take up the life-style of a particular group whose actions one was trying to under-stand, but there is no reason why the insights that this gave you when you became a member of that group should be communicable to anyone else. These arguments have been specifically addressed to survey research, claiming that it is incapable of approaching the meaningful aspects of social action. In Chapter 5 we shall look constructively at precisely how surveys set about achieving that difficult task, but we shall not address some of the general criticisms head on. They have centred around the measurement of social phenomena and their con-version into variables; they have insisted that the interview is a social interaction as much as any other, and is open to all the interpersonal effects that are found elsewhere in social life.

Survey research uses the language of variables. A variable is a parameter which has one and only one value for each case, and which varies across the population. Numbers are usually assigned to the categories in the process of coding, but these categories need represent nothing more than a nominal level of measurement. (It is interesting to note that this use of number to differentiate is probably its original function; see Struik 1956.) In other words, all that the translation into variable language requires is that when we code something, we must minimally be able to distinguish between a characteristic being present and being absent, which is not really an overstringent requirement. Coding something as a variable 'measured' at a nominal level is doing no more than describing it, making the rules for the description as explicit, systematic and comprehensive as possible. The possibility of making one of the codes 'inapplicable' means that all the cases can be described on one coding system.

There are three prominent critics who have concerned themselves in different ways with measurement problems in surveys, Cicourel, Blumer and Phillips.

Cicourel, in the first chapter of *Method and Measurement* (1964), gives an extremely stringent set of rules for how variables should be constructed. Using the language of measurement derived from psychophysics, he argues that scientific models should be explicit axiomatic theories where the relations between the variables should have a functional form isomorphic to some mathematical system. As he quite correctly notes, explicit theories of this precision are never found in the social sciences. His criticism is directed against attempts to construct a scale with ordinal and interval properties from social data; you have to be able to prove that the thing that you are measuring has the properties that you are trying to measure, rather than just assume that it does. He calls this literal measurement as opposed to measurement by fiat. He rightly notes that some techniques of scaling impose unidimensionality rather than demonstrate its existence, but does not acknowledge the fact that there are other techniques which aim to test this very assumption. The reason why survey research fails to be scientific in his terms is not because his rules are ridiculously stringent, of course, but because social life is mediated through shared meanings.

Cicourel seems shocked to discover that social scientists, when they develop their scales and variables, are not merely reflecting the properties of social phenomena objectively and literally in their measures, but using a commonsense understanding of the meaning of this act or institution for the actors involved. As we shall see in Chapter 5, there are several ways to approach these social meanings in a reliable fashion in a survey. There are some situations in which one can ask people for their reasons directly. There are some subjective variables which can be measured quite successfully. It is possible for outsiders to reliably agree on the meaningfulness of events. These solutions all call for careful and painstaking piloting, but Cicourel seems to imagine that the need for piloting proves his point that the social researcher cannot assume that the commonsense meanings are common to the subjects and the researcher.

This argument has had a popularity among social scientists that I have never been able to fully comprehend. This book is still the most popular book on the reading lists of methodology courses in British universities (Marsh 1979); my heart sinks when I try to imagine what students make of the rather tortured arguments. It is cited in support of the view that surveys have inherent positivistic flaws by those who would consider Cicourel's demand for rigorous measurement of this type even more positivistic. His remarks have force when directed to some attempts at deriving ordinal or interval scales from social data; they also have force with regard to the many surveys that are performed without adequate pretesting and piloting. Not all survey research is of this type, but even if it were, Cicourel would not be able to argue that it has to be that way. One single counter example would be enough to knock his card-house down.

Other critics have focused attention on the problem of interpreting the very 'obvious' variables that survey researchers use. One frequently cited critic is the symbolic interactionist, Herbert Blumer. In two key articles in the 1950s attacking contemporary views of social theory, he argued that until the variables that were being used in the theoretical endeavours were what he called 'generic' variables, nothing interesting would ensue (Blumer 1954 and 1956). Blumer held that we should not be trying to correlate observables, but showing the relationship of one basic attribute of social life to another. He cites as an example the concept of age. When we discover that age is related to some attitude, we need to know, not that age was defined as the answer to the question 'How old were you on your last birthday?', but rather whether the important thing about this correlation is the effect of stage in the life-cycle, generation membership, or epoch (Berger 1960). Blumer is convinced that survey variables will never be able to capture the 'intimate and inner-moving complex of meanings' which underly social processes, but Lazarsfeld or Rosenberg would have responded by suggesting either that the complex variables should be broken down into their components or that intervening variables should be introduced to delineate how any independent variable is producing its effect.

One important derivation of these arguments has been a criticism of the use of structured questionnaires. The first thing to say is that criticisms of questionnaires alone cannot damn surveys as a whole, for questionnaires are not the only systematic method of data collection. Anthropologists have investigated the existence of cultural universals by coding features of various societies (Murdock 1967). Sociologists of the media have made correlations between different factors coded from magazines (Funkhouser 1973). There have been studies of police behaviour where the unit of analysis was the police–citizen interaction and where the method of collecting the data was observation, not interview (Reiss 1971). In situations where it was not possible to conduct structured interviews, researchers have coded the information that they needed afterwards from tape-recordings of the interviews (Brown and Harris 1978). So the criticism of surveys that equates them with structured questionnaires is just ignorant. (However, if you have ever had to go through even a small number of tape-recorded interviews, transcribe them and then code them, you begin to realise why structured questions are so useful when they can be justified. This is why that is the most common way of collecting data.)

But it must be said that structured questionnaires are used too readily, and with insufficient thought; many, perhaps a majority, are inadequately designed and piloted, and, too often for comfort, are not an appropriate way of collecting the information that was required for the problem at hand. It is a damning reflection on survey research as currently practised that no book exists specifically to guide researchers through the pretesting and pilot stages of a survey.

There are huge difficulties with standardised question-wording, but we should note, in passing, the irony of surveys getting blamed for the difficulties that arise in asking questions which are sensitive to minor changes in wording; surveys have highlighted a problem that must exist in any form of data collection which relies upon the answers to questions, and it is quite mistaken to assume that anything less problematic ensues from more informal 'negotiated' interactions in a pub over a pint of beer. Many of the subtle meanings in different adverbial qualifiers, for example, have only been discovered through their use in survey research and through experimenting with different forms of wording in a split-ballot (Bartram and Yelding 1973), so there is no reason to suppose that a 'very' uttered in a pub is any less problematic.

There is no doubt that 'bias' in question-wording has often been dealt with in a very simplistic, not to say 'positivistic', fashion. It has been conceptualised as a deviation from the 'true value' which every individual has in answer to any question which may be tapped accurately or with error (Hansen *et al.* 1951; Alwin 1978). Payne, in an otherwise sensible book on questionnaire design, defines an un-biased question as one which does not itself affect the answer (Payne 1951). But what is this supposed to mean? Does it mean that the answer would be an utterance that the same person would have made spontaneously? Clearly not, for any utterance is spoken for a reason, with the intention of communicating something; spontaneously, there is no reason why people surveyed should desire to convey this information without a reason. The definition is absurd, for we ask questions precisely to get utterances slanted in a particular way. Payne continues: 'one thing has always stumped researchers, and will stump us for a long time to come: having observed different results with different types of questions on the same subject, we still cannot agree on which of the different results comes nearest the truth'. With a definition of truth like his, who can blame researchers for being stumped?

Research into the effects of different forms of question-wording has been pitifully meagre, until recently. Now researchers in both Britain (Kalton *et al.* 1978) and in the USA (Schuman and Presser 1981; Bradburn and Sudman 1979) are investigating these problems systematically. The results of this research do not have to be inter-preted as distinguishing 'true values' from 'errors' but rather can be broken down into research on the various ways in which the social context of the interview and the task required of the respondent have an impact on the type of responses that are given. This research will not enable us to remove these effects, as the 'true value' paradigm suggests is its goal, but should improve our understanding of the interview as a process of social interaction and enable us to design interviews which achieve higher degrees of communication between the interviewer and the respondent. Reactivity is a fact of life in social research. We cannot get away from the problems by positing a notion of an underlying true value and blaming the respondent to the question when she makes a 'response error'.

Critics of interviews, however, have frequently gone much further than this in their criticism of structured questionnaires. Instead of conducting the painstaking research required to pin these problems down, some critics have instead proposed that we abandon this attempt to get at the social world, and indeed 'abandon method'. The development of the ideas in two books by Derek Phillips is a good case in point of this kind of thinking. In his earlier book, *Knowledge from What?* (1971), Phillips reviews some of the problems that have been shown to exist in communication in interviews. He reminds us that attributes of the interviewer can have their effect on responses given to this interviewer (although he is somewhat selective in his reporting of the literature, and does not review the findings of many who have concluded that interviewer characteristics are not an important source of difficulty in interviewing). Attributes of the subject may lead to problems, especially when the subject tries to please the interviewer, or is apprehensive about the likelihood of an evaluation of performance resulting from the responses given in interviews, or tends to agree to anything the interviewer says. Human beings need social approval, not just for themselves as people, but also for the views that they hold. The physical setting of the research can have important effects on responses, claims Phillips (although here again his evidence is weak and has not generally been borne out). And perhaps most importantly, respondents have expectations of what is required of them, and will try to get clues about what it is that the interviewer or researcher expects.

In this first book, Phillips argues quite plausibly that interviews are often used when they are not the most appropriate method of data collection, but he concedes that there are occasions when they are the best way of collecting information – when details of past activities, private activities, motives, beliefs, or attitudes are under study (a long list!). They generate data that is standardised, amenable to statistical treatment and can be generalised. If triangulated with other methods they have their uses. But by the time he wrote *Abandoning Method* (1974), a curious cocktail of Kuhn, Winch, Wittgenstein and Feyerabend was having an effect on him, and he concludes that social scientists, being no special breed of human beings, should stop trying to pretend that they have any peculiar claim to social knowledge, and should rely on the method of introspection, and try to look at the world 'through their own eyes' rather than through the scientific instruments which are currently clouding their vision. In effect we are back to the ridiculous idea of Payne that it is possible to perceive the world without the instruments of perception.

At least Phillips openly admits that he has changed his mind between his first and second books about the possibility of using survey methods. There is a much deeper ambiguity in *Method and Measurement*. Cicourel admits in the introduction that he takes a rather extreme position on the need for literal measurement in his first chapter, and claims that the subsequent chapters show that he does not in practice make these stringent demands on the different research methods; he is not proposing that 'sociologists stop all further research and measurement until the basic categories of daily life have been clarified and their numerical properties ordered axiomatically'. But, he insists, nor is he arguing that these methods could simply be improved. He is rather seeking 'clarification of sociological equivalence classes at this level of basic and substantive theory' and he intends to do this by improving 'the methodological foundations of sociological research' (1964: 3).

To judge whether he achieves these grandiose (and none too clear) aims, one turns to his chapter on the use of fixed format questionnaires. 'Standardised questions with fixed-choice answers provide a solution to the problem of meaning simply by ignoring it', declares Cicourel; survey researchers treat the meaning of events and situations as 'self-evident'. Some clearly do, but any reader who thinks this is true for the entire class of survey researchers should turn now to Chapter 5 and read the account of the two years George Brown and his team spent designing scales which could assess the threat associated with events that happened in their subjects' lives. Cicourel elaborates (1964: 109-11) nine rules which would need to apply before one could treat the results of fixed questions as meaningfully valid.

(1)   Every response would have to be explicable theoretically.
(2)   Pretests would have to have been done.
(3)   The social researcher would have to know the situation so well that the responses to questionnaire items could be read as indicators of a social process.
(4)   Question and response would have to use familiar language the meaning of which was not to be altered by context.
(5)   Clock time must agree with actor's experience of time.
(6)   Meanings of questions would have to be understood identically.
(7)   Researchers need a theory of meaning to show how (4) and (6) have been achieved.

(8)   The forced nature of the questions would have to be removed.
(9)   It is not just enough to say that the words must be understand-
      able but the meanings which respondents have must be
      translated to the social scientist's language by means of invariant
      correspondences.

There are two themes underlining these rules. The first is perfectly
acceptable, namely, that all the small decisions about coding and
grouping that are made in the course of the research should (*a*) be
recorded and (*b*) be defended according to some theoretical rationale.
To the extent that Cicourel can be read as arguing for a much greater
discussion of these points of detail, his contribution could be very
positive. But his insistence that the questions should be understood
identically and not open to different interpretation according to
'particular relevance structures' is much more problematic. He is not
just asking for unambiguous questions; every textbook that has ever
been written on questionnaire design suggests that this is a good aim.
When treating peope's beliefs and attitudes, there is a very thin line
dividing the meaning people endow social objects with and their feelings about them. When you ask people their attitudes to the EEC,
they are *not* all really responding to the same stimulus, because they
all have different associations with this object. The researcher will be
keen to discover precisely how views of the EEC vary according to
'particular relevance structures', if I understand the term correctly.
And one interesting method of eliciting the assumptions respondents
make about events and institutions is to probe precisely what they
mean by and associate with particular stimuli. Stressing the need for
invariant meanings capable of being coded by explicit literal rules of
correspondence is effectively saying that this type of research is
simply impossible, until indeed the basic categories of daily life *have*
been clarified and their numerical properties ordered axiomatically,
whatever he says he is arguing.

Structured questionnaires are not the only way of collecting
systematic information from a cross-section of cases, but they
constitute a very popular way of doing so. They always run into
difficulties with unanticipated definitions and responses, as Cicourel
points out, so, to succeed, they rely on very careful piloting (for a
painstaking example from the National Readership Survey, see
Belson 1968). Neither do they have a monopoly on the problems of
meaningfulness of social action. They have problems of their own
which require more thought and research than they have been given
to date. But discussions like this are cited in defence of the case that
the problems are insurmountable. Certainly, Cicourel never went on
to show how it could be done, or to elaborate a theory of meaning
which could achieve his fourth and sixth rules.

The Atomist Fallacy

Another way that surveys might be shown to be inherently positivist would be to prove that they committed one to a particular level of analysis. You would be forgiven for thinking that the fallacy historically associated with positivism through the writings of Durkheim and Comte was that of holism, of assuming that there was anything real about properties of whole groups of societies independent of properties of members of those collectivities. But the majority of critics have levelled the charge of atomism:

> Their fundamental source of information is a sample of individuals. The questions asked in these studies are put in terms of the psychological reactions of individuals. Accordingly, the assumption is required that the historical structure of society, in so far as it is to be studied in this way, can be understood by means of such data about individuals. (Mills 1959: 79)

This charge that surveys are fundamentally incapable of perceiving structural effects has reverberated through many of the criticisms.

But it simply will not hold water. To be sure, it is a danger, as the best survey practitioners have recognised: 'Quantification, so important in providing evidence in support of generalizations, has often produced an artificial atomism of the organized social structures under investigation' (Blau 1957: 58). But it is corrigible. First, if there is to be only one level of analysis, the unit does not have to be the individual, as we have seen. It could be the household, the firm, a society, village, or even units of time. The danger involved in only looking at collectivities is dealt with in the traditional criticisms made against holism: it reifies social processes, and suggests that there is something real and tangible about social forces independent of individual actions. But these criticisms can be met by designing a study so that the measurements are made at the appropriate level of analysis, and the effects of processes at one level on outcomes at another can be empirically tested.

There are a wide variety of ways in which variables can be related to one another at different levels and lead to a hierarchical dataset. It is very important that researchers specify how they hypothesise their relationships take effect. If, in a random cross-section of workers drawn from many different workplaces, we found a negative correlation between shift-working and class-consciousness, it could be because

(1) working shifts makes individuals less likely to develop class-consciousness regardless of what other people in their factory do;

(2) people on shift work come from factories where shift work is done; under these conditions the whole factory fails to develop class-consciousness, shift-workers and day workers alike;
(3) shift work is more common in particular industries which for some historical reasons unrelated to shift work directly have had a non-militant tradition.

In other words, it could be an individual effect, a contextual effect, or a global effect, or a combination of these (Lazarsfeld and Menzel 1961). On a simple cross-section we could not pin down which. There is no need for *ad hoc* rationalisations made after the event to explain why the negative correlation resulted. Such arguments can be very dangerous, as Hauser has shown (1970). But if the competing explanations can be anticipated, with some careful thought a study could be designed of several factories and workers within those factories to illuminate some of these interesting questions.

The sociology of organisations has pioneered the collection of data on how individuals relate to other individuals, the creation of various aggregate indices and the comparison of group effects with individual effects held constant. Blau stressed as long ago as 1957 that features of the group of organisation as a whole, aspects of its *Gestalt*, could also be brought into the picture alongside aggregated features of the collectivity, and many industrial sociologists have taken up these methods.

But hierarchical data structure is not the only answer to the charge of atomism. We can also collect data on individuals and their relationships with other individuals. In studies of diffusion of new information among doctors, Coleman, Katz and Menzel set out to discover the views of doctors' friends, as well as the doctors themselves, through a technique known as 'snowball sampling' (Coleman *et al.* 1957). They picked a random start, and then got each doctor they interviewed to tell them the names of his closest colleagues. Coleman (1959) has summarised the various sampling and analytic strategies open to the researcher who wishes to avoid the pitfalls of atomism.

It must be pointed out that the statistical apparatus for handling the analysis of such data is rather underdeveloped; the problems of sampling inference and degrees of freedom are very complex. Furthermore, the only user-friendly computer software available for survey analysis at the moment requires that the data be rectangular, that is, a straightforward case by variable matrix, to be processed by looking for relationships between variables, not between cases. If you have a survey that has information stored hierarchically, converting this into rectangular data matrices can be tedious, although guides do exist on how to do this (Sonquist and Dunkelberg 1977). We can look forward to the next generation of software which will make available to 'naïve users' the advantages of more sophisticated methods of handling hierarchical and relational data. When we can move from individual to household to village or from worker to factory with great ease, then perhaps this potentially exciting way of handling data will become more popular. There are gains to be made from studying institutions rather than having to infer their effects from individual data. This is why, for all its faults, *Fifteen Thousand Hours*, a study of twelve London secondary schools and the children in them, is such a tremendous step forward in the endless debate on the effects that the education system has on children (Rutter *et al.* 1979).

Attack on Positivism from the Rationalists

Another way to make the charge that surveys are *inherently* positivist would be to argue that drawing causal inferences from patterns in data suffered from one of the flaws associated with Kolakowski's four rules mentioned earlier. If one did not recognise the role of theory and assumptions in drawing inferences from correlations, then that practice could potentially commit these mistakes, but again, it does not intrinsically. Indeed, it is the positivist who, because of the empiricism inherent in the first two postulates of positivism, cannot accept that the aim of science is to uncover the causal relationships between things. Ideas of cause and mechanism, indeed the very idea of necessity, is an abstraction erected by theory. It is the positivist who must deny the difference between correlation and causation. The empiricist Karl Pearson spelt this out very clearly in his *Grammar of Science* (1892).

None the less, it is on attempts at causal explanation in surveys that a group of anti-positivists whom I shall characterise as 'rationalists' have focused their attack. If I am to be guided by a survey of texts most frequently mentioned in British social science courses in selecting representatives (Marsh 1979), I would pick Hindess's *Use of Official Statistics in Sociology* (1973), and the work of David and Judith Willer. Since the publication of E. P. Thompson's withering attack on the Althusserian rationalism of Hindess and Hirst (Thompson 1979), readers may be referred to that. The fact that Hindess does claim that he is making suggestions about how empirical research should be done should not conceal the basically anti-empirical stance of his philosophy.

So the Willers will have to do the honours. The two texts for consideration are one by David Willer published in 1967 entitled *Scientific Sociology* and one by both David and Judith Willer published in 1974 called *Systematic Empiricism*. Both books ostensibly claim to hold that a science of society is possible; they argue that it will not be achieved by the current use of 'systematic empiricism' and will only be accomplished by a rationalist theory-building activity. Both books claim that this rational science will make use of empirical evidence, but will do it through abstraction, not through generalisation, through logically produced categories, rather than empirically or operationally defined variables, by providing explanations unlimited in scope of applicability to particular times and places, rather than by providing historically specific descriptions. What a wonder this science will be to behold – and quite unlike any other science! When this conception is examined more closely, it turns out to be a fake. It is no accident that the first book, while claiming to be a description of what a Scientific Sociology is, is more an attack on what it is not. And the second gives not one clue of how Systematic Empiricism is to be avoided if the empirical world is to be approached.

The picture painted of a social science in *Scientific Sociology* is familiar. There is the familiar denunciation of survey research as being inherently atomist in that it inevitably treats individuals. There is also an 'attack' on random sampling, proposing instead that we should perform 'scope sampling', aiming not to make generalisations about a finite set of individual cases, but to establish 'conditional universal truths' about human affairs. Return oh ye gods of absolute truth! (In fact, all they really require is disproportional stratified sampling to ensure that a sufficient number of cases have been collected to ensure that the applicability of the hypothesis under investigation can be properly tested in widely differing circumstances.)

The best thing about *Systematic Empiricism* is its opening statement, that is is wrong to confuse 'empirical' with 'empiricist'. After that, it slides pretty sharply down a slippery slope into historical inaccuracy (the section on Pearson and Fisher's contribution to the statistics for testing causal hypotheses is factually inaccurate), high-handedness and arrogance (all experiments, surveys and techniques of scaling are dismissed, as are the contributions of Pearson, Fisher, Hume, Mill, Russell, Hempel, Popper and Blalock, often in a sentence), and confused argument (cf. Hindess 1977 for similar arrogant dismissiveness). While claiming to present a fundamental critique of the epistemology of systematic empiricism, in the chapters which aim to debunk traditional research practices, the criticisms that are in fact proposed are very traditional and well known. Their argument against experiments boils down to the old chestnut that they cannot come up with valid empirical generalisations because of the trade-off between naturalness and control. (Field experiments are not mentioned.) The arguments against scaling assess its achievements by the traditional criteria of dimensionality, stability and order. And surveys are held to be an example of systematic empiricism because they cannot demonstrate causality.

Yet it is not clear why they should consider this last point to be a criticism, since they believe that the very terminology of causation is further evidence on the mistakes of systematic empiricism. They believe that science is not a set of statements about natural regularities; indeed, it does not even need to presuppose that there are any, according to the Willers. Scientific laws are definitional, analytic and man-made, and so any notion of cause in theories which claim to be a statement about necessity in the outside world is incorrect. They assert that theories aim to make 'determinative statements' which predict outcomes universally across time and space; how they think theories can do this without some notion of a world that is caused, however, is beyond me.

The view of science that is put forward is utterly implausible. 'Science . . . ignores what is and what was, often denying observation in order to generate theoretical postulates.' There is a very weak clarion call to radical sociologists to get out of the conservative way of thinking of systematic empiricism, and liberate themselves from the tawdry world of reality. 'Science assumes no empirical truths, and thus is not restricted by them.' How very much easier it would be to do sociology (or be a radical!) if one could sit back on this assumption. When the only truth is truth by definition, and when science has no empirical content, but is rather a logical structure, relating to the empirical world by abstraction, there is indeed no need for a concept of cause. It is highly significant that both this strongly rationalist account of science and the Althusserian version propagated by Hindess and Hirst is driven to arguing that causes do not exist. Extreme empiricists have been driven to the same conclusion. The reason for this coming together is that it is only the language of cause which unites logical and natural necessity; empiricists deny the former and rationalists the latter.

Criticisms of Survey Methods of Causal Inference

Ironically, the criticism that comes nearest to the mark in sustaining a charge of positivism comes from those who have not questioned the value of the canons of science. They have doubted the ability of the survey on the fourth of the five rules of scientific procedure, namely, in its ability to test propositions in a systematic way. They point to the inherent weakness in drawing causal inferences from a correlation with controls established *post factum* as opposed to an experiment which sets up controls through randomisation (Stouffer 1949; Madge 1953; Hauser 1969).

It is true that some methods proposed to draw inferences from correlational data have been frankly positivist. Fisher believed that his tests of significance would provide some kind of automatic theory-generating process that did not require judgement or the intervention of the scientist. This eccentric view caused a rupture with Pearson in the end, who believed that to reject a null hypothesis was *ipso facto* to accept an alternative hypothesis of some kind. There are a wide number of data-dredging techniques in the multivariate armoury which will search your data for pattern for you, from stepwise regression to AID (automatic interaction detection). The existence of cheap computing, which gave such a spur to the development of causal modelling technology, can be badly misused: you can crosstabulate ALL against ALL as easily in SPSS as you can do something more thoughtful, and then you can select those interesting tables (that is, those with a significance level of less than 0·05) to reconstruct a story for. With any luck there will be about one in twenty of them! (Selvin and Stuart 1966).

The fact that these blatant misuses of survey data are possible does not mean that they are inevitable. The techniques of elaboration, to be discussed in the next chapter, can be used by those who have theories about the way the world works which they want to test, and who are not prepared to restrict their constructs to apparent observables. Such researchers do not derive their theories in any automatic way from the data, but rather use the data as a test, albeit a limited one, of a theory they have already formulated. The theory dictates which variables to introduce into the analysis, and to that extent such endeavours are not positivist. But we have already noted the problems with any passive observation programme: you never know that you've brought in all the right variables. There is no way of undermining this objection. The Lazarsfeld/Rosenberg techniques show how to introduce test factors to see if the relationship one is looking at holds up under different situations. But the sample size dictates limits to the number of variables one can control, and there may be a host of variables that one has not suspected (or thought about too late!) whose impact is not tested. The precise nature and direction of the causal relation has to be assumed, for it cannot be tested.

The power of intervening directly in the world, in order to know it, cannot be improved on. As Mao said, if you want to know the taste of a pear, you must eat it. Or, as Kurt Lewin said, if you really want to see if you have a handle on leadership, try varying it. Experiments may run into difficulties working out which variable to control, as with the man who couldn't work out why he was getting hangovers; he drank scotch and soda, vermouth and soda, brandy and soda . . . and concluded that the problem was the soda (Kish 1959). But at least he would have realised his mistakes when he just cut out the soda. The survey practitioner might not!

The objection cannot be undermined, but it can be overridden, at least for the time being. For, until the Utopia of community social science is on the agenda, the range of phenomena open to experimentation is lamentably restricted, on both practical and ethical grounds. Far from being the cadillacs of research design (Acland 1979), in reality experiments are driven into laboratories where their subject matter is constrained and their realism is questionable.

On the other hand, it might be (and has been) argued that if the researcher cannot practically or ethically intervene in the social world she wishes to study, inferences should be drawn from the attempts of the politicians or administrators to so intervene. When a policy change is made in one area, what consequences flow? The attempt to investigate this kind of question has been termed a 'quasi-experiment' (Campbell and Stanley 1963), and the activity of evaluating the social world as it changes is known as 'action research' (Halsey 1972).

This style of research seems to differ from both classical experiments and from surveys, and this seems to contradict my earlier remarks about these two methods exhausting the logical possibilities of methods of drawing causal inferences. Can 'quasi-experiments' not meet both the objections to laboratory experiments and the drawbacks to inferences from surveys? The answer, alas, is that they are more likely to run into the drawbacks of both and the advantages of neither. They do not represent a 'middle ground' in a continuum between experiments and surveys. The power of the experiment as a tool of research lies in the creation of a genuinely comparable control group through randomisation. The 'quasi-' bit of the term comes from the fact that control is never adequately achieved. Moreover, since the assessment of the effects is so often dependent on one case, and since the practical difficulties of measuring all the other factors at the time which might have produced the effect, from the passage of time *per se* to the Hawthorne effect, are so great, the result is often a rather inadequate survey. It most often takes the form of drawing inferences from a time-series, where the 'cases' are units of time, but the logical problems are the same.

In short, there is no obvious alternative to survey research in most situations. If you cannot intervene in the social world yourself, and you are chary of drawing very strong or general conclusions from those quasi-experimental situations where others have, you are forced back to considering variation as it occurs.

The attack on Science

Inferring processes of causation from patterns in the final outcome is a dangerous business. It is here that surveys run most risk of being positivist, but this is not taken up in that debate. This is because the emotional centre of anti-positivism is rejection of the values of science. Science is held to be a cloak for unwarranted, ideological claims, and a new term, 'scientistic', has been coined to convey the sense that these claims do not have the validity claimed for them. Critics of this kind cannot berate surveys for not being like experiments, because if surveys are 'scientistic', experiments are worse. This is ironic because, in one sense, experiments have a truly radical potential; they can create variance which had not previously existed, whereas surveys are much more restricted.

The line between science and scientism has got very blurred in these debates. There is a great deal of unease among sociologists about using the former term to describe their activities, almost as if there was something embarrassingly naïve in believing oneself to be engaged in a scientific pursuit. The good old idea that knowledge itself (science comes from 'scientia' – Latin for knowledge) is neutral, and can be put to good or bad ends, used or abused, has suffered a temporary eclipse (Griffiths *et al.* 1979). The 'New Left' position is that the knowledge that can produce such barbaric technology as the nuclear bombs which destroyed Hiroshima and Nagasaki, or the defoliants which denuded North Vietnam, is not just being misused, but must be fundamentally evil in itself. It was hard to argue that the knowledge could be used differently when supposedly socialist countries were using it in the same way to build bombs. In fact, this position represents a new form of technological determinism; the argument boils down to the idea of there being something fundamentally wrong in the technology.

The 'use–abuse' model was hard to extirpate in the natural sciences, but it has been given up freely by social scientists, especially by the 'radicals' and the New Left. It was not that they were doing research which was being put to grossly immoral ends. They did not disagree with the reforms which were so connected with social research, although many doubted the value of 'reformism' as a political programme. Their objection was that the term 'social scientist' appeared to allow some human beings, mostly an élite in universities (a *numerical* élite anyway in British universities to which only 6 per cent of the relevant cohorts go), to claim superior knowledge about such basic issues as why people marry who they do and so on. Moreover, the idea of knowledge for knowledge's sake in the social sciences has never cut much ice, and the 1960s generation of social scientists owed little allegiance to the ruling authorities.

We can now begin to discern that the 1960s and 1970s New Left phenomenon was partly a reaction to the seeming truth that capitalism had solved its recurrent problems of crisis. You could no longer criticise capitalism for failing to produce the goods; postwar social democracy clearly was providing health and education, as well as a wide range of consumer goods. Instead you had to criticise the goods. Part of the student movement of the late 1960s and early 1970s was talking about sociology teaching in universities being the inculcation of bourgeois ideology (Blackburn 1972). But now the continuous flow of goods seems as though it might be drying up, as health and welfare service are cut, manufacturing industry slumps and sociology departments are closed. Once more, the old idea that the relations of production might actually be a fetter on the means of production is beginning to re-emerge. It seems as though current capitalism cannot in fact utilise the science and technology that the 1960s generation criticised as inherently bourgeois and ideological.

In Chapter 6 we shall examine the various ways in which survey research is put to manipulative uses; we shall find it necessary to distinguish between the abuse of genuinely powerful survey techniques and the undoubtedly scientistic claims of opinion polling. But we have found no way to make the charge that surveys are inherently positivist stick. We have tried looking at it from a wide variety of angles, and find that the arguments will not come together. Most of the texts considered have been American, although there do exist British examples (see Pawson 1978, for example); they have, however, had a far wider impact in Britain than they have had in the United States. Speculating on the cause for the popularity of the accusation of positivism, one is forced to look beyond sociology to wider cultural values. But a stronger refutation of the anti-positivist's position would be to find some examples of surveys which will illustrate some of these points, and it is to this that we now turn.

4

Adequacy at the Level of Cause

This chapter and the next will examine the extent to which surveys can provide explanations of social phenomena which meet Weber's requirement that they should be both causally adequate and adequate at the level of meaning. In reviewing the different criticisms of survey methodology in the last chapter, it was pointed out that the process of drawing causal inferences from surveys is problematic and indirect; we know that a correlation does not equal a cause, but we shall see in this chapter how far down that road it is possible to push it.

The Concept of Cause
There has always been a fierce controversy about the usefulness of the very concept of cause in most areas of life – in the natural world, in the social world, in the moral world. It has intensified this century because of developments in physics that seemed to threaten its mechanical basis. There is not the space, and I have not the competence, to get involved in that debate, but there are some observations that must be made to facilitate the discussion in the rest of the chapter.

(1) It is important to accept (and indeed the language of not just everyday discourse but most scientific discourse accepts) that causes do really exist out there in the world; they have been called the 'cement of the universe' (Mackie 1974). They are not just epistemological concepts designed to help us work out what is going on.

(2) The central idea of a causal relationship is that one event, or state, or variable, *produces* another outcome in the course of time. When we come to study causes, we should be able to specify a starting-point to this process, the length of time it takes for the process to work and the end-result. If we wished to take the matter further, we could always inquire into the cause of the cause, or we could decide to investigate in more depth the nature of the process to discover how it was that the cause was producing the effect. A satisfactory causal *explanation* will always be relative to the question asked; medical science may be satisfied for a while with the explanation that a particular bacillus is the cause of tuberculosis, but eventually someone will want to know where it comes from and how exactly it wreaks its havoc.

(3) Causation is not the same thing as complete or unique determination. Indeed, the concept of unique determination in the social
world is rather strange to contemplate; the world in which it operated
would be a strangely metaphysical place. Imagine if all men were
black, working class ... and voted Labour, and all women were
white, middle class ... and voted Conservative. It is doubtful if a
concept of cause would even arise in a world like this. Things
would probably just be accepted as being the way they were.

We must be prepared to conceive of multiple causality as a
property of the external world, and reject Durkheim's dictum that
each effect has one and only one cause. It is, of course, still possible
that, with further conceptual elaboration, it could be shown that
different causes are producing different types of effects; indeed, it was
with this idea in mind that Durkheim enunciated his general
principle about the desirability of aetiological classifications. But, to
repeat, our causal theories are always provisional, never perfect, and
always open to refinement. Furthermore, as we shall see in the next
chapter, if we hurry prematurely to an aetiological set of categories,
we may cut ourselves off from ever exploring other, perhaps more
fruitful, lines of causal inquiry. There is no harm, and a lot of good,
from assuming that we have a situation in which there are many ways
to produce a given effect. They may not all operate in the
same way – some may be necessary preconditions, other things may
act as catalysts, other factors may influence the way in which the
effect is produced, others may be sufficiently strong to produce the
effect on their own. Moreover, some of these causes may change in
themselves within one individual (like age), some may be open to
change from outside (like political opinions), while others may not be
changeable at all (like sex). To call a wide variety of factors
multiple causes of a given effect is not to say that either their logical
status or their practical implications are the same. But it is to say that
if we believe that they are all working together in some way to
produce an outcome, then we shall have to take them all into account
in our survey.

Hundreds of books have been written and thousands of
philosophers have whiled away millions of hours ruminating on what
causation really is. It was worth devoting some time to considering its
nature, because it has proved so tempting to fall into an operationalist
position and to argue that causation amounts to the method of
recognising it, that it is *defined* as constant conjunction in time, as
Hume put it, or some modern equivalent.

Inferring Causes from Variation
The core notion in the scientific pursuit of an explanation of how
things work is the concept of variability. Experimenters and survey

researchers alike draw their inferences from observing variation, but they do so in radically different ways. To illustrate this point, consider an experiment performed to compare the different perspectives that actors and observers of a social process bring to bear; the subject matter of the experiment is also of more than incidental interest to us (Jones and Nisbett 1971) The researchers experimentally varied the monetary incentive which they offered a series of student-subjects in return for showing a visiting professor around the university. The students had been randomly assigned to one of three groups, so that the researcher could be confident, within limits, that the amount of variability within each of these groups in any characteristic you care to mention was the same, and that there was no difference other than chance between the groups. The researchers then artificially produced a variation between the groups by offering the first group a paltry sum, the second group a moderate amount and the third group a lot of money. They then observed the differences that this produced in response patterns, and, sure enough, very few of the low-incentive group agreed, about half the moderate group agreed and virtually all the high-incentive group agreed.

The most striking thing about this experiment is that the subjects, when questioned afterwards about their motivation for complying or not, never mentioned money, but instead tended to produce a variety of situational explanations – 'I had nothing to do that afternoon', for example. Another group of students who watched the interactions were asked why they thought the student had or had not complied; they did not mention money either, but produced more dispositional explanations – 'she's a helpful sort of person'. These constant and different biases in actors' and observers' accounts of behaviour are of great interest to social psychologists, but I use this experiment as an illustration because it also makes the point that only the social scientist who has deliberately set out to see the full variation in the phenomenon under investigation is privy to the true causal explanation. Social scientists do not have to claim to be a special breed of human beings, or to have greater powers of insight, to offer explanations which can be more valid than the actors'.

The inferences that an experimenter draws from variations in the 'effect' between the treatment groups are direct and watertight. There may be differences of interpretation over precisely how the cause produced the effect, but that *something* about the experimental treatment produced the observered differences is, within the limits of the laws of probability, certain. How can patterns in a survey produce proof of a causal process operating through time, starting with a cause and ending up with an effect?

The simple answer is that they cannot. But just because there is nothing in the cross-sectional evidence to clinch a causal argument does not mean that such evidence cannot help corroborate a hypothesis. Finding a correlation between smoking and lung cancer in no way proves that smoking causes lung cancer, but it does mean that the hypothesis cannot be ruled out. If we have reason to believe that it is a plausible connection, and if we can demonstrate to critics of the theory that the correlation holds up even after we have controlled for the factors that *they* believe to be responsible, the argument gets stronger and stronger.

Models

The key to the correct use of survey data to provide corroborative evidence of a causal process is in the adoption of a model. The concept of a model has had a very wide usage in the social sciences, sometimes referring to a system of abstract concepts at a more general level than a theory, sometimes used interchangeably with the notion of a theory but usually implying formal propositions of some kind, sometimes meaning a statistical model of the $Y = F(X)$ variety. A model adopted to summarise, formalise and generalise a causal process can be derived from any of these sources, so no more precise definition will be given. The hallmark of scientific uses of surveys is the amount of rigorous thinking, logical clarity and argumentation that goes into the development of causal models before one ever tries fitting them to survey data to see how adequate they are. It is the model that stands between the researcher and unbridled empiricism in the attempt to draw causal inferences, for it forces the researchers into explicit theory-making activity. No body of data suggests a unique model of its own structure to the researcher, and no one model can ever be shown to be the one and only way to make a good fit to the data (Tukey 1977).

There are some striking examples of how the model may be improved by hard thinking at the pre-empirical stage. The quality of debate about mobility analysis has been greatly improved by the increased attention that has been paid to models of mobility in recent years. For example, from the very first postwar studies of mobility it has been customary to compare observed mobility against a baseline model of 'perfect mobility'. The perfect mobility model is the ordinary model of statistical independence of rows and columns in a contingency table. In effect, it says that the chance of a son or daughter falling in a particular occupational group is the same whatever the occupational group of their father. Keith Hope, however, has shown that perfect mobility is not a simple concept but a compound (Hope 1981). One of the elements is a model which fits the same occupational distribution to fathers as to children, and this is the true base model of mobility analysis because it simply allows for the fact that some occupational categories have more people in them than others. The second element is a model which looks at differences between the origin distribution and the destination distribution and tells us how much mobility is required to transform the one into the other. This analysis of perfect mobility into its elements enables us to quantify structural mobility in the same scale of importance as other aspects of mobility, and it typically reveals that between a quarter and a half of mobility 'variance' is due to structural factors.

Sex-role stereotyping is another area which needed some clarification of the relevant models before good empirical analysis could be performed. Looking at changing attitudes of American parents to the sex-appropriate behaviour of their children, Duncan (1979) argues, you are not so much interested in the changes in the marginal responses to individual items (asking whether girls should help to clean the house or boys to wash the car), but in the growth or decline of consistent response structures to the questions taken as a whole. When a model is fitted which fits parameters specifically to account for 'traditional' and 'egalitarian' ideologues who answer all the questions in this light, much more interesting trends in sex-role attitudes are revealed.

Models are no more than intellectual crutches, designed to support and encourage theoretical activity of a complex kind. They allow us to keep several ideas in the air at once, and examine the relationships between them, but their value is lost on many social scientists when they are cast in the form of a series of equations. There is nothing particularly honourable or sacred about algebra; its value lies in allowing us to pursue the purely logical implications of relationships between variables. But since so many people (including seasoned statisticians) had difficulty following the logic of vast systems of symbolic relationships, and often made elementary logical errors in drawing deductions from such systems, when path analysis popularised the use of the pictorial causal flowgraph in multiple regression analysis, many people began to see the potential for using a model as a way of formalising their theoretical activity (Duncan 1973).

Modelling Causal Processes by Means of Flowgraphs

The principles of representing causal models by means of flowgraphs are not restricted to the mathematics of regression theory, however. They have a much wider relevance, and later in this chapter I shall illustrate how coefficients can be found for the arrows in such flowgraphs from the humble percentage table. In the meantime, let us explore a little the logic behind these graphs and the principles on which they work. (For a much fuller discussion, see Heise 1974, Stinchcombe 1968 and Davis 1971 and 1976).

The causal model is centrally linked to the concept of multiple causality, to the idea that more than one cause can independently contribute to the same effect. The existence of an 'effect' is denoted in flowgraphs by an arrow running from one variable to another (often represented as a dotted line if the effect is negative). Moreover, it makes explicit an important insight of multiple causality: variables are hypothesised to produce some outcomes directly while producing others indirectly by a chain reaction, A causing B, which in turn causes C, which causes D, and so on. In this instance, we talk about A having a direct effect on B but an indirect effect on D. The more thought goes into specifying such systems of multiple causality in advance of data collection the better; it is no good having a flash of brilliant insight about the intervening variables in a causal process at a later stage if you failed to collect information about these variables in the first place.

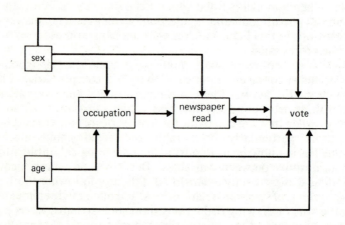

Model 4.1   *Causal model for voting.*

Let us imagine that we had come up with Model 4.1 as a model of the causal inputs to deciding how to vote. What is the model saying? Start by looking at all the things it shows as influencing vote. Men and women tend to vote differently; different age-groups have different voting patterns; the job that you do influences your party choice – it is well known that labour parties attract more manual and industrial workers than conservative ones. But propaganda plays its part too, and the final adoption of a party is significantly influenced by the newspapers you read. Which way you vote will be some compound of these four influences, according to this model. Moreover, each cause is represented as having an effect *independently* of other causes; regardless of one's occupation, preferred newspaper, or sex, the older you are the more likely you are to vote in a particular way.

The model also suggests that your support for a particular party in an election itself has an important influence on the kind of paper you choose to read; the Tory supporter will prefer the *Daily Express* to the *Guardian*. There is a feedback loop between newspaper readership and vote which needs to be taken into account before thinking of vote as a stable end-state phenomenon. There are other influences on newspaper readership as well in this model; one's sex and occupation influence the type of daily newspaper one reads – a fact which editors and advertisers know well. Thus sex affects vote both directly and indirectly through occupation and newspaper readership, for the jobs open to you depend strongly on your sex and when you were born.

If we can find a way to assign a positive and a negative pole to the variables in the system, then we can include another piece of information in models of this kind, namely, whether variables have an enhancing or suppressing effect on later variables. Only age in our model suggests an obvious positive–negative dimension, but this can be added for the other variables by selecting one category out for treatment. In this model, if we assign female and Conservative to the 'positive' poles, then we can say that sex has a positive effect on vote. This is quite straightforward to represent with dichotomies, but with polytomies the models start to look a little more complicated. (Interested readers can pursue this further in Davis 1976, where there is an excellent discussion of polytomous percentage tables.)[1]

These models represent pictorially a fundamental point about the workings of the world-out-there, namely, that things are both effects of preceding events and causes of subsequent ones. Engels might have been writing an introduction to a textbook on multivariate analysis when he wrote:

> [W]e find that cause and effect are conceptions which only hold good in their application to the individual case as such; but as soon as we consider the individual case in its general connection with the universe as a whole they merge, they dissolve in the concept of universal action and reaction in which causes and effects are constantly changing places, so that what is effect here and now will be the cause there and then, and vice versa. (Engels 1976: 27)

Until now, we have only considered the qualitative statements suggested by flowgraphs like this – 'occupation is one cause of vote', or, more realistically expressed in the language of probabilities, 'being female makes you more likely to vote Conservative'. There are two reasons for wanting to get more quantitative than this. The first is to answer questions such as 'How *much* more likely are you to vote Conservative if you are female?' and 'Which is the *more important* determinant of vote: sex or occupation?' (see Blalock 1961). These are interesting questions, although secondary to the qualitative ones, and are enormously hard to produce technically adequate answers to.

The second reason is rather more subtle. Although the causal logic is individual, we are going to use data from a cross-section of individuals to decide if an effect exists from sex to vote. We reason that, if being female does increase one's propensity to vote Conservative, if we look at a population at one point in time we shall find a higher proportion of female than male Conservatives. This correlational evidence presents itself in numerical form. To assess whether a direct effect exists at all from sex to vote, then, we shall have to see if there is still covariation between these two variables after occupation and age have been controlled in some way. We can now see why it is hard to produce a technically accurate answer to the *size* of the effect – it is utterly dependent on the adequacy of the causal model in telling us which variables to control.

Without discussing at this stage any of the technicalities for producing the coefficients to summarise the causal strength of the arrows, there are two common principles of causal models of this kind which will simplify the task both conceptually and mathematically if they can be made to apply. We are looking for coefficients that can be added together to produce a composite picture of the different causes of voting behaviour, which would allow us to compare the effect of sex and occupation, for example. This is the 'additive rule' of flowgraphs. Secondly, in order to get a measure of the strength of indirect causal effects, it makes sense to be able to multiply adjacent paths, so that, if the effect of A on B is 0.3, and the effect of B on C is 0.5, then we can say that the effect of A on C via B is 0.15. This yields the 'multiplicative rule'. These two rules, in combination, allow us to add up all the ways, both direct and indirect, in which one variable can affect another.

If we think of all the variation in voting being unity, then we should add a fifth arrow into it to represent all the other causes of vote that we have not included in the model, variously called the residual or error term. This is nearly always the largest coefficient in the model; it is common for models to explain between 10 and 20 per cent of the variance in the dependent variable. For the coefficients on the other arrows to mean anything, we have to assume that the residual causes operate randomly, and that no important systematic effect has been omitted.

Social scientists take themselves too seriously in that they often call the residual variance 'chance', and put a strong construction on what this means. Jencks (1973) concludes that fate is the major determinant of success in the school system in America because the causal models do not explain much of the variance. Blackburn and Mann (1979) conclude that chance determines people's placement in the labour market more decisively than do their skills or personal qualities. But this is to give the concept of chance a positive meaning it operationally does not have; in fact, it usually is a negative reflection of our ignorance – the residual tells us that there is a certain amount of variance whose origin we have not pinned down with our model. It is always relative to the state of knowledge at the time.

The small amount of variance explained is not cause for general alarm or despondency. It need not lead us in the footsteps of Derek Phillips to abandon method.[2] How much variation in the location of leaves which had fallen off a tree would remain unexplained after a survey of these leaves had taken into account the laws of gravity? Quite a lot. It might even be held to be a reason for great rejoicing among those sociologists who are concerned above all else to insist that human beings have free choice; the types of variables that are considered determinants in causal models are not the results of very obvious choice processes – age, sex, religion, and so on. A relationship should be described as 'strong' or 'weak' relative to the size of correlations usually found, and conventions need to be laid down about what to regard as a strong correlation. Davis has suggested a set of adjectives that might describe associations (but only on Yule's Qs) of various sizes which might be a starting-point (1971: 50; see also McNemar 1946 and Hyman 1955: 191).

Finally, if such a diagram as our putative model of voting were to appear in the pages of a sociology journal, it would almost certainly contain an arrow linking age and sex. This may seem absurd; there is no way in which *a priori* reasoning would lead you to think that there could be a causal effect of age on sex or vice versa. But since the coefficients are derived from a cross-section of cases, the arrow represents the descriptive statement about a population that women tend to live longer than men and so give rise to a correlation between age and sex. It is important to remember this fact about a population that we wish to use to derive other coefficients from. I did not include the arrow in the hypothetical example, because I wanted that to be considered as representing the 'true' effects on voting for any individual.

For any one person, of course, this model would be a hopeless oversimplification of the processes which had been at work in the past and were still operating to produce a particular vote. There is nothing in this model which captures important political experiences, the unique impact of discussions with family and friends on one's world outlook, and so on. One justification that might be given on this model is that it contained all the processes that are common to most people. (Even then there are howling deficiencies – there is no mention of education, or religion, or trade union membership; there might be nothing common enough to various political experiences for a generalisation to be in order, but we might have included a variable which summarised the partisan tendencies of any individual's most close daily contacts.) Our concern for what is generalisable to the population as a whole comes from our belief that what is general is of sociological interest, and from the fact that we shall derive the coefficients to apply to the causal arrows from our knowledge of the population as a whole

The difficult technical problems of *deriving* these coefficients must be kept separate from the simple logic of these models. Our example purports to represent the actual process of determination which leads one individual to vote in a particular way; it is a (philosophically) realist model. This is why we are always concerned about the causal order of our variables; if the model was not an attempt to summarise individual processes, but was just a descriptive summary of correlations in the population, we would not have to worry about the causal order of class and newspaper readership.

The logic is 'individual' when the unit of analysis in the survey (the most common case) is the individual; if a survey had been performed of schools, then the logic would be about causal processes in individual schools. However, as we noted earlier, even when the unit of analysis is the individual person, variables can always be introduced to show the effect of various social or ecological agencies on the individual.

If the values of the coefficients are to be derived from the known population values for these variables, then the biggest problem is going to come to models of this kind when the causal processes at work are not common to all subgroups in the population but differ in some systematic way. Our original model said, in fact, that age would be an important direct and indirect influence on voting behaviour, but that after you had taken it into account, you could add a separate amount for the effect of occupation and newspaper readership. In fact we know that this is not the case. Throughout this century, systems of political allegiance in Britain have been moving away from class- or religion-based politics and towards a more issue-oriented framework. The crucial question to ask of young workers today is not so much whether the job they do is manual or non-manual, or if they are Church of England or Non-conformist, but whether they think that the trade unions have too much or too little power, for example. Given that political allegiances crystallise fairly young, younger people are more affected by changing currents in politics than are their parents, and so we cannot hope to find one model which will sum up the effect of job on vote across the whole population.

Statistically speaking, this means that we suspect that there is an interaction or non-additivity in the system. The operational definition of an interaction is a situation in which the relationship between two variables depends on the value of a third. But, pursuing the realist's argument, what it asserts is that, underlying this, the processes of causal determination in the external world are not the same for all members of the population. Interactions cannot usually be represented in flowgraphs. Some multiplicative relationships can be coped with by transforming the scale of measurement of the variables, such as a log transformation. But the change of scale that might promote additivity in one part of the model might not work in the rest, so, in general, the only way to cope with interactions is to draw up a separate model for each of the categories of the variable that is causing the interaction. Indeed, most analyses of political allegiance are forced to give separate accounts of different age cohorts and the influences upon them.

Notice that I have been very careful up to now to express the reasoning on the basis of the causal model, and not on the basis of the existence of correlations in any particular dataset. I argued that if sex does have a direct effect on vote, then we should find a correlation between sex and vote after controlling for the other variables; I did not say that if we find such a partial correlation in the data we should thereby infer the existence of such an effect. There is no need to be an absolute purist in these matters; we can all smile at the folk myth among statisticians of a colleague who would only calculate those correlation coefficients that he had decided to investigate before-hand, and had posted to himself in a sealed, dated envelope to prove to the world that he had *a priori* reason to suspect would be significant. Provided we understand the dangers inherent in *ad hoc* reasoning, we can pursue hunches generated later in the process of data analysis. But the vital thing is to realise that the validity of any particular coefficient is dependent on the correctness of the causal model as a whole. If it is mis-specified, then the coefficients that we calculate will be absolutely meaningless, however many stars for statistical significance they can command.

We have already stated some of the required properties of the co-efficients on the arrows. They must be capable of being multiplied together to produce indirect paths of causal influence and of being summed to estimate the total causal effects. If we are prepared to make one further assumption, their calculation will be quite straight-forward. Unfortunately, as with most of the powerful assumptions of statistics, it's a big one. We have to rule out reciprocating causal systems. Going back to the hypothetical example of the effects on voting, we must rule out the feedback loop between newspaper readership and party preference. However plausible such a loop may be in reality, if we are not prepared to say that, at the end of the day, the net effect is preponderantly from newspaper to vote rather than vice versa, we shall never be able to estimate coefficients for the arrows from a cross-section of people.

The mathematical reason for this is that any sample will only yield *one* coefficient to express the extent to which vote and newspaper readership covary unless we apply advanced techniques which require artificial assumptions (see below). There is, underlying this technical difficulty, the conceptual point that if you just freeze reality at one point in time and examine the picture, you will either be look-ing at a point in the reciprocating process when everyone is only on one half of the loop, or, more probably, by looking at a cross-section of individuals at different stages in the reciprocal process, you will be getting an estimate of where such a feedback process will 'settle down'. To understand this concept of a loop 'settling down', it is only necessary to remember the multiplicative and additive rules of flowgraphs. Suppose we can isolate the loop, and, further that we can know the correct coefficients to assign to it, as in Model 4.2. How do we work out the total effect of newspaper on vote? Well, it is the direct effect, 0·3, plus an infinite series of 'indirect' effects, $0·3 \times 0·2 \times 0·3$ (0·018), and $0·3 \times 0·2 \times 0·3 \times 0·2 \times 0·3$ (0·00108), and so on; this will 'settle' at around 0·319, which is the coefficient we would expect to find expressing the dependence of vote on newspaper at any one point in time.

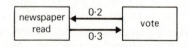

Model 4.2   *Looping the loop.*

Once we make this final assumption and rule out feedback loops, it is possible to show that both regression coefficients and percentage differences have the properties required by our additive and multi-plicative rules.[3] The direct effect of X on Y, net of any connecting paths through Z, is given by the partial regression coefficient of Y on

X controlling for Z; alternatively, it is the average of the differences in %Y between X and not-X in both Z and not-Z conditions. Both regression coefficients and percentage differences are asymmetric measures, that is, they take on different values depending on which variable you decide is causal and which caused. The values obtained will also depend on which variables it is deemed necessary to control; in trying to estimate the direct effect of X on Y, any variables which offer an alternative connecting path between X and Y must be controlled, but those which do not can be ignored. So, the conclusion once again is unmistakable: the value of all the coefficients depends utterly on the correctness of the model.

Assigning a Causal Order to the Variables

How, then, do we decide how to place the variables in a particular order? The forlorn search still continues for a way of torturing the data into revealing its order to us, but the results, like those of other forced confessions, are not very reliable. One such is a technique known as 'instrumental variable estimation' (Wonnacott and Wonnacott 1970). It claims to be able to solve the problem of having reciprocal causation in survey data by calculating the value of one of the arrows between two reciprocating variables net of the effect the other way round. How does it achieve this miracle, when, as we have noted, surveys only yield one measure of the covariation? It does it by making unrealistically strong assumptions. If you wish to calculate the effect of Y on Z, you have to find an 'instrument' which is a third variable with the following properties:

- it must have no direct effect itself on Z .
- it affects Y either directly or through a variable which does not affect Z
- neither Y or Z influence it
- it is uncorrelated with the error term of Z.

You of course can have no evidence that the variable you choose as the candidate has these properties, because of course it will appear to be associated with Z even when controlling for Y. You just have to decide that the appearances are illusory, and your assumptions about what is going on are preferable. It is a fascinating piece of statistical reasoning, because if such a variable could be found, then indeed it would solve the problem of causal systems with loops in them, and this would be very convenient. But candidates for such variables do not thrust themselves forward in the ordinary course of social research.

Another obvious way of ordering the variables is to make use of the time-dimension to causality, and to reason that if X occurs before Y,

X must be a cause of Y. *Post hoc ergo propter hoc.* Unless we do a longitudinal survey and go back to the same individuals for repeated questions after an appropriate interval, we do not strictly know the time ordering of the variables in a cross-section, but, of course, we can always ask. If you look at any survey schedule you happen to lay your hands on, you will find many of the questions are, in one way or another, memory questions. What was your father's occupation? When did you last buy a packet of Colgate toothpaste? Have any of your family had a serious accident in the past year?

Insufficient methodological attention has been paid to the problems of validity with questions such as these. Respondents' ability to recall even quite major events can be error-prone. Telescoping may occur, so that a respondent remembers an accident but outside the period asked about (Maclean and Genn 1979). People seem to 'remember' others' behaviour by remembering one feature of it and then associating with it features that fit the first in a stereotyped view of behaviour (d'Andrade 1974). Respondents to the Family Expenditure Survey dramatically underestimate the amount they spend on drink and tobacco and respondents to the General Household Survey overestimate the number of baths they take per week. And, if Freud is to be believed, people don't so much forget things as repress them, making the things they do remember a less than representative cross-section of events. Despite the decades of work put in by experimental psychologists into understanding the processes of perception and memory, they are nowhere near being able to formulate decent advice for questionnaire designers on how to tackle the problems.

Survey researchers struggle on, building up a body of experience about how to ask memory questions (we know, for example, to ask 'when did you last . . . ?' rather than 'how often do you . . . ?') but not finding a way to codify it and cumulate experience about it. Moss and Goldstein (1979) have brought together a collection of papers on this topic which confirm the subject-specificity of existing research, and the failure of experimental psychology to help out to any extent.

However, even if the past events are recalled with total accuracy (or if a longitudinal survey is conducted to collect the required information nearer the time of its occurrence), there are still two stumbling-blocks to using time to order variables. One is that the variables may not represent events as such, but ongoing aspects of a situation – the condition of housing lived in, the number of sibs, marital status, and so on. Until these situational variables are clarified and we may know how exactly they have their effect and what the starting- and finishing-point of such a process is, it will be impossible to use time alone to order, say, housing conditions and marital status.

More importantly, to argue *post hoc ergo propter hoc* is to commit a logical fallacy. The same conscious faculty of human subjects which allows them, conveniently for the survey researcher, to recall events in the past, means that they have the capacity to anticipate future events and take account of them *before* they happen. Teenage girls may have certain expectations of marriage and motherhood which influence their choice of subjects and performance at school, for example.

But if we are prepared to reason in this fallacious way, another ingenious way of torturing the data has been devised, known as 'cross-lagged correlational analysis'. The claim is that it allows a researcher to order two variables, X and Y, if there exist measures of each of them at different points in time. The idea is that if X causes Y rather than vice versa, the correlation of X_1 with Y_2 will be much bigger than X_2 with Y_1 (see Model 4.3). (You also check to see that the simultaneous correlations of X_1 with Y_1 and X_2 with Y_2 are smaller than the first cross-lagged correlation and larger than the second.) But all this only works if, besides all the usual assumptions about causal models of this kind, you assume that the measurement interval is the same as the causal interval, and further that the fact that the value of the variables change between measurements reflects real change in the variable, and not just unreliability of measurement. The fact that these assumptions are so rarely met explains the lack of enthusiasm for this technique in social science.

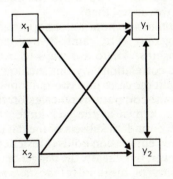

Model 4.3   *Cross-lagged correlations.*

At the current state of our knowledge, in fact, refined techniques for measuring the timing of variables and varieties of econometric trickery will not replace theorising as the way in which the ordering of one's variables is accomplished. Theorising could be in the grand tradition (arguing about the causal primacy of Protestantism and the rise of capitalism, for example). It could be thinking hard about which influences in life tend to be stable and unchanging (like religion of upbringing). Or it could involve reasoning about the likely independence of various events (as we shall see in the example discussed in detail in the next chapter). (Hyman 1955 still provides the best discussion of the different reasons employed by sociologists to resolve these ordering problems.) Nor is it possible to see how technical refinements could solve the problem, for it is essentially philosophical, as we have discussed before. If all you do is watch variation, however meticulously, as it actually occurs, without trying to intervene and manipulate it, you are always open to being misled by neglecting to take all the relevant factors into account.

The Logic of Survey Analysis

Whatever type of theory we are talking about, then it is not to be found located in the dataset itself. This is not, however, to argue that the process of specifying and elaborating a full causal model will always be done prior to data collection. The more that sociological craftsmen become accustomed to thinking about how they intend to analyse survey data in good time, the less likely they are to end up kicking their data in vain at a later stage and blaming their tools for what is in fact their own fault. But it is inevitable that new ideas will strike a chord at some point during the analysis, and we must not emulate the purist mentioned earlier by refusing to consider these new hypotheses, especially if we are fortunate enough to have the variables on which we can test them.

Only the unscrupulous go hunting, snooping and fishing by cross-tabulating ALL against ALL and then concentrating on the significant relationships. There are ways to avoid the dangers of lighting on 'chance correlations' by this method: the most straightforward way is to split the cases into two random subsets, explore the first and check out the correlations revealed on the second. A more complex technique, known as the jack-knife, involves essentially exploring all possible random subsets of the data and seeing in how many of them a given correlation holds (Mosteller and Tukey 1977). The problem, however, is not really the danger of the 'chance correlation' but the sterility of the kind of *ad hoc* arguments that are drummed up to explain them.

The trouble is that such *ad hoc* arguments can produce directly contradictory results. Suppose I told you that people who wore seat-belts were more likely to have a crash in the first place (regardless of severity of injury). You would probably reply that one didn't need sociologists to tell us such elementary truths; dangerous drivers see more need for seat-belts than others, and anyone who puts on a seat-belt is lulled into a false sense of security. If I tell you that people who wear seat-belts have fewer crashes, this will again be obvious; safety-conscious people wear seat-belts more often and drive more safely. So a survey into the effects of seat-belt wearing on driving behaviour would have to try to anticipate both of the 'obvious' explanations and design questions which would give more weight to the final interpretation put on the results; perhaps this would be done by getting an independent measure of safety-consciousness. (See Lazarsfeld 1949 for further discussion of 'obvious' explanations.)

It is not unscrupulous to have a good idea, an insight into the possible way in which one variable is having an effect on another, or a pang of doubt that a plausible prior variable may be entirely responsible for the visible correlation. In fact, such ideas may actually be inhibited by rushing at a dataset with one's head lowered, model polished and gleaming in one's hand. If you look at the way sociologists actually work, they often ask of a bivariate relationship, why is there a correlation here? and work productively by gradually elaborating this relationship at the kernel of their model, thinking, refining their ideas, rejecting and including variables one at a time.

This is not the only way in which they can work. Some entire projects are built around a rather different question such as what are all the causal influences on delinquency? (the question which Hirschi and Selvin set out to ask themselves in their excellent book which they subsequently renamed *Principles of Survey Analysis* because it made so many methodological points so clearly); another question sometimes asked is, what are all the consequences, throughout a person's lifetime, of the education that they have received? (the question which Hyman, Wright and Reed (1975) asked of an enormous body of US data).

However, the elaboration of a bivariate relationship is a suffic-iently popular approach for a school of survey analysis to have arisen around it. Rosenberg (1968) identifies common steps in the process of testing and elaborating a relationship between two variables and we shall now leave hypothetical examples and conclude the chapter by tracing them through on an example from an analysis of British elections that has been ably conducted by Butler and Stokes and reported in *Political Change in Britain* (1974).

(1) The original correlation. The classic original correlation which most voting studies of British elections have considered is the relationship between social 'class', defined as the distinction between manual and non-manual jobs,[4] and support for the two main twentieth-century parties, the Conservative and Labour Parties. Unlike many other liberal democracies, the major lines of cleavage between the parties in Britain has been this one of occupational

culture, rather than religion, race, or region; this is the starting-point for any analysis of the influences on electoral behaviour in twentieth-century Britain.

Table 4.1   *Class Basis of Party Support in 1963 – Frequencies*

	Non-manual	*Manual*	*Total*
Conservative	198	199	397
Labour	60	502	562
Total	258	701	959

Source: All these tables are based on data in Butler and Stokes 1974. In some cases enlightened guesses have been used to reconstruct base Ns.

Model 4.4   *Simple class–vote model.*

The association at the kernel of the model is, then, this class–vote relationship, as shown in Table 4.1. In order to use these results to fit the first stage of our model (as shown in Model 4.4) we have to remember that we are assuming that vote depends on class, not vice versa, and so we should run the percentages within the categories of class, calculating the proportion[5] of the non-manual stratum who vote Conservative, rather than the proportion of Conservatives who are non-manual. Table 4.2 shows that the difference in the proportions voting Conservative in the two occupational groups is, indeed, quite striking. (Since the proportions voting Labour and the differences in these proportions are just mirror images of the proportions voting Conservative, we shall in future concentrate on only one category – the 'positive' category – of the dependent variable.) We can assign the value ·483 to the coefficient in our model from class to vote. By adding a couple more values to the table, we can get a good insight into how the model is working. It says, effectively, that there are 0·483 more non-manual than manual workers who support the Conservatives. But there are still some manual workers who support the Conservatives – 0·284 to be precise. Since their behaviour is 'unexplained in our model, we can use this proportion to represent the residual effect on voting. Finally, if we remember that 0·269 of our sample is non-manual, then we can perform some arithmetic on this model. Look at Model 4.5. We can now 'predict' that the proportion of Conservative voters in this population, with 0·269 middle class people, will be 0·284 + (0·269 × 0·483), i.e. 0·414, which is correct for 959 ÷ 397. Isn't that neat?

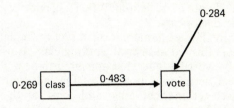

Model 4.5   *Class–vote model with coefficients added.*

The strategy in the rest of the steps will be to break the original Table 4.1 down into sub-tables (or sometimes called partial tables) to re-examine this relationship under different conditions. There are many different reasons for creating sub-tables, many different types of variable to stratify by and many different possible outcomes, so it will not be possible to exemplify each exhaustively. The following is intended only as a sketch of one possible line of reasoning.

Table 4.2   *Class Basis of Party Support in 1963 – Percentages*

	Non-manual	*Manual*	
Conservative	0·767	0·284	difference (d) = 0·483
Labour	0·229	0·716	
	1·000	1·000	
Total	(N = 258)	(N = 701)	

Source: See Table 4.1.

(2) *Is the relationship spurious?* The second step in the Rosenberg logic is to check that this relationship is not spurious, or to establish what part of it is spurious. Of course, in one sense, once you have established that there is an association there, it really exists, and there is no way that you can then argue that it doesn't. The adjective is really being applied to the validity of drawing some kind of causal inference from the association. The classic example of a spurious correlation is that of the correlation between the number of storks and the number of babies born in particular regions of Sweden.

Anyone above the age of 6 would probably suspect that this correlation was not being produced by a causal connection between the existence of storks and the existence of babies, and would search for third factors which, when controlled, would show that the original relationship had been spurious. The urban/rural factor is the classic explanatory factor in the above correlation; in rural areas, both humans and storks are more fecund. When you control for this factor, the relationship disappears.

Methodism, the largest Nonconformist sect in England, was born among the newly formed industrial working class. It would be quite reasonable to be worried that what appeared to be a class effect on vote was in fact a spurious product of the fact that most of the Noncomformists get manual jobs, and most of them also vote Labour. (We have been looking at the share of the major parties up to now, and ignored the smaller third parties; in fact, among the middle class this is a serious omission, for middle class Nonconformists are the major source of support for the Liberal Party.) However, Butler and Stokes show that when you look at the various religions separately, there is still a strong class difference remaining, so we are justified in assuming that the heart of the model is about the relationship between occupational and political culture.

If the test factor is prior to the relationship under consideration, and if, after its introduction, the relationship disappears, then we are justified in applying the label 'spurious' to the original relationship. If, after controlling for income, the relationship between class and party were to disappear, we should not want to call this a spurious association, for income is a large part of the very distinction between manual and non-manual jobs. Hyman's book on survey analysis has a very good section on uncovering spurious associations, and goes into this point in much more detail (Hyman 1955; see also Simon 1954 for the classic paper introducing this operational notion of spuriousness).

(3)   Component variables. The next step in the procedure of elaborating the relationship between these two variables is to see if the measures of the variables cannot be further refined, broken down into their component parts to reveal a sharper statement of the relationship. The party one finally comes to vote for cannot hope to reflect the full complexion of one's political views. One obvious way to enrich the analysis would be to establish whether support for a particular party can be seen as a cluster of political beliefs or issues that the party is identified with. The evidence presented by Butler and Stokes suggests that it is not possible to break down vote into support for constituent issues on which the party is seen to have policies. There are issues on which the British electorate sees a

difference between the Conservative and the Labour Party – the Conservative Party is seen to be more in favour of the monarchy, less in favour of nationalisation of industry, more likely to keep the nuclear bomb. But any attempt to interpret party support congruence between the party's stand on various issues and the voter's own position on these same issues fails at the first hurdle. Moreover, while voting for one party is a fairly stable phenomenon, Butler and Stokes discovered that very few people have consistent views on policy issues from year to year. So it would appear that vote cannot be broken down into component issue support; it is not simply an amalgamation of views. This is a very important thing to have discovered about our key variable, and should lead into other directions to explain what it 'is' in more detail.

Breaking one's variables down into their component parts should not be confused with causal reasoning; it is rather an empirical concomitant of conceptual analysis to which the survey researcher must pay great attention.

(4) Antecedent variables. Depending on the type of problem being investigated, the next step could be to go one step back and inquire into possible factors that give rise to the causal variables. It is interesting to ask what determines the type of job one takes. Although this question was not the main focus of the study, Butler and Stokes's data allow us to examine the effect of the regional structure of employment on opportunities for different types of jobs. London and the south-east have very many more white collar jobs than does the north. We can see from Table 4.3 that regional variation in the occupational structure will be one causal influence on the jobs open to individuals to take. There was no point in controlling for vote in this model, because we are arguing that vote comes after the causal influences of region and class, and so we would not expect it to have any influence on this bit of the system.

Table 4.3   *Proportion of Middle Class within Region*

	North	South
	·24	·32
	(N = 609)	(N = 350)

Source: See Table 4.1.

But one thing we should consider is that there may be an impact of region on voting independently of class. In other words, we may introduce antecedent variables to try to show what gave rise to the first variable, and decide that we should check at the same time that this variable was not producing a spurious correlation between the two. This distinction between the fourth and second steps of the process of elaboration is often blurred in practice.

Is the correct model (a), (b), or (c) in Model 4.6? Example (a) models the case where an antecedent variable is introduced to show how the first variable came about, whereas (c) is an example of the introduction of a test factor which shows that the original relationship had been entirely spurious. The situation in (b) suggests that there is an element of truth in both (a) and (c), where region is part of the explanation of class, and part of the explanation of vote in its own right.

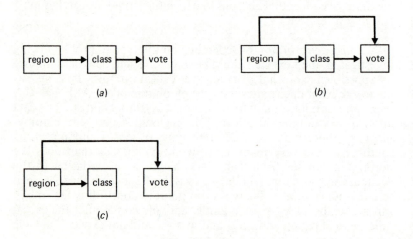

Model 4.6   *Alternative models for region, class and vote.*

In fact, (b) proves to be the most plausible model. Table 4.4 demonstrates that there is still a strong class relationship in both of these regions – 0·48 difference in the north and 0·47 in the south. But there is also a small effect coming from region itself; living in the south makes 0·06 more vote for the Conservative Party among the middle class, and 0·07 among the working class. We shall see later how these coefficients may be applied to our three-variable model to build up a more complete pattern of the effects upon voting.

Table 4.4 *Proportion Voting Conservative by Class and Region*

	North		
Non-manual	*Manual*		
0·74	0·26	$d=0·48$	
(N=146)	(N=463)		
	London and South-east		
0·80	0·33	$d=0·47$	
(N=112)	(N=238)		

Source: See Table 4.1.

(5) Intervening variables. The next step in the process of unravelling a cause–effect process is often to try to pin down exactly how the outcome is produced by the cause. As we said earlier in this chapter, there is never one definitive answer to this question; we can always probe a mechanism or a process more deeply, introducing more and more refined intervening variables to explain the outcome.

One important question to ask about the link between class and vote is the extent to which it is mediated through the individual voter's consciousness, or whether we shall have to provide other types of explanation, such as the impact of occupational culture on voting habits, to explain the association. Butler and Stokes asked their respondents which class they themselves *thought* they belonged to. This did partly explain the class effect, for the effect of class on vote among those who thought of themselves as belonging to the same class was weaker than the original correlation. None the less, it did not disappear entirely, so this intervening variable does not completely interpret the relationship.

Note that in each of these steps, the mechanics of what we do are exactly the same. We apply a test factor to the original relationship and stratify the original association within categories of this factor. But the conclusions we draw from what we find depend entirely on whether it is introduced as an intervening or antecedent variable, to test the relationship for spuriousness or to interpret its process more fully.

(6) Conditional relationships. When we controlled for region, and then re-examined the effect of class on vote in the separate regions, we discovered that the effects were only slightly different – 0·48 in the north and 0·47 in the south. The additive assumption of flow-graphs was applicable. But this is not always the case; sometimes the relationship between two variables is conditional upon, that is, varies within, categories of a third. This is called an interaction – something

that is a headache from a technical point of view but most exciting from the standpoint of substantive sociology. When such conditional relationships are revealed on stratification by a third variable and on observing different *d*s in the sub-tables, a separate causal model must be specified for each condition or category.

One of the most interesting and important examples of an inter-action in British electoral support comes when we compare the class alignment of different cohorts. Political loyalties among the oldest cohorts surveyed are determined most strongly by religion rather than occupational stratum. The strength of the class-vote relation-ship grows, and is strongest for those generations who spent their young adult life before the Second World War. Since then, the most recent cohorts are basing their political allegiances not on religion or even so much on class, but on single issues. We cannot hope to find one model that will generalise the important political influences for all time in Britain, so the analyst turns to elaborating a set of separate models for the different generations. Far from being something to be rued, the insights yielded by noticing interactions and specifying the conditions under which they hold can be very rich. Notice that inter-actions are easily *spotted* in tables; with multiple regression, we might effectively be performing an average on very different relationships, not even suspecting an interaction, and we would never know about it unless we went out to look for it. Only the cynical will consider this an advantage with multiple regression techniques.

(7)   Conjoint influences. The last step in the procedure suggested by Rosenberg is to construct what he calls 'systems of conjoint influences'; in other words, we should attempt to bring variables together simultaneously, and present a total picture of the way in which they interrelate, in the manner that we did with the fictitious example earlier on in this chapter. In a sense, the introduction of a test factor for any reason points the way towards the construction of a system of interrelating variables. This is perhaps, therefore, not so much a step in the process as the final assembly of the earlier findings.

One of the most depressing things about British survey work at the moment is that so many reports are presented showing only bivariate relationships. One can perhaps forgive the classic surveys of the 1960s for not being adventurous in their style of analysis; surveys such as Goldthorpe, Lockwood *et al*'s study of the affluent workers of Luton (1968), or Runciman's (1966) study of how the notion of relative deprivation explained why people accepted inequality, rarely went beyond bivariate relationships, although imaginatively designed and written up.

But the surveys of the 1970s have not been any better – sometimes the standard seems to have declined (with some signal exceptions).

Gallie published a book entitled *In Search of the New Working Class* (1978) in which he compares 'automation and social integration' within oil enterprises in Britain and France. The analysis consists of presenting each of his items of information – on income, hours worked, and so on – singly for each plant that he studied. Roberts *et al.* (1977), in a survey of two areas in Liverpool in which they investigated perceptions of class, do their analysis by correlating a series of different attitudes with a series of different 'objective' background factors, each taken on its own, and conclude that there is a *Fragmentary Class Structure* (or should it really be fragmentary survey analysis?). Newby's *Deferential Worker* (1977) totally relies on single or bivariate relationships. Every table in Blackburn and Beynon's *Perceptions of Work* (1972) shows various perceptions of work broken down by the type of shift worked. I do not cite these studies because they are particularly weak; on the contrary, they have all had a significant impact on British sociology. They are just representative of a genre of survey analysis. Part of the problem seems to be that surveys are still being conducted with inadequate sample sizes, sometimes as a result of a one-person effort, rather than using any larger institution to do the fieldwork; the result is that there are simply not enough cases to build up systems of conjoint influence in the way Rosenberg suggests.

Up to now, third variables have been brought into the analysis in order to highlight features of the original two-variable correlation of interest, to check it was not spurious, to elucidate how the causal effect occurs, to show precisely what it was about the original variable that produced the causal effect, and to show what gave rise to the original variable. But we have already noticed on several occasions that one may also introduce a third variable to see if it is another independent variable operating on the dependent variable. Going back to Table 4.4, you will remember that the same table yielded information about the effect of region itself on voting. The model that looked like the most plausible fit to the data was the model in which region and class both affected vote independently of one another, and where region had an effect on class. How may the results of Table 4.4 be incorporated into this model and show the relative influence of all the variables?

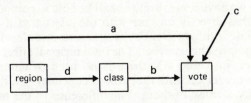

Model 4.7   *Conjoint influences on voting.*

Model 4.7 shows the full model of the conjoint influences upon vote. The value of path b will be some kind of average 0·47 and 0·48. Since they are so close we do not need to worry about the precise way of averaging them giving proper weight to each figure; instead we can call the result 0·475. Similarly, the value of a is an average of 0·06 and 0·07, to which 0·065 is a reasonable approximation. Now, if we recall some further information we have about this table, we can build a model which can predict the proportion of Conservative votes in the same way as before. There is another arrow, c, coming into vote, emphasising that we have not got all the Conservative voters pinned down with these two variables; there are still some people who live in the north of England who are working class and vote Conservative. The value for that residual path will be 0·26, which is the proportion of Conservative voters among northern working class members of the sample (see Table 4.4). The final piece of information that we have to recall is what proportion of our sample actually do live in the south as opposed to the north, and are middle class. You can reconstruct the Ns from the previous table, and you get 0·365 for the proportion in the south and 0·269 for the proportion middle class. Now we can write an equation to predict the total Conservative vote; if P stands for probability:

$$P(\text{Conservative}) = c + P(\text{South})\,a + P(\text{Middle})\,b$$
$$\text{so: } P(\text{Conservative}) = 0·26 + 0·365 \times 0·065 + 0·269 \times 0·475$$
$$= 0·412$$

In fact, if you go back to the original Ns and calculate what the total proportional vote for the Conservative Party in this sample was, on my figures, the result is 0·414. So this is a very accurate 'prediction'. The reason it is not perfect is because of the averaging process that we used to remove the minor differences between the ds. If there had been interactions of any size in the model, we would have found this result much more wide of the mark.

Finally, we still need to put a value on the path d from region to class; when we have done this, we shall be able to compare the effect that region has directly on vote with the effect that it has through being associated with different class structure, and class in turn being an important influence on vote. The total regional effect on class was already given in Table 4.3; there is no need to control for vote, because our model assumes that vote is dependent on the other two variables, not a cause of them. The difference in the proportion of middle class people between the north and London is 0·08.

Now, looking at Model 4.8, we can make the comparison between the two different ways in which region has an effect on vote. Directly it makes a 0·065 difference, but it also makes a direct difference of 0·08 on class, which in turn makes a 0·475 difference on vote; multiplying these two paths together, we can say that the indirect effect is 0·038 – not a large amount. Furthermore, we can add these two effects together and obtain a total effect of region on vote of 0·103; this is approximately what we should have found if we had started out with the simple two-variable relationship of region by vote.

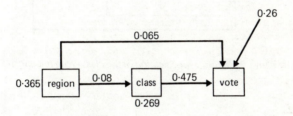

Model 4.8   *Filling in the coefficients for Model 4.1.*

Table 4.5   *Proportion Voting Conservative by Region*

	London and South-east	North
	0·374	0·483
	(N = 350)	(N = 609)

Source: See Table 4.1.

The *d* in Table 4.5 is 0·109, which is once more in very close agreement to 0·103. This model, complete with coefficients, now tells us in a visually punchy way about the system of 'conjoint influences', as Rosenberg calls them, which go into voting, assuming class and region are the only two influences which it is necessary to consider. Of course, we know already that a more complete model is really required. Perhaps we need something like Model 4.9 for each age cohort.

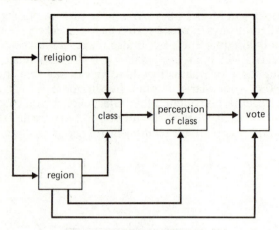

Model 4.9   *Further specification of the class–vote relationship.*

In sum, I believe that this sequential logic represents a valuable approach to survey analysis that more powerful and computerised routines still have not replaced. If one were to take the range of methods currently used in British social research to be exhaustive of the possibilities, one would be faced with a ridiculous methodological choice. Either, as in the surveys that I cited in the last section, the analysis consists of showing every single variable broken down by one other variable (usually the same one). Or one processes all one's variables simultaneously through a computer-based package programme which will spew forth unstandardised and standardised regression coefficients, each with its standard error, level of significance and number of stars, in a trice.

The gradual elaboration of a more complex model allows a fruitful interaction between one's existing ideas and the data. Despite the prescriptions of the Poppers and Hempels of this world, practical scientific reasoning does not only consist of making deductions from theories. However inadmissible it may be as a form of proof of one's theories, induction certainly has some role to play in the process of generating ideas. To turn up one's nose at exploring fully anything more in the expensive survey data one has collected would be folly indeed; there might well be insights to be obtained from having a good look at other relationships in the dataset and puzzling over them. (Rosenberg's last chapter gives a good account of the discovery aspect of surveys; see also Merton 1968: 157–62 on what he calls 'serendipity'.)

Surveys certainly do impose on researchers a most awkward time-table. Properly designèd, anticipating rival causal explanations as far as possible and building in ways to test them, surveys can provide evidence for and against different causal models. This evidence is not proof, however; it is only as good as the model is.

Notes: Chapter 4

1 The following discussion has been deeply influenced by the ideas of Davis (for example, 1976).
2 It is interesting that Phillips makes a big fuss about how little variance is normally explained and also about how unreliable sociological measures usually are. He fails to remark that the latter may strongly attenuate the correlations used in the former (1973: 7).
3 The percentage difference, as Jim Davis drew to my attention, is just a regression coefficient between two 0,1 variables.
4 I cannot support the idea that these two occupational strata constitute classes in any important sense. However, the word has become so widely used in this sense that I find myself bowing to convention.
5 I use percentages and proportions interchangeably – I like talking about percentages but I prefer calculating proportions.

5

Adequacy at the Level of Meaning

Two Sociologies?
Marx complained in his first thesis on Feuerbach that the idealists
had managed to get a monopoly on viewing human beings as active
and creative. He put the blame on the materialists like Feuerbach
who gave the ground away because they were not prepared to treat
subjective states as real and has having a real impact. It is a complaint
that could well be made about current sociological practice. We saw
in Chapter 3 how the devotees of the New Idealism (Gellner 1974)
insisted that subjectivity and intentionality constitute the social
world; they had no difficulty in capturing the active and creative side
of human existence, but failed to recognise the extent to which that
creative capacity was constrained. To dub them idealists (in the
philosophical sense of the word) is not unfair. Yet the current
'materialists' have often let them get away with it through concentrating on causal explanations which fail to show the rational, understandable components of social action. The aim of an explanation is
not just to show high correlations between variables; sociological
explanations would almost always turn out to be a terrible flop anyway on these grounds. It must also show how the actions of the people
involved were the actions of conscious human beings, reacting to an
environment, trying to make sense of it and pursuing various goals in
their actions with more or less success. Only explanations which take
cognisance of the meaningful aspect of social action will satisfy us as
human observers.

From reading much of the current methodological literature, it
would appear that there are two different methods, appropriate to
either causal explanations (surveys) or meaningful explanations
(participant observation). It seems as though we are being asked to
make a choice between two packaged sociologies which come in
hermetically sealed wrappers. Inside each there is a view of the nature
of social man, a theory of knowledge and a suitable method of study.
In an article explicitly arguing this, Alan Dawe (1970) delineates
two sociologies which have emerged from the Enlightenment. One
takes as its central problem the estabishment of social order, and
erects a vocabulary of social systems which derives individual
intentions and consciousness from the central societal value systems,
and the other takes as its problem the libertarian question of how

humankind can achieve control over the institutions that it creates, and uses a vocabulary of social action, will, intention and meaning. At the heart of these two sociologies, he argues, is a different view about the relationship of man to society. These in turn give rise to different ways in which it is appropriate to investigate the social world, the former seeing it as more appropriate to take up the tools of natural science and use them to look at subjective meanings as internalisations of externally imposed social norms, and the latter leading to understanding or 'Verstehen' as the key method of the social sciences, in its attempt to get inside subjectivity of individual actors' definitions of situations.

Having delineated the two sociologies, Dawe suggests that the distinctions between them comes down to an irreconcilable conflict of fundamental societal values, of security versus freedom, and that you must therefore just choose between them. However, the way in which he sets up the terms of the debate means that your choice is actually not that free! Dawe argues very convincingly that the very core of the concepts of subjectivity, will and action, cannot be derived from the language of the social order approach; in its attempt to synthesise action concepts into social system terms by deriving their meaning from social norms, the concept of subjectivity loses all its force and coherence. But he does not equally argue that, in viewing social systems as the result of interactions of individual unit acts, the social action approach cannot derive a plausible account of the social system. There is a confusion between the title of his article ('The two sociologies') and a statement in the article that 'sociology has developed on the basis of the conflict between them'. If the two sociologies were as hermetically sealed in their language and their problematics as Dawe maintains, how would debate and interaction between the two be possible?

The fact is that there is no logical reason why we should be forced to select neat polythene bagfuls of social philosophies all at once, as indeed all the major social theorists were centrally trying to show. Your research, your choice of subject and method, your operationalisation of key concepts, and so on, is not determined by your epistemology and implied ontology. What you discover is also determined, although not completely, by the nature of the social world. You cannot just choose whether to view man as active or passive. (Which would *you* choose, incidentally? It's not much of a choice.) You cannot just choose whether social institutions come before or after individuals. You cannot just choose whether or not individuals have got 'free will'.

I argued earlier that the issue of 'free will' had been badly framed in most traditional accounts. Clearly human beings make choices, not just between different evaluations, but also between different courses of action and between action and non-action; being conscious, we have the capacity to imagine a situation that does not yet exist, and to try to create it or prevent it. Causes and intentions are not incompatible. Certainly, if will were indeed free, and I could intend and achieve whatever I wanted, then there could be no question of assimilating the two notions: events would be either willed or caused. But we recognised earlier that people may make history, they may exercise choice, but they cannot choose the conditions, the avenues of possibilities open to them. To the extent that there are constraints on unbridled will, part of the apparatus of causality will be needed to explain the structuring of these constraints. Freedom, as Engels argued, is the recognition of necessity; conversely, oppression is often the product of unrecognised constraints. That is the paradox at the heart of some of the most exciting sociological explanations; studies which can show the double-sided nature of the human condition, creating as well as experiencing social structures, are the most satisfactory ones to read. The best sociological questions are those which aim to investigate the conscious, the subjective, the creative aspects of human action and to delimit the extent to which they are the key determinants of a given outcome.

The adoption of the 'plastic man' bundle of goods which views society as a constraining force over man is only politically conservative *if and to the extent that it is untrue*. But the setting of the terms of debate in this sealed-off form precludes sociology from ever asking the crucial questions of whether the constrained nature of social man is a reality or not. It is very important for us to break out of the methodological conventionalism of which Dawe's article is but one example. Survey research is definitely seen as part of the 'plastic man' package, incapable of utilising any of the insights derived from the 'active man' package. The aim of this chapter is to show that by opening up the bags, and by combining the logical elements of the survey method with the method of Verstehen, we can begin to construct much more satisfactory explanations for social phenomena.

Weber's Injunction

It was Weber who argued that explanations would only be satisfactory if they were 'adequate at the level of' both cause and meaning. The strength of Weber's point is his insistence that motives and intentions are 'causal hypotheses' whose adequacy must be empirically established. It holds that the task for the social sciences is to provide such evidence.

Without adequacy at the level of meaning, our generalisations remain mere statements of *statistical* probability, either not intelligible at all or only imperfectly intelligible; this is no matter how high the probability of outcome ... and no matter how precisely calculable in numerical terms it may be. On the other hand, from the point of view of its importance for sociological knowledge, even the most certain adequacy on the level of meaning signifies an acceptable *causal* proposition only to the extent that evidence can be produced that there is a probability ... that the action in question *really* takes the course held to be meaningfully adequate with a certain calculable frequency or some approximation to it (whether on average or in the 'ideal' case). (in Runciman 1978)

In other words, the mere fact of a high correlation between, say, Protestantism and capitalism, while being a necessary part of an explanation, doesn't yield sociological knowledge until the reason for the connection is made intelligible to us. Nor will we be convinced that the ideas of a particular kind of Protestantism encouraged the development of capitalism on intuitively appealing grounds; we shall want to see the correlation established. The key question now is whether survey data is bound to yield only 'statements of statistical probability', or whether it can make its correlations meaningful.

Unfortunately Weber did not give much of a clue about how this is to be accomplished. The original statement is vague, opening the door to such difficult problems as unconscious meaning. We are told that all social action is meaningful, and that behaviour performed without a motive is not of interest to sociologists, but it is not clear what is ruled out by this, for Weber's category of 'affectual action', or action undertaken for instinctive or emotional reasons, is still called action. It is sufficiently ambiguous for interpreters of Weber's work as different as Schutz and Parsons to disagree profoundly about what he meant. There have been several broad responses among survey researchers to Weber's call for using Verstehen or understanding in explanations, to which we shall now turn. The approaches differ in whom they believe the meaning should be supplied by and how much and what type of evidence is required before one can validly attribute meaning to an action. In the last chapter we reviewed a procedure which aimed, step by step, to establish an adequate causal explanation. Unfortunately no such neat formula exists (or probably could exist) for making surveys provide a convincing explanation of the meaningful nature of the action for the actors involved.

Facesheet Sociology
One early response to the idea that Verstehen had a part to play in sociological explanation was to argue that it only had a part to play in generating hypotheses, and was quite unnecessary in explaining or assessing the success of an explanation (Abel 1948). The dominance of that point of view must have something to do with the swing to a

very phenomenological interpretation of Verstehen in more recent years. But an inspection of journal articles over the last thirty years will reveal that at no point did sociologists ever actually give up trying to present their correlational studies as plausible, cogent explanations as well as causally adequate ones. The majority of the arguments about the meaning of actions or events for the participants, however, are supplied from outside the research context, with no justifications whatsoever from the data.

Over the years, there has developed a practice which we can usefully term 'facesheet sociology', which uses a rather mechanical algorithm for coming up with sociological explanations. A dependent variable, an 'explanandum', is selected on some theoretical but more usually practical grounds. Experience has taught survey researchers that most variables correlate with some of a series of background variables, and so these are routinely included on the 'facesheet' of every survey – sex, age, social class, occupation, education, ethnic origins, religion, and so on (Davis 1979). The explanation then consists of correlating the dependent variable with clusters of these background variables, showing that women are more satisfied with their jobs than men, or that manual workers tend to vote for the Labour Party. The more variance in the dependent variable that can be accounted for by these background variables, the better the 'explanation'. But however high the correlations are between the background variables and the explanandum, they are most unsatisfactory as sociological explanations on their own, for they beg the questions, *why* is sex correlated with job satisfaction? or what *makes* workers remain loyal to a particular party?

The way most facesheet sociology is dressed up into a readable article is by supplying a meaningful dimension of analysis from the outside. (The unreadable articles are those where even this is not done.) We may be told that sex 'explains' job satisfaction because women are brought up to have lower aspirations than men, or that occupation 'explains' vote because the Labour Party has always actively cultivated its cloth cap image. But the assumed meaning of the relationship, how it works mechanically or symbolically, is not in the data but laid on top of it. It was commonly understood by early writers on surveys like Wells (1935) that this was inevitable. They thought that surveys could only yield correlations and the interpretation of these would have to be supplied by intensive interviews with a handful of respondents to supply the qualitative insights.

The problem is that we have no evidence that the supplied interpretation of the correlation is in fact the explanation for the correlation. There may be good answers to the questions, why is X correlated with Y? There have been ambitious, if rather unsuccessful, attempts to show that the choice of facesheet variables and the success that they have represent an implicit theory of socialisation (Baldamus 1976). But in traditional facesheet sociology these questions are not brought out into the open and theorised prior to data collection so that the mediating explanations themselves can be tested.

And these explanations have a very *ad hoc* quality. There is rarely any justification of which of the background variables it was necessary to introduce. Religion is always brought in as an explanatory factor in Irish mobility studies, but its absence is never commented on in British studies. This suggests that there is some meaning attached to religion in Ireland that does not hold in Britain (which accords with what we feel we know of Irish society), and sociological explanation will only make headway when it has managed to pin that element down.

However, in suggesting that this type of sociology is not adequate for providing convincing accounts of human action, I do not mean to suggest that we should stop collecting facesheet data, and carefully checking in any analysis that we do that the inferences we draw are not spurious because of the effect of intercorrelations with background variables. It may even be that reflection on the generalisable findings from facesheet sociology will provoke better research designs to test some of the arguments that seem to be implicit in interpreting these correlations. A useful start in this direction has been made by Davis (1979) who has examined the cumulated results of NORC's General Social Survey to see what generalisable statements can be made about the intercorrelations of background variables and their impact on dependent variables; this allows him to assess the average total effects of such things as age, race, religion, and so on, on a wide range of attitudinal data.

Indeed, it is often the correlation between a background variable and a dependent variable which first stimulates the curiosity, as Rosenberg (1968) points out. Rather than supplying the interpretation from outside, we can turn to 'elaborating' the relationship to unpick precisely how it has its effect, and this process will often involve the introduction of intervening variables which show the subjective link between the two. It is significant that Rosenberg describes a relationship as having been 'interpreted' when the introduction of an intervening test factor reduces the partial association to zero. Correlations that are 'meaningless', that don't appear to 'make sense', should not be abandoned as useless but unpicked, interpreted (see Hirschi and Selvin 1973, ch. 10). Of course, logically there is nothing to prevent endless elaboration through the introduction of more and more refined intervening variables, so Verstehen, instead of being relegated to the role of a useful hypothesis generator, plays a central part in the disentangling of an explanation *by telling us where we can stop*, by allowing us to judge at what point we have teased out a sequence of events that makes the action of the participants plausible (Leat 1972).

Facesheet sociology provides the problem for explanation more often than it provides the solution. The interpretation must come from the data, not from the outside. What kind of variables are going to provide correlations which satisfy us as explanations rather than puzzle us and provoke us into asking why this is going on? There is no one answer to this question, but it is generally true that they are pieces of information which allow us, as observers, to get an idea of what the subjective experience of the actor must have been like, and of what that actor might have been reacting to or trying to achieve in the circumstances.

These are the variables that pose the very difficult measurement problems; in fact, the problems are considered insurmountable by some, who, believing that subjectivity is inaccessible, turn to intro-spection or try to find solace in phenomenological styles of research. Now let me say immediately that I am not arguing that measuring subjective dimensions poses problems that are the same as those of measuring externally verifiable conditions. In the last analysis, the subjective *experience* is unknowable to anyone but the actor (Nagel 1979). None the less, the thing that organises subjective experience is meaning, and this is given through social rules and conventions and through language. These social meanings are common stock and are available to the social scientist. There are problems in justifying that one has accurately tapped this meaning; validity has no application to completely subjective phenomena, and the researcher is forced back on to various reliability measures. Since there are no outside ways of checking that people really do find satisfactions derived from family life greater than those derived from work, in the way that one could check their age, the sociologist will have to find other ways of claiming to know something of that subjectivity.

There are basically two ways of getting access to those meanings. You can either ask the actor to supply them to you, or you can read them off the actor's situation, behaviour and 'naturally occurring' speech.

Asking Actors to Supply Meanings

(1) Reason analysis. The social sciences took a step forward on the day when researchers decided that it was worth asking people to account for their own actions, decisions and motivations. If you want to know what gives rise to a decline in fertility, an increase in geo-graphical mobility, or variation in child-rearing practices, then one obvious way to proceed would be to ask the actors involved why they limited their family size, what brought them to move, or what they were trying to achieve in bringing up their children. The develop-

ment of the questionnaire as an instrument of data collection, and the growing acceptance of the idea of a respondent as opposed to an informant, encouraged this strategy for sociological explanation. But asking actors to supply the reasons for their actions runs immediately into many difficulties.

These problems were considered to be so overwhelming by one of the founding figures in British market research, Harry Henry, that he was stung into writing a paper in 1953 that has remained a classic, entitled 'We cannot ask why'. In a series of examples, he compares the reasons that people cite for buying particular products with inferences that can be drawn about their purchasing behaviour from comparing buyers with non-buyers, and concludes that the actors are simply not a reliable source. The reasons that people give for buying *any* baby food are remarkably similar, regardless of the particular brand, and the researcher must use statistical analysis to uncover the real determinants. He is scathing about the possibility of using depth interviews to uncover motivations, a technique which he considers more appropriate to social anthropology, 'that harlot among the social sciences' (1953; 1971: 310). While he thinks that the problems of prestige bias are probably more severe 'in the woman-dominated cultures of the North American continent than . . . in the more stable atmosphere of Europe', he argues that it is a problem even in (macho?) Britain, and researchers here should also eschew this approach to understanding the determinants of action.

It is very important to decide whether the major problem is that actors don't know why they act as they do, or that it is hard to elicit these reasons. To the extent that we decide actors simply don't know, then, in Weber's terminology, we are no longer dealing with subjectively meaningful action but mere behaviour. Determinants of action which are unknown to the actor are not going to make the behaviour 'understandable' to the researcher when they are uncovered through statistical analysis, either. However, it is not as simple as that. There is a spectrum from consciously known, perceived and communicable to the literally unknown, and this spans through the murky epistemological waters of the subconscious. In a book on the *Hidden Injuries of Class*, Sennett and Cobb (1977) argue that the psychological damage inflicted by class society is so great that attempts to get at it by asking direct questions will come up against the Freudian syndrome of repression and denial. Deciding whether to characterise this as a problem of actor's access to the explanations, or actor's ability to communicate them, reveals that the distinction between the two problems is not as watertight as we may previously have thought.

An influential school of social psychology holds that the problem is one of access; it has tried to demonstrate that the rules of evidence and logical inference used by actors and outside observers to decide what produced a piece of behaviour are essentially the same. It is argued that actors do not have any privilege in access to explanations of their behaviour. If you ask actors to reflect on the determinants of their behaviour, they appear to produce *a priori* culturally plausible explanations (similar to the explanations observers might produce) and only use their private experience to check that it does not blatantly contradict the facts.

In a review of a wide-ranging series of successful experiments, where the subjects were questioned after the experiments to see if they were aware of the effect the manipulation had produced, Nisbett and Wilson (1977) conclude that in most cases they were not. They cite Maier's classic experiment where subjects were set a problem of tying two pieces of rope dangling from the ceiling, where they were too far apart to hold both at once. One solution to the problem – fixing a weight to the end and setting it in motion – rarely occurred to subjects without a cue from the experimenter, but when questioned afterwards on how they got the idea, the common reply was, 'It just dawned on me' (1977: 241). In another experiment, the authors demonstrated a strong 'position effect' in selection from a set of consumer goods, yet subjects were unaware that they were tending to pick the last thing they had seen (1977: 243).

Nisbett and Wilson draw very wide conclusions from these experiments – 'the evidence indicates it may be quite misleading for social scientists to ask their subjects about the influences on their evaluations, choices or behaviour'. But there are a couple of points to note here. First, they are talking about what they term 'higher order cognitive processes' which appear to be a rather small and rarified subsection of all cognitive processes. Just because a respondent is not aware of a position effect on choice does not mean that the choice was utterly irrational. Secondly, these experiments present an unusual kind of actor–researcher relationship; the researcher does indeed know the true (and often trivial) cause in this experimental situation, which explains why A rather than B did X, but the actor has to search his or her stock of explanations, assuming that it is a more usual context. This should not be taken as evidence for arguing that survey researchers have nothing to gain from asking people why, for example, they emigrated. Still, the studies alert us to the fact that there are a range of constraints on actions which will not necessarily be perceived any other way than by statistical comparison.

At the beginning of the last chapter, we discussed an experiment designed to show the situational and dispositional biases in the accounts of actors and observers respectively. On the face of it, it seems strange that actors are the ones to attribute their actions to external constraints while observers attribute them to personal qualities of the actors; it is almost as if actors are denying their ability to choose while observers are according it to them. But a little thought reveals that actors well understand the importance of Engels's idea that freedom is the recognition of necessity. One way for them to preserve their experience of personal autonomy and ability to act rationally is to emphasise the way in which their actions were a response to a given environment. The fact that there are unperceived constraints on action, as Nisbett and Wilson showed, doesn't undermine this point. The reason actors don't attribute their own behaviour to personality traits is probably because this goes against their existential perceptions of themselves as free to react in any way they wish to a situation. But why should observers look for dispositions in actors, especially when there is scant evidence of major variation between people in these personality traits? It might be that observers mainly see most social actors in only one 'role' and so fail to perceive the rich variation in personality of most other people. Anyway, the observer who perceives personal traits of 'hostility', rather than merely 'hostile acts', also gains a sense of predictability and control over the environment.

What does all this tell us about the survey researchers' likely success at extracting valid reasons from those involved? The first point is of course that people with the opportunity to see a range of cases are not just ordinary observers, having access to a type of explanation not available in any other way. But, secondly, like other observers, they may be likely to attribute actions to dispositions rather than to rational responses to circumstances, and the popularity of attitude and personality models for which there is little empirical support would seem to suggest this. Asking the actors may act as a corrective and ensure that those factors are supplied. We are alerted by these experiments to the common biases of both actors' and observers' attributions, which we can take into account when evaluating the reasons they provide. Thirdly, actors as such do have privileged access to their own experience but not to all the determinants of their own behaviour. However 'plausible' or 'adequate at the level of meaning' their responses are, they still may not be causally adequate. Their reasons are often much better informed and are interesting in their own right, but have no logical status over any other explanation. If for any reason there are difficulties in getting the required information from the actors themselves, there is nothing against using observers to supply the social meanings.

In summary, we cannot agree with Henry about the use of actors' reasons. Actors *do* know a great deal about why they behave as they do, and we must not eschew the insights they have. But we shall treat them with circumspection. As with so many of the sweeping criticisms that are made of survey research, this is better seen as a caution against asking why-questions inappropriately or badly, over-interpreting the results, rather than a reason for abandoning the attempt.

But even if we reject the idea that there are principled objections to thinking that actors have access to their motivations, there are still formidable problems attached to eliciting them. Just consider for one moment how many jokes and quips rely on a misunderstanding of a why-question: why did the chicken cross the road? (to get to the other side) or why do you drink beer? (because I can't eat it), and so on. We cannot imagine why the inquirer needed to be told the answer; that much is taken for granted. But why-questions which just demand an explanation in a totally unspecific way run into this problem, because an explanation involves the reduction of curiosity and there-fore the replyer has to assess what makes the questioner curious. These jokes make us laugh because they reveal something of the replyer's perception of the inquirer and the tacit assumptions operat-ing. It appears that even children are highly sensitive to the inquirer's reason for asking a particular question. If they think that they are in some kind of test situation, they search for clues about what the problem is supposed to be, and react very differently from when they are playing. There have been some dramatic reversals of Piagetian experiments when they have been conducted through play (Sinha 1978). It has been discovered that one excellent way of piloting individual questions is to ask the respondents why they think the researcher asked that particular question (Belson 1968). The task for the sociologist who wants to know why people restrict their family size or whatever is to make it absolutely clear to the respondent what she is curious about and why.

Survey researchers have faced these problems for many decades, and many of them have come to the conclusion that the bald question 'why?' should never be used. But they have elaborated a set of tech-niques known as 'reason analysis' in order to try to overcome some of the obvious criticisms (Kadushin 1968). Since the determinations of decisions and actions are so complex, as we saw in the previous chapter, the sociologist must try to specify in advance the variety of different types of the determination she is interested in, and ask about each separately. Reason analysis always involves the elaboration of an 'accounting scheme' of different types of determination. The researcher has to construct a model of all the different types of input into a decision or outcome she expects to be relevant, and then draw up a series of questions that inquires about each in turn.

For example, a model for ascertaining reasons for buying a particular product might break the determinants down into (a) influences towards action (for example, the advice of friends), (b) attributes of the product (for example, colour) and (c) impulses of the purchaser (for example, a regular habitual purchase) (Lazarsfeld 1972). Since the reasons for a decision will not be common to all respondents, the interview schedule for an inquiry about motivations must be quite flexible and adapted to the concrete experience of the respondent. It will almost always require an experienced interviewer to conduct a depth interview (– perhaps it is appropriate for the 'harlot among the social sciences' to have come up with the method most suitable for 'soliciting' reasons!).

But undoubtedly the most complete and most influential model of action that has been elaborated in sociology is that proposed by Talcott Parsons. Actually, he did not just propose one, but in the course of his intellectual development and interactions with Shils and Bales, he proposed a series of different models. These could be treated as 'accounting schemes' for reason analysis. In *Toward a General Theory of Action* (Parsons and Shils 1951, ch. 2) the authors consider action most clearly conceptualised as being 'oriented' towards 'objects'. As they explain, 'action has an orientation when it is guided by the meaning which the actor attaches to it in its relationship to his goals and interests' (1951: 4), and there are two major ways in which such meaning is invested in objects. First, the actor or actors may have *motivations* with regard to the objects, either believing them to have particular properties, or just investing emotion in them. Secondly, they may make *evaluations*, according to standards of truthfulness, appropriateness, or rightness. However, as Kadushin (1968) notes, this scheme 'has been used more frequently for developing typologies of actions and institutional norms than as guides to the analysis of concrete decisions', and this is probably why Rex (1961) and Giddens (1976) have criticised the theory of action for being over-deterministic.

(2)   The search for general orientations of actions. Many sociologists who have used Parsons's 'action frame of reference' have concentrated on producing explanations of behaviour in terms of value orientations, making sense of people's behaviour through tying it down to their way of ordering their priorities in life. A wide variety of different pieces of empiricial research in Britain, for example, grew out of David Lockwood's classic paper on three different 'orientations' to society that were to be found in Britain, the traditional proletarian, the deferential and the privatised (Bulmer 1975). The most famous of these were the *Affluent Worker* studies of the workers in the rapidly expanding town of Luton, in which Goldthorpe and his colleagues argue that work behaviour must be understood as a product of the workers' overall orientations to life, not as a response to technology or as a personality need-fulfilment. There are a group of workers, they argue, who work for pay, not job

satisfaction, who fail to form close work groups, who have con-
tractual, money relationships with the boss, who have an
instrumental approach to the union and who see advance in terms of
domestic standards of living, not in increased occupational satisfactions. Their point is that this instrumental worker is pursuing a very
different life project from the traditional worker, and failure to
understand the different evaluations they place on different parts of
their lives will lead to misunderstanding much of their work
behaviour.

But, despite the theoretical importance of this argument, the
Affluent Worker studies started life as part of a very different research
project about the 'embourgeoisement' of the working class, which
made Luton a particularly critical area to test the original thesis in,
but a poor location for a study of the independent importance of
instrumental orientations. The authors do not attempt to measure
the orientations directly, but rather are prepared to use patterns in
revealed preferences – that is, actual choice – as evidence of the
principles underlying those choices. Luton cannot be said to be a very
good place to look at variation in orientations, of course; if one only
defines an orientation in terms of revealed preferences, then, partly
by definition, the Luton sample is instrumental. (Even only looking
at revealed preferences, strong criticisms can be made of the extent to
which their data do adequately establish the instrumental orientation, for most instrumental workers as they defined them were not the
ones who did large amounts of overtime, or who got the most pay, for
example. Those studies which have tried to avoid the circularity of
much of the argument about revealed values by measuring orientations directly have often shown orientations to have weak
explanatory power. Blackburn and Mann (1979), in a study of the
operation of the unskilled labour market in Peterborough, examined
the extent to which workers' aims in the labour market are coherent
and stable. They found only limited evidence that there are stable
differences in preferences which are brought into play when workers
try to understand and evaluate their own work experience; they failed
to find evidence of clearcut orientations to work such as 'economistic'
or 'searching for intrinsic satisfaction'.

I am not arguing here that the direct measurement of values or
general orientating principles in people's lives is wrong, but simply
that it is extremely hard to do well and to introduce convincingly into
an explanation. There have been studies, mainly in the USA, which
show that there are enduring structural differences in values between
different subgroups of the population (Glenn 1967), but the attempts
to show how these cluster or relate to structured groups of beliefs have
not been very successful, even on such prominent values as
Conservative–Liberal (Converse 1964) or on the Left–Right

spectrum (Butler and Stokes 1974: 328–31). Values, rather than being stable and coherent, are often highly labile and wide open to bias in elicitation (Fischoff *et al.* 1979). There is even some suggestion that the more topical, specific attitude items, where the marginal responses fluctuate over time, are more explicable in terms of background variables than are the more general questions about people's values; the correlations between background variables and concrete items on racial matters or freedom of speech, for example, are much higher than the correlations with qualities looked for in a job. This means that values have little chance of entering as intervening variables to provide the subjectively convincing link between the background and opinion items (Davis 1979: 42).

Rather than admit to the measurement problems, researchers seem to prefer to attribute the failure of their measures to correlate with other beliefs to the respondent's inability to see the implication of one set of ideas for another. They talk of 'fragmentary class consciousness' (Robert *et al.* 1977) or distinguish in a rather supercilious manner between 'ideologues' and 'non-ideologues' (Converse 1964). But often the attempts to measure these values are very thin. Compare, for example, the richness of Durkheim's concept of anomie, the state of insufficient regulation by social norms, and the batteries of 'anomia' measures that have been devised for use in surveys (see, for example, Seeman 1959). Critics of these superficial measures have objected to the reduction of such a full and theoretically rich concept to questions about feeling hopeless (Horton 1964). In short, it is in principle possible to establish the existence of values and orientations independently, and to avoid the circularity which comes when they are inferred from behaviour. On the other hand, their greater stability has never been adequately demonstrated, their power as intervening variables is not sufficient for them to provide the bridge of interpretation between background variables and specific dependent variables and they have never been very adequately measured. They are not the panacea to the problem of action, nor have they proved to be the basis of a generalisable set of propositions about the sources of a wide variety of different types of action.

So there are severe difficulties both in getting actors to account for individual actions, and in discovering any broad goals that people are pursuing which could account for their actions. They are not always insurmountable, but they require very careful survey design.

Meanings Supplied by the Researcher: the Social Origins of Depression

There are, however, situations in which the researcher may feel that the actors cannot validly provide the data for a plausible account of their own behaviour. This does not mean that we must abandon the search for a meaningful explanation in these circumstances. The individuals may still be reacting in an understandable way to events that have happened to them, even though they are not in a position to explain this to a researcher. In such circumstances the researcher will have to read the meaning into the events. The example that I have chosen to treat in more detail in this chapter is one that is forced to pursue this strategy because it seeks to explain depression, and the actors were not felt to be suitable informants, as we shall see.

Depression is ostensibly a deeply individual state of mind, considered the domain of the psychiatrist more than of the sociologist. But in *The Social Origins of Depression* the authors, George Brown and Tirril Harris, set out to show that broader social forces must be brought into any account of why people get depressed. The book consists of a powerful demonstration that a particular set of 'life events' have the power to provoke such a feeling of hopelessness that they can induce clinical depression. Its success as a piece of sociology is that by the end of the book the reader is convinced that these are the causal factors, but also has a strong sense of how understandable it is that depression should result from these stressful 'life events'.

It is a theoretical project strongly reminiscent of Durkheim's *Suicide*. Although the life events are not actually described as inducing anomie, they strongly resemble that theoretical construct, in that both consider change itself to be an unsettling factor. It is also cast in the same *methodological* mould as *Suicide*, in trying to account for an individual, subjective phenomenon by social factors. But it is a vast improvement on *Suicide*. The meanings of events are measured directly, not assumed. The subjects themselves are approached directly, producing individual not ecological correlations. Durkheim's confusions about multiple causality and aetiological classifications are corrected. In short, through careful operationalisation of the central concepts, through the breaking down of complex variables into component variables, and most importantly through the systematic measurement of social meanings through paying attention to the context in which the subjects – all women – live their lives, Brown and Harris achieve an utterly plausible explanation of depression.

If inferences are to be made from natural variation, it is very important that the cases in one's study are as unbiased a cross-section of the population that one wishes to generalise about as possible. How is a sample of people suffering from depression to be generated, when it is possible, and indeed this study confirms, that the condition is not even recognised by large numbers of people suffering from it? If a sample had been generated from those who had sought help from agencies which might then have provided a list, the result would have contained the biases that are known to result from selective recognition of suffering and selective referral processes which bring people into contact with their GPs or with hospitals. The only solution was to conduct a careful screening survey, and this was confined to women living in the Camberwell area of London for logistic reasons, since depression is much commoner in women than it is in men.[1] Several comparison groups were also sampled, in- and out-patients of psychiatric hospitals, a group of women being treated for depression by the GPs and a sample from the Outer Hebrides, but I shall restrict my discussion to the Camberwell sample.

The authors note that the survey 'has great potential, but, with some exceptions, its promise has not been fulfilled' (1978: 13). They attribute this failure to problems with measurement, and bemoan the reliance of many researchers on 'some form of the standardised questionnaire, with dispiriting pretensions to measure almost anything by means of a few, often fixed choice questions' (1978: 10). Their solution is to combine the advantages of intensive interviewing for adequate measurement with extensive sampling for valid causal inference. Once again, we can see that depth interviewing is often required for the production of meaningful explanations.

There are several difficulties associated with classifying individuals as depressed: (1) It is not uniformly an actor's category. In fact, most depressed people tend to talk about their 'nerves'. (2) Everyone undergoes mood changes, and suffers grief at some point in their life. The difference between this and clinical depression is a quantitative one of intensity, duration and extent of distress, but where does one draw the line? (3) The very idea that it is an 'illness' has been attacked, on the grounds that the medicalisation of mental illness robs people of their moral responsibility. The answer to the first problem is that this means that the task of measurement is more difficult, not *ipso facto* impossible; to accept actors' characterisation of their own states uncritically would mean that the extent of un-diagnosed depression, or biased referral processes to the agencies which provide relief of various kinds, could not be investigated. Interviewers' judgements have to be carefully calibrated to ensure that they would make the same diagnosis on the same case. The definition of depression used was one based on symptoms, and the evidence about the existence, timing, intensity and duration of these was collected systematically by something rather like a standardised clinical history, drawing the lines as far as possible in the same place as psychiatrists. To the objection that mental illness should not be treated on the 'medical model', the authors can point to the fact that there certainly is a recognisable group of symptoms which commonly occur together, and deserve some label; they can also point to the fact that these bring such distress and suffering with them that they often do have the effect of preventing the person from carrying out a particularly active or free life. But, in the last analysis, they argue that whether you chose to call depression an illness or not does not really affect the research. One can show that a constellation of symptoms commonly occurs together, such that one can identify a syndrome whose existence is not dependent on the label.

In deciding whether to concentrate on symptomatic definitions of depression, the authors take a strong line against aetiological classification. Durkheim was convinced that classifications had to be aetiological and not morphological, as he termed them; in other words, when you made a classification, your aim should be to separate things with different causes, not just things that seemed to be different. It was something along these lines that Plato meant when he said that the task of concepts was to carve reality at the joints. The problem about an aetiological classification system, especially in an exploratory phase of an inquiry, is that it can preclude the types of relationship you can find between the variable thus classified and other variables. This is especially true with depression. If you characterise a person as either 'endogenously' or 'reactively' depressed, you are committed to looking for one set of causes in the first case and another set in the second case. If by so doing you have indeed carved reality at the joints, this may not be serious, but there is no evidence that this distinction goes to the heart of two different processes generating depression. There are many possible models of depression aetiology and symptomatology, as Ni Bhrolchain (1979) has shown; differentiating between them is impossible if the aetiology and symptomatology are confused in the classification system.

So, the interviewer in each case inquired and probed about experience of a wide range of symptoms, sleep disturbance, weepiness, depressed mood, changed eating patterns, muscular tension, obsessional symptoms, and so on, over the past year, in order to collect sufficient information to decide whether the person was either chronically depressed or had had an onset of depression during the year. As a fact-finding inquiry of the Booth/Rowntree variety alone, this survey would rate highly. They uncovered an amazing incidence of depression among the population of Camberwell. Seventeen per cent of the women were 'cases' – in other words, they clearly had a disorder that psychiatrists would have agreed needed treatment, in the past twelve months, and a further 19 per cent were borderline (1978: 57). If the women were working class and had children under the age of 6 at home, then the percentages went up to 30 and 20 per cent respectively.

Research in many different places has suggested that 'life events' are of central importance in provoking an onset of depression. But, so far from arguing that these events are external determinations diametrically opposed to subjective states and desires, the authors argue, in sympathy with the Verstehen tradition, that it is the meaning that these events have for the subjects that gives them their causal force in provoking an onset. But how is this meaning to be established? The difficulties of viewing actors as having privileged access to their own motivations are compounded when the subject is depressed. Brown and Harris reject the idea that the method of introspection is the only one capable of yielding meaningful attributions; they claim that it is possible, if an outsider has enough detail, to see how a typical individual would react under similar conditions. The dispute that has raged between the phenomenologists such as Schutz and positivists like Durkheim has not been over *whether* one should use such judgements about the meaningfulness of an experience for somebody, but *how much* information is required before that can be done (Brown and Harris 1978: 89). If there do indeed exist common social meanings attached to institutions and events, then it should be possible to get at them in a reliable manner; the validity of such attributions does not depend on the respondent's acquiescence in the attribution.

The argument of *The Social Origins of Depression* is that it is life events which pose severe long-term threat to the individual that cause depression. In evolving measures of such life events, Brown and Harris make a generally valid methodological distinction between units and qualities, and argue that the two must be measured separately. Whether a life event has occurred to a respondent or not must be assessed in a manner that is uncontaminated by the degree or quality of emotional response it provoked. Establishing whether a respondent lost her job in the preceding year is a separate task from estimating the degree of anxiety associated with a loss of job.

Parsons argued that all concepts can be crudely divided into units and qualities. A unit is part of reality, and it makes sense to talk about units existing in their own right, although Parsons opens the door to abstract units which do not necessarily have physical existence. Once we have decided what the units are, it is possible to characterise these units by means of various analytic concepts, general properties which are only observable in the particular. In short, units are what things *are*, and analytic concepts are the qualities that units *possess* (Parsons 1949: 27–41). This is a distinction with general validity, not just in a particularly subjective emotional area.

The twist that Brown and Harris add to this discussion is to argue that one should be searching for units and qualities which are distinct, but yet related to some extent. 'If the correlation between unit and quality is too low, we risk collecting a good deal of data of little intrinsic interest; if it is too high, we will run into the kind of circularity that we set out to avoid' (1978: 345). Separating out the unit from its analytic qualities at all stages of the process of measurement prevents the kind of circularity mentioned earlier. If, to take an example, we can separate the unit 'changing job' from the anxiety which might be associated with it, then we will be able to examine the statement that changing job leads to higher rates of anxiety. If we have not made this separation, empirical investigation will be impossible.

It is important that investigators make this basic distinction in their conceptual framework, but the distinction has to be carried forward into the measurement task, which is quite difficult when the qualities are meanings which are intimately bound up with the events, and when the outcome is depression. Let us consider first the recording of the units, the incidence of life events.

There is always a danger that knowing that a bout of clinical depression followed a particular event would induce the respondent to remember it particularly or an interviewer to record it. The authors cite a study of Down's Syndrome mothers before the chromosomal basis of the syndrome was discovered, which claimed to demonstrate a relationship between stress and the syndrome, because the mothers reported such an increased rate of stressful events occurring during pregnancy. What probably explains this high reportage of stressful events was the mothers' searching for some clues which might explain the birth of a 'mongol' baby (1978: 75–6).

It was said in Chapter 2 that many surveys go into the field inadequately piloted, and that many of the criticisms which set themselves up as being fundamental arguments against the whole method in fact apply only to poorly piloted or unpiloted questionnaire work. Nothing of this criticism can be applied to this particular study. The final instrument used to establish the existence of a life event consisted of a lengthy set of questions checking among both depressed and non-depressed individuals whether they had changed job, moved house, been ill, and so on, to try to cut down selective memory by the depressed. These questions took two years to develop. Tape-recorders were used not just on the pilot survey but also in the main study, so that the whole research team had the chance to comment on the coding used, and thus to improve its reliability. To check the validity of these questions, additional reports were obtained from relatives on the first fifty cases, and agreement between the two was very high. This is how they ensured that depressed people would not report more things happening to them than non-depressed people, simply by virtue of being depressed. Great attention was paid to timing to avoid respondents bringing events forward into the period of interest.

Respondents may exaggerate the unpleasantness of life events that occur to them, particularly if they are depressed. The qualities associated with life events were therefore measured separately, by getting raters to judge how threatening and anxiety-provoking such events would be to the average person. Thus the meaning of the event was supplied by having very full information about the context of each woman's life including her hopes and plans, and by outsiders judging the seriousness of the event in that context (for a fuller discussion of this see Brown 1981). The people who did the rating from the tape-recorded information were not told whether the respondent got depressed, and the intercoder reliability of the judgements were checked. The reliability proved to be very high after training, and after rules had been established about what should and should not count. They did also ask the respondents themselves how they felt, to see how these responses compared, and the correlation was fairly high. The resulting scales are models for how social meanings may be reliably measured. Our critic, Cicourel (1964: 107), asked: '[C]an we assume that the interviewers, ethnological "scouts", coders, data analysts and the director of the social science research are all employing the same theoretical frame of reference and interpreting each event, respondent, etc., identically?' His answer was negative, but this is precisely what a carefully designed and controlled research project has as its goal; even if it cannot hope to succeed completely, it can make a good attempt. If one stuck too closely to Cicourel's argument the best would certainly become the enemy of the good.

The coders did not establish the meaning of these life events independently of the context in which they occurred, which you will remember was a large component of the complaint of the ethnomethodologists against survey research. The raters had to judge how threatening to an individual in her particular circumstances any given event was; to be rated as severe it had to necessitate a general reassessment of life and its meaning, and the threat that it posed to the woman had to be relatively long-term. Childbirth was not normally rated severe unless it happened in a context of bad housing and shortage of money. In one case the death of a mother-in-law shortly before the birth of a woman's child was rated as severe because the mother-in-law had been relied on to babysit to allow the woman to return to work. The fact that the meaning of an event is context-dependent does not preclude establishing meaning objectively and reliably if sufficient contextual information is available to the rater.

How do severe events provoke depression? By definition, they are those events which pose long-term threat to the individual, and as such only constituted 16 per cent of all events. Brown and Harris next looked for the *components* of these events, and the great majority turned out to involve a loss or disappointment. This is compatible with a psychoanalytic theory of grief. The loss need not be of a physical object or person. It could be disappointment or symbolic loss, such as the loss of someone's conception of her relationship with her husband on discovering that he had been unfaithful. Breaking the events down into component parts thus revealed the symbolic mechanism whereby severe life events have their causal impact.

We can summarise the lessons to be learnt from this study about systematic measurement of qualitative, subjective, meaningful aspects of social life as follows:

(1) Categories used in social research do not have to be demonstrated to be actor's categories.
(2) It helps if one can show clusters, or syndromes, of attitudes, emotions, or whatever.
(3) Where the intuitive judgement of outsiders is required, great care must be taken to demonstrate that there is consensus; inter-coder reliability is vital.
(4) Explanations of the form

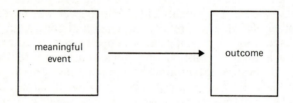

run an omnipresent risk of circularity:

(a) the outcome may lead the respondent, the interviewer, or the researcher to imbue a previous event with meaning it did not have at the time;
(b) the outcome may have been *defined* in such a way that only particular events could possibly explain it;
(c) if the event is purely subjective, it may be impossible to distinguish it as an external, separate event.

These lead to the following rules of guidance:

(a) make measures of units and their qualities as independent as possible from measures of outcome, aiming for a moderate correlation between the two;
(b) avoid aetiological classifications.

(5) Complex variables should wherever possible be broken down into their components for sharper clarity.

The authors combine these carefully measured variables into a model of depression, which is also adequate at the level of cause; this study is an eloquent refutation of philosophical arguments that causes and meanings are incompatible in one explanation. The starting-point for much research on the aetiology of depression came from establishing, contrary to common assertions that it is a middle-class phenomenon, that it is much more prevalent among working class than among middle class women. This study replicated the findings from other epidemiological studies. Table 5.1 shows that 7 per cent more working than middle class women get depressed in a given period. One might be tempted to remark that the association was not very strong, but one would be suspicious of the independent measure of class if the correlation was much higher. This is the zero-order relationship that many studies have tried to decompose, if possible to 'explain'.

Table 5.1 *Proportion Depressed by Class*[2]

	Working class	Middle class
	0·124 (N = 209)	0·052 (N = 210)
	$d = 0·072$	

Source: Brown and Harris 1978: 168.

As we have already been told, life events are hypothesised to cause depression, and Brown and Harris had measured these carefully, separating the measurement of the events from the measurement of their symbolic impact. But, even after establishing independently that these events did happen more to depressed people, it could still be that the events were effects rather than causes of depression. The interviewers were therefore instructed to probe to see if there was a possibility that the life event had been induced in some way by the depression; if, for example, a woman was one of a whole section made redundant, this constituted an 'independent' life event, but if it could have been incipient depression that brought about the job loss, it was not so counted. Three-quarters of the events were labelled as independent and one-quarter as possibly independent, but since the relationship between both and depression was similar, it would appear that one can rule out the hypothesis that the direction of causal force was from depression to life events. Once again, we are forced to conclude that only sociological *reasoning* will allow us to decide which variable is cause and which effect. This solution of trying to establish which is the independent variable is vastly superior to the magic tricks of the econometricians that we touched on in the last chapter.

Life events occurring at one discrete point in time were not the only adversity these women faced. There were also a series of ongoing difficulties – a son's taking drugs, a damp flat – which were included as potential factors in provoking depression. They had to have been ongoing for at least four weeks, and their severity was rated contextually in the same manner as life events. Those difficulties which were rated as severe enough to cause unremitting distress, and which had lasted at least two years (and which did not involve any health problems as these were considered separately), were classed as major difficulties.

The weight of problems that these women faced makes depressing reading itself! It cannot be adequately summed up by the raw statistics that the sample between them suffered 1,400 events involving sufficient disruption to their lives to arouse strong emotions, or by knowing that one-sixth of the women experienced an event that brought with it long-term threat, or that half were experiencing enough difficulties to cause them marked distress. Table 5.2 shows the summary association between provoking agents (severe events and major difficulties) and depression.

Table 5.2   *Proportion Depressed by Provoking Agents*

	No severe event	Severe event
	0·016 (N = 255)	0·201 (N = 148)
	$d = 0·186$	

Source: Brown and Harris 1978: 168.

The next thing the survey analyst must investigate is whether this could explain the class differential. Could it be that working class women suffer more depression because they suffer more severe life events? To examine this hypothesis, we must look at all three variables in conjunction. Table 5.3 shows the joint association of these three variables. We can see that this is part of the explanation of class differentials in depression – working class women do quite simply have more happening to them to make them depressed, and the effect is stronger among the working class ($d = 0·229$) than among the middle class ($d = 0·120$). But there is still a class difference remaining among those who experience one of these provoking agents. The next task is to elaborate *how* the life events operate symbolically, and hope that this will further illuminate why more working class women get depressed.

Table 5.3   *Proportion Depressed by Class by Provoking Agent*

Working class		Middle class	
No provoking agent	*Provoking agent*	*No provoking agent*	*Provoking agent*
0·018 (N = 112)	0·247 (N = 97)	0·014 (N = 143)	0·134 (N = 67)

Source; Brown and Harris 1978: 168.

Brown and Harris's theoretical formulation owes a lot to Durkheim, and the central importance that he placed on the regulation of individuals by society. Their argument is that depression is brought about by life events which are perceived by those to whom they happen as constituting a threat of some kind, most often because they involve the loss of something valued. Any changes of a sufficiently all-embracing kind can enforce a consideration of what one's life is about, and can threaten one's sense of the meaning of life. When this happens to those who are already vulnerable through some factor in their situation, the anomie that develops is sufficiently acute to engender depression. Vulnerability to depression, they argue, is associated with factors which have the effect of lowering one's self-esteem. Not having a job, having lost one's mother at an early age, lacking an intimate relationship with a partner and having three or more children under the age of 14 at home all seem to place women in this condition of vulnerability, and Brown and Harris argue that they can all devalue a woman's sense of her own worth and thus reduce the resources available to cope with difficulties.

In other words, the life events, through inducing change, force people to reflect on their life as a whole and its inherent meaningfulness. When they occur to people whose self-esteem has been run down for some time because of some aspect of their situation such as having to chase around after young children at home, or failing to get support from a close relationship with a partner, these people are very much more likely to experience such profound worthlessness, hopelessness and meaninglessness that they get depressed. In principle, it would have been preferable to have had a direct measure of self-esteem, but there is no way in which that could have been assessed independently of depression.

Thus the authors refine the undifferentiated concept of an independent variable as a causal factor and acknowledge that some variables must be treated as directly producing effects, and other as facilitating agents, affecting susceptibility to the causal process. (They also introduce a third type of cause, those factors which influence how the cause will 'express itself' – here as determining the type, intensity, and so on, of the symptoms which form.)

Table 5.4 shows the joint effect of one of the vulnerability factors, lack of intimate confidant, and provoking agents on depression. It shows that a life event has a larger effect on the proportion depressed among people in a vulnerable condition ($d = 0.29$) than among people who are not vulnerable ($d = 0.09$). It is not just that a profound sense of hopelessness overtakes one when awful things, things involving loss of some kind and therefore threatening, happen. Indeed, the authors argue that if you can weather these storms you not merely survive but might feel good, for reward can be gained from the idea of having withstood adversity. But similarly, they hypothesise that if treasured ideas are lost and the feeling of hopelessness is generalised because the subject has a low sense of her own worth anyway, then the result is usually clinical depression.

Table 5.4 *Proportion Depressed by Provoking Agents by Vulnerability*

Vulnerable		Not vulnerable	
No severe event	*Severe event*	*No severe event*	*Severe event*
0·03 (N = 62)	0·32 (N = 76)	0·01 (N = 193)	0·10 (N = 88)

Source: Brown and Harris 1978: ch. 11.

Central to this theoretical argument is a statistical one involving a substantive interpretation of the concept of an interaction (Everitt and Smith 1979). The definition that they used was one that we have been using, namely $d_1 - d_2$, a difference in differences of percentages. Here we can see from Table 5.4 that the effect of an event on vulnerable women is 0·29, but on non-vulnerable women is only 0·09, which we can call an interaction. But suppose we concentrate instead on the rates; we find that in both vulnerability conditions ten times as many people with severe events as without severe events get depressed which does not square with our intuitive idea of an interaction – an effect only working under certain conditions. How are we to choose whether we are right to call a woman in one of these situations 'vulnerable' (Tennant and Bebbington 1978)?

The question at issue is this: if someone, instead of being married and childless, were suddenly to find herself with three young children and husbandless, would she be at greater risk of depression than she is at the moment if something went wrong? At the moment, her chances of getting depressed go up from $\frac{1}{100}$ to $\frac{1}{10}$ if something happens, but they would go up from $\frac{1}{30}$ to $\frac{1}{3}$ under the changed circumstances. Although in each instance this amounts to a tenfold increase, she still has little to worry about in practical terms from being in a 'vulnerable' state *per se*, but a lot to worry about if something befalls her while in that state. It seems reasonable to describe certain situations as making the person involved 'vulnerable'.

Table 5.5   *Proportion Depressed by Provoking Agent by Vulnerability by Class*

	Vulnerable		Not vulnerable	
	Provoking agent	No provoking agent	Provoking agent	No provoking agent
Working class	0·34 (N = 56)	0·07 (N = 30)	0·12 (N = 41)	0·00 (N = 82)
Middle class	0·25 (N = 20)	0·00 (N = 32)	0·09 (N = 47)	0·02 (N = 111)

Source: Brown and Harris 1978: 359.

Table 5.5 shows that the lack of a class effect in depression among those with no provoking agent is borne out here; there are only two very small Ns cancelling each other out, so we shall concentrate attention on those who have a provoking agent. Vulnerability has a 0·22 effect among the working class and a 0·16 effect among the middle class. Likewise, being working class has a 0·09 effect among those with a provoking agent and a negligible 0·03 among those without. Now we have reduced the question of the class difference in the proportions who get depressed to a simpler issue: why is there this 9 per cent difference between the middle class and the working class among those who are both vulnerable and who have experienced a provoking agent? Brown and Harris show that it comes in fact from the different severity of vulnerability in the two class groups; of 19 depressed working class women in this situation, 10 were in a condition of 'severe' vulnerability, having three or more of the vulnerability conditions, whereas only 1 of the 5 middle class women was.

Conclusion

Making sense of social action in a valid manner is very hard, and surveys have not traditionally been very good at it. The earliest survey researchers started a tradition which continues today of bringing the meaning from the outside, either by making use of the researcher's stock of plausible explanations, derived from history or

psychology or wherever, or of bringing it from subsidiary depth interviews, sprinkling quotes derived from there liberally on to the raw
correlations derived from the survey. Survey research became much
more exciting to the sociologist when it began to include the
meaningful dimensions within the study design. We have looked at
two ways of achieving this in this chapter. The first involves asking
the actor either for her reasons directly, or to supply information
about the central values in her life around which we may assume she
is orienting her life. The second involves collecting a sufficiently
complete picture of the context in which an actor finds herself that a
team of outsiders may read off the meaningful dimensions, carefully
checking that they are doing so in a consistent manner. The second
method is the only one available when the subjects are not capable of
communicating the meaning of their actions validly. In the example
we have just discussed in detail, it might be argued that getting
depressed is hardly a form of social action in the sense that Weber
meant by that. But we should turn this argument round; the mistake is
to think that it is only action that is human and understandable –
reactions are too.

The problems we came up against in this chapter are indeed
immense. Very often it is impossible to boil the interview down to a
structured questionnaire, and researchers have painstakingly to post-
code the qualitative information that is collected. It is hard to ensure
that one has included a question to test every possible interpretation
of the relationship or to cover all possible aspects in the 'accounting
scheme'. Extensive piloting beforehand, not just of the data
collection but also a trial analysis of the results, is the only solution. It
is when surveys are unpiloted, and when major interpretations of the
results are only hit upon after all the data has been collected, that one
finds researchers being forced to bring the explanations in from outside. Once again, there is a danger that sociologists will sympathise
with philosophical arguments about the *a priori* impossibility of
reconciling causal and meaningful accounts instead of resolving to
pilot their surveys better next time.

Notes: Chapter 5

1 Because the subjects of this study are all women it can say nothing about the effects
   of being female, for there are no males for comparison, thus putting paid to some
   rather ignorant 'feminist' criticisms that have been made of Brown's work. If people
   object to the restriction to Camberwell, let them replicate it elsewhere.
2 The discrepancy between the $\frac{37}{419}$ (8·8 per cent) depressed here and the 17 per cent
   reported on p. 114 comes from the fact that the 17 per cent were the total number
   depressed in the last year, whereas this percentage only refers to those cases in which
   onset occurred during the last year and excludes chronic cases for whom tracing
   aetiology would be very difficult.

6

Political Applications of Survey Research

There is a common belief, among sociologists at least, that there is
something intrinsically manipulative about survey research: the
words often used to describe it come in particular from the vocabulary of Frankfurt Marxism – 'scientistic', 'technicist'. It is this
political resonance of positivism which has the strongest power to
explain the sociologists' neglect of the survey method. The aim of
this chapter is to investigate the source of this belief and the validity
of its claim. First, however, some confusions in the conception of the
'manipulation' involved have to be clarified.

There are two quite distinct ways in which surveys, or social
science in general, have been held to be manipulative. The first,
which can be called 'abuse of power', recognises that knowledge
about the social world, in an analogous way to knowledge about the
natural world, gives power to those who own or control it, and hence
gives them the wherewithal to put it to ends of which one may
approve or disapprove. The second, which may be called 'ideological manipulation', asserts that the so-called 'knowledge' about
the social world is not knowledge which is grounded in outside
reality but is an ideological reflection of some kind, created through
artefactual or reified means, whose acceptance furthers particular
interests. You cannot make both these criticisms at once: either
some particular piece of knowledge is powerful enough to endow its
owners with a real basis for action when they intervene in the world,
or it is artefactual and serves as the basis for various ideological constructions. There has been a tendency to present both criticisms of
surveys, especially opinion polls, alongside one another without
facing this contradiction. (See Lessnoff 1977 for a discussion of the
Frankfurt Marxists in this light.) Surveys of objective or subjective
phenomena raise the possibility of the abuse of power, whereas
opinion polls are the correct object of a criticism of artefactuality.

Definition of Survey and Poll

First, however, there is a definitional problem of classifying an
opinion poll as distinct from the kind of survey, often of subjective
beliefs and attitudes, of the kind discussed in the last two chapters.
The distinction between a survey and a poll is sometimes made by
academics to elevate the status of their activities by gracing them

with a Latin-root word, as opposed to an Anglo-Saxon one (Schuman 1979); as such, the distinction is pointless. But one can make a distinction between two different *ideal types* of research, a distinction not based on location (university versus market research company) or methodological sophistication, but on the function which the survey performs, and the differing orientations which ensue. A survey is performed to better understand something. The claim for an opinion poll is that it can be part of a process of democracy. I stress that the argument is about ideal types; any particular piece of research is likely to have elements of each. There are dangers in using the potentially teleological language of functionalism, but we may follow these rules:

(1)   Orientation to the subjects of the research. In a survey, the individuals are treated as informants. They are people who have to be interviewed because only they can provide the details about aspects of their inner psychological life that the researcher is interested in, or because they are the most effective source for other data. In polls, the respondents are treated as citizens, and interviewer instructions on how to elicit a response from a doubtful member of the general public usually suggest that the interviewer should stress that it is important for everybody's views to be recorded in order to give a fair picture of what people think.

(2)   Orientation to the data. The responses that are given in a survey are treated by the researchers as 'data', and this immediately prompts the question: *who* gave them, under what conditions, with what significance? The theoretical task is now to interpret them. If 63 per cent of people in a survey opine that big business is too powerful today, then the only factual element that the researcher is prepared to treat as given is that 63 per cent of people, when interviewed in their homes and asked the question 'Many people think big business is too powerful today. Do you strongly disagree, fairly . . .', said that they agreed or strongly agreed. The process of interpreting the results to such questions in a serious attempt to look at attitudes is to search for clusters and structures of beliefs, and to see if it is possible to interpret the responses to such a question as lack of overall political trust, or some such construct.

In a poll, the responses are treated as votes. Crossing the 50 per cent line is important, because the aim is to be able to make statements about what the majority think. If 63 per cent of the people believe that big business is too powerful, this is tantamount to a referendum on the subject, and the suggested consequences of these responses is that somebody should act on them. The people have decreed what the problem is, and it is for the government to act as an executive and find a way of fulfilling the decree of the people.

(3) Orientation to action. Inconsistency between attitudes voiced in an interview and subsequent behaviour is not problematic, or surprising, for the survey researcher. Indeed, one often finds that the inconsistency itself is the most interesting part of the research findings. Verbal methods 'may be used to get at what people think, or at least what they think they think, but not at what they actually express in social situations' (Galtung 1967: 112). But in polls, this inconsistency is glossed over. All the respondents are treated as citizens with clearly articulated and rationally considered views about some aspect of policy; what they say and what they do are presumed to be in harmony.

(4) Orientation to policy. The policy consequences of survey research are not determined by the very nature of the inquiry. It might well be that the most important policy conclusion to be drawn from much research into the political attitudes of the adults of Great Britain would be that these are open to various changes. Platt, in an excellent article on policy consequences of survey research, reminds us that David Donnison's research into public attitudes towards comprehensive schools demonstrated that attitudes were most favourable where such schools already existed (Platt 1972). He drew the conclusion that there was fear of the unknown, and that if comprehensives were introduced into areas where current opinions against them were running fairly high, the result would be a diminution in the opposition.

The policy consequences of polls are not presumed to require reflection. What reason could there be for not bowing to the will of the people thus expressed? There are more cautious statements made by the pollsters on this topic, but they relate to occasionally *disregarding* 'the will of the people'. Democratic rhetoric has become so fully absorbed into the political idiom of our society that no one needs to bother pointing out this aspect of polls, it seems, although the newspapers occasionally report their results in the format of calling on the government to respond.

(5) Orientation to the audience. The audience of survey results is either a community of social scientists or a community of policy-makers with specific interests in knowing the views of a group or 'public'. The success of the survey does not lie with the popularity of the results, as is the case with the opinion poll. The audience of poll results is ostensibly the political authority, but it is often the very citizen body whence the original opinions came.

Abuse of Power

The control over information in the division of labour is becoming increasingly important, and some have even argued that the changes provoked by the centrality of information-processing are so profound that a transformation of the mode of production is occurring; whereas capitalist society is organised around the institution of private property, post-industrial society is held to be organised round the axial principle of theoretical knowledge (Bell 1971). This extreme assertion is untenable; the value of knowledge itself is still only finally realised through the production and sale of a commodity. None the less, it is increasingly the case that those who can privately own information about society potentially gain many advantages of increased control over individuals and situations (Hopkins 1973). Survey-based knowledge is no exception to this.

Market research holds a central place in the reproduction of capital in most advanced capitalist countries. The more separate the decision to produce and the decision to buy become, the greater is the need of the producer to collect systematic information about the buying habits of the potential consumers, either to guide production or, more commonly, to plan advertising approaches. Much of this information comes from surveys, and many contributions to survey methodology and to psychological and sociological theory have been made by market researchers – quota sampling, motivation research, developments in attitude scaling and the theory of consumer behaviour, to name a few. As automatic auditing becomes more widespread through use of the computerised bill at the point of sale used for stock control and sales information, we may expect these surveys to concentrate more on the subjective aspects of product preference and decision-making. Industry pays hard cash for this information because it believes it provides a solid and testable base for decisions. Whether you decide that this use of social information for commercial decision-making is a form of manipulation that is acceptable or not depends on the balance of beneficial and harmful effects you see in the procedure, weighted by your judgement of the beneficial and harmful effects of alternative ways of making decisions about production and distribution. At any rate, it is a highly visible feature of 'modern' society, and one which has attracted a critical literature of its own, both popular and academic (for example, Packard 1957; Williams 1976).

There are, however, less widely known features of modern market research. In the words of Leo Burnett, 'Proliferation of brands and mergers have brought on a growing need for corporate advertising. No brand can be given the support it needs, and corporate identity is becoming more important as a seal of approval' (cited in Worcester 1972). In order to know how to present itself to various publics, first research must be done into how the relevant publics view the corporation. These include consumers, shareholders, the City, opinion leaders, potential employees, the local community, suppliers, the 'trade' and employees (Worcester 1972). The purpose of such research is not just to plan the advertising but also to give general guidelines on how the organisation that sponsored the research should behave towards the various publics – in how to handle employee relations, on what to say in public pronouncements of the company, on how to present something to the shareholders, and so on. The aim is not to put into practice whatever the relevant publics say they think is or should be the case, but usually to influence the public's views in some way or another.

Corporate image research is conducted regularly in Britain; MORI and ORC have pioneered these techniques, but other market research companies now also do this style of research. Several major international corporations sponsor cross-national surveys to monitor the visibility of their products and attitudes towards their company image. Moreover, some surveys in the USA have recently been concerned with attitudes towards corporate profits in general, without specifically concentrating on the image of one particular company; from time to time, for example, Union Carbide sounds out the American people's attitudes towards profits, company taxation and government regulation of industry. The kind of money required to do this research and to mount the subsequent advertising campaign is not the kind of money available to most groups in society. It is important for people to know that large corporations are using their money not just to try to sell their products, which everyone is aware that they do, and has grown rather cynical about, but also to defend certain political images, programmes and positions.

The creation of survey-based information to aid decision-making is not restricted to production and distribution, but has extended to such areas as jury selection. The principle of trial by jury is that twelve citizens should be invested with the responsibility for weighing evidence of an accused's innocence or guilt. As the boundaries of citizenship have been extended to include women as well as men, propertyless as well as propertied, non-tax-payers as well as tax-payers, so the pressure has built up on the legal system to draw these boundaries in once more, to exclude those of 'unreliable character'. Systematic vetting of jurors in certain types of cases has become routine (Thompson 1980). Now, however, surveys are being used by parties to litigation to enable them to exercise their right to contest jurors in the most effective way they can, and to try out the appeal of various lines of arguments.

In a civil case in the USA, a drug company, Eli Lilley, was sued for marketing a drug which had been taken during pregnancy by women with a history of spontaneous abortion. A majority of the female offspring of such pregnancies subsequently developed cervical cancer. Eli Lilley commissioned Seasonwein Associates to conduct a survey to discover whether a jury was likely to acquit, with a view to deciding whether it should settle out of court or not. If the matter reached court, the company had a profile of the kind of individuals who were most likely to acquit, so that it could conduct jury contestations in the most effective manner, and it also gave the defence a dry run of the kind of arguments that were most likely to sway the opinions of the jury. This research has to try to simulate the process of attitude formation accurately, so detailed questions are asked to test respondents' reactions to alternative points of view. (Eli Lilley were forced to pay heavy damages in the end.) Researched jury contestations have become so widespread in the USA that a group of left-wing activists have compiled a manual which goes into full detail on how to do this kind of research (Shapley 1974). It tells those activists worried about the morality of such research that they can rest assured that the other side are doing exactly the same thing, and that not doing it would be to start with a disadvantage.

Another interesting development in the use of survey research in the legal sphere has been the enjoinment of the Advisory, Conciliation and Arbitration Service under the 1975 Employment Protection Act to discover the true opinions of the employees of any establishment where there is a dispute about whether a union should be recognised. This statutory provision for testing opinion has brought with it the inevitable legal commentary on how such opinion should be sounded, since management in more than one such dispute challenged the results of the surveys done by ACAS on various technical and quasi-technical grounds (Reeves 1979, Reeves and Harper 1981).

There was a sampling problem, if you like, in a dispute at Grunwick's photographic processing laboratories, because the management would not allow ACAS access to any employees, other than those still employed during a long strike. In another dispute involving an insurance company and ASTMS, the management hired an opinion polling firm to give expert evidence which claimed that the employees could well have voted for union representation simply because that was the first option on the list, or because ASTMS was the only union mentioned by name. Methodological problems in these surveys are hotly contested. Judge Browne-Wilkinson ended up having to rule about the likely existence or non-existence of such effects in surveys (Reeves 1979, Appendix 3), and rapped the research company acting for management (MORI) firmly over the knuckles for misrepresentation of their evidence.

Many different quasi-governmental and public bodies are actively engaged in survey activities of various kinds, and this is not always the traditional welfare state research investigating the physical and moral well-being of the people. Before the 1975 referendum about whether Britain should remain a member of the European Economic Community, some rather careful research was done by National Opinion Polls into the effect of different ways of wording the final referendum: see Table 6.1. These findings are of course consistent with many interpretations. They might reflect a deep trust on the part of the British people for the recommendations of their government. Or the fluctuations in percentages depending on wording could reflect the fact that this is an issue on which the British people did not have deep feelings at the time. A scientist would wish to explore the differences to try to gain further insight into public opinion. A politician might draw rather different conclusions!

Table 6.1   *Wording Effects in EEC Referendum*
            Difference between % Pro and % Anti among Intending Voters

Do you accept the government's recommendation that the United Kingdom should come out of the Common Market?	+0·2
Should the United Kingdom come out of the Common Market?	+6·2
Should the United Kingdom stay in the Common Market?	+13·2
Do you accept the government's recommendations that the United Kingdom should stay in the Common Market?	+18·2
The government recommends the acceptance of the renegotiated terms of British membership of the Common Market. Should the United Kingdom stay in the Common Market?	+11·2
Her Majesty's government believes that the nation's best interests would be served by accepting the favourably negotiated terms of our continued membership of the Common Market. Should the United Kingdom stay in the Common Market?	+16·2

Source: Butler and Kitzinger 1976: 60.

It has been estimated that the Britain into Europe lobby spent over £30,000 on surveys exploring in depth the knowledge of voters about the EEC, and the way in which they were phrasing their anxieties (Butler and Kitzinger 1976: 257–8). The anti-Marketeers had neither the same resources nor equivalent expertise at their disposal, and it was not until they were assured of a government grant for their campaign that they were able to do any research. When they did, all they could afford were four quick surveys, which merely confirmed their gloomy impression that they were going to be defeated.

It could be argued that the political issues raised by this type of survey research are just microcosms of the issues raised by the differential access to power and wealth in society. Those without the money are denied access to many survey findings, and therefore denied the possibility of gaining this powerful knowledge. We may have grown inured, as a society, to inequalities of wealth and power, to the point where we treat them as natural. But there is this difference with information: the private ownership of social knowledge offends against the values of the scientific community. These values, to be sure, demand recognition of originality, but the rewards are largely symbolic. To the extent that this research is private, often covert and not intended for wider circulation, objection must be raised. The demands for privacy and confidentiality are inadequate as a response to the 'information explosion', and must be replaced by the demand for more open access to information which is used in the public arena (albeit with proper individual safeguards).

Ideological Manipulation

However, it is not the abuse of powerful knowledge that has formed the basis of many sociologists' misgivings about the potential that surveys offer for increased control over citizens. Indeed, professional debate has fallen behind on this score, partly, no doubt, as a result of the lack of conviction that the results of many surveys could ever give anybody any power! The entry of 'the views of the electorate' into many political debates by means of superficial opinion polls has exercised many people, however, and we must now turn our attention to this. Opinion polls must be sharply differentiated from the surveys discussed earlier in this book, and from the market research activities discussed above. They can legitimately be called manipulative, but in the second, ideological sense.

Consider the following poll. In July 1978, when proposals to nationalise agricultural land were under public discussion, the Country Landowners' Association, an organisation representing the interests of large landowners in Britain, commissioned a poll from the British Market Research Bureau (*The Times*, 31 July 1978). They released to the press a report on the basis of this research, which concluded that the population as a whole was opposed to the government's proposals. The question asked which formed the basis of this report was: 'How strongly do you agree or disagree that it is important for a free society that agricultural land should be privately owned?' The overwhelming majority appeared opposed to nationalisation, But we know that people will endorse almost any way of furthering the emotive concept of a 'free society' if it is not defined, and no alternatives are given. In the survey itself, we discover that less than one-tenth knew of the government's proposals. Respondents were also asked many other questions. They were asked, for example, if they thought that private ownership of land puts owners in a more privileged position; more than one-half agreed and less than one-third disagreed. These results were not reported. (For other examples, see King 1979.)

This raises an entirely separate set of ethical and political questions which are peculiar to opinion polling. While appearing to be highly scientific, objective findings, in fact these polls can be the rich person's petition. The function of these hypostatised representations of 'public opinion' is not to *reflect* that opinion, but to intervene as a lobby into the political process. Later in this chapter I shall discuss the real targets of this lobbying; they may appear to be figures in authority, but instead it is more often the 'general public' itself that is the intended audience, and polling is part of an attempt to construct a social consensus.

Methodological Weaknesses of Opinion Polling
The distinction made above between a survey and an opinion poll was not made on technical or methodological grounds; it was a distinction between functions. The journalistic function of polling does lead, however, to some important methodological ramifications. Reliability and validity of the instruments of research are central questions for anyone wishing to treat the results scientifically, and for this reason sociologists and social psychologists have been very chary of the interpretation to be put on the answers to single-item questions. Indeed, McNemar argued as long ago as 1946 that they should be abandoned in favour of multiple items which could be demonstrated to form a scale, although it must be conceded that there has been too little attention paid to the fundamental *measurement* issues involved in the development of scaling techniques. Single-item measures are often volatile, low in test-retest reliability and susceptible to minor changes in wording, as we saw in Chapter 3. But their very volatility makes them more open to manipulation by pressure groups seeking to find a form of words which will demonstrate normative consensus to be on its side. In the example above of the Country Landowners' poll, the fact that the word 'free' exercises a pull of its own in a question enabled them to present these scientistic representations of the public mood.

One can delimit contributory factors to the high volatility of these single item opinion measures by asking three questions:
(1) *How much information is available to the respondent?* Many researchers have shown that respondents' knowledge of the detailed workings of the formal political machinery of representation is slim. Only one-half of the electors in this country can name their MP, and only around one-fifth know where he or she stands on various issues

(Butler and Stokes 1974: 355). One should not conclude from this that the electorate is stupid. After all, when it comes to parliamentary decisions, what really counts is an MP's party affiliations; the over-whelming majority of people know what party their MP belongs to. None the less, it does mean that asking people detailed questions about aspects of the machinery, the personnel and proposed legislation, almost certainly produces over-crystallised responses which would never have been voiced outside the interview situation. People find it hard to admit that they do not have knowledge about the workings of the political system, and so will give opinions on various topics even though they have little knowledge of the subject under discussion.

The really shocking findings of the 1940s that over 70 per cent of people would give a verdict on an entirely fictitious Metallic Metals Act (Payne 1951) have not been replicated; only one-third of Americans risked an opinion on the repeal of the (fictitious) Public Affairs Act 1975 (Bishop *et al.* 1980). None the less, the proportions of people who give the response 'don't know' is always so much higher when a no-opinion option is formally presented that one must conclude that, in its absence, one might be misled about the fixity of respondents' views. Furthermore, there are (albeit fairly rare) instances where the inclusion of a 'don't know' category changes the correlation between the opinion item and another variable, so serious scholars must treat this issue carefully (Schumann and Presser 1977).

(2)   *How salient are these opinions for the respondent?* Who can say precisely why asking people if they would allow speeches against democracy to be made in their locality would be a very different question to asking them if they would forbid it? Yet there is a con-sistent 15–20 per cent of people who would not be prepared to allow it, but on the other hand would not forbid it either (Schuman and Presser 1978). This is a robust finding which has been observed since the Second World War. The only conclusion that it is possible to draw from findings of this kind is that people are responding to the words 'allow' and 'forbid', and the connotations that they evoke, rather than the more central idea of speeches against democracy. Attitudes about 'allowing' seem more salient for some people than attitudes about 'speeches against democracy'.

(3)   *How intensely does the respondent feel about this?* This is the question most frequently asked by those who argue that public opinion cannot really be measured by an unweighted sum of individual opinions. It is not easily resolvable. Schumann and Presser (1978) tried to account for the gap between public opinion in the USA on gun control which is strongly in favour and legislation which is permissive, by looking at the intensity with which respondents held their views; one explanatory hypothesis argued is that the anti-

registration group held their views much more strongly and this had more influence over legislators. Ironically they discovered that if they measured intensity on a traditional Likert scale, asking people how strongly they felt on a 0–5 scale, the registration proponents seemed to feel more strongly. However, if they asked whether gun control would be an issue on which respondents would choose candidates in an election, it was the views of the anti-registration group which seemed more intense.

The moral of this story is that we have a long way to go before we can claim to have understood anything but the most elementary facts about question-wording effects. A good deal of *ad hoc* evidence is being collected, but few general rules have been forthcoming. Even purpose-built studies to investigate the effects of a specific problem in question-wording are often inconclusive. Despite intensive research, no general rules are available about which method of administration of questions – personal interview, telephone, or self-completion survey – is best for threatening questions; the results are even specific to the type of threat (Bradburn, Sudman *et al.* 1979).

Polls produce unsatisfactory and inconsistent evidence on key topics, due to over-reliance on single-item attitude measurement. This issue of precisely how items should be grouped together to search for dimensionality inherent in them is one of lively academic debate; I do not wish to give the impression that the difficult technical and conceptual issues in the construction and interpretation of scales have been conquered (see Turner and Martin forthcoming, Ch. 3). Opinion polls, however, do not attempt to tackle them. These single-item questions are cheaper, make better headlines and their marginals are more easily pushed around to support a specific point of view. These volatile answers to weak and unvalidated questions are then treated as *vox populi* and a place is claimed for them in the political process which ignores all the conceptual and technical difficulties involved in their production and use.

Opinion Polling and Democracy

The claims that have been made for political opinion polling have not been modest. George Gallup has said that the 'modern poll can, and to a certain extent does, function as a creative arm of government', and refers to political opinion polls as a 'sort of American equivalent of a vote of confidence in the government' (Gallup 1972, 1948) Teer and Spence, authors of the authoritative work on political opinion polling in Britain (1973), claim that polling has become an essential part of modern democratic government; without it, others have argued, the leaders would not know the opinion of the general public from whom they derive their support (for example Webb

1980). There is general support among British pollsters for Irving Crespi's contention that such polls act as 'continuing election' and for Gallup's observations that they allow a 'bright and devastating light [to beam] on the gap which too often exists between the will of the electorate and the translation of this will into law by legislators' (both cited in Roll and Cantril 1972).

These views have not been without critics. The criticisms have, however, been of two very distinct, perhaps even opposite, types. The first we may call the elitist view, for, while it is correct in its analysis that the activity of public opinion polling leads to propaganda efforts 'to shape the very opinion that is being so assiduously courted' (Nisbet 1975: 166), its main criticism is that true 'public opinion' which can express the common interest of a community can never be reduced to the shallow aggregate of crowd belief 'rooted in fashion or fad, and subject to caprice and whim' (Nisbet 1975: 68). There is a long history to this point of view. It was perhaps first forcefully expressed by Burke in his famous speech to the Bristol electors where he outlined the importance of representative democracy as opposed to popular control, but one can see the same themes in *The Federalist*, in de Tocqueville, in Bryce and in many twentieth-century political commentators. What drives these arguments is a fear of democracy and democratic principles leading to 'mob rule'; the people, it is claimed, cannot decide what is in their corporate best interests.

The solution, for Nisbet and for others before him, is to distinguish between the popular opinion of the mob from the public opinion of 'a body of men [*sic*] . . . agreed on the ends and aims of government and upon the principles by which those ends shall be attained' (Lowell 1913, cited Nisbet 1975: 185). Public opinion is thus often not differentiated from legislative outcome; if a law is passed prohibiting alcohol, that is deemed as evidence that public opinion has crystallised on this topic. Making this spurious and elitist distinction between the real people and the people as a corporate nation (who decides what the interests of the corporate nation are, I wonder?) does, however, have the effect of turning these eighteenth-century Tories against the democratic claims of opinion polls. One can accept the conclusions without buying the elitist view of the impossibility of less manipulable forms of expression of 'popular' interest.

But there is a second objection to reading public opinion directly off the polls. Public opinion is aptly named, for it refers to a climate of opinion, a set of views that are in the air at any one time, the subject of conversations between people in public places, and usually the focus of controversy. It is not some metaphysical entity which is latent in the corporate body public until expressed by legislative decision. It is, rather, to do with what is being talked about; understanding the dynamics of public opinion formation involves understanding pressures on people to speak or to stay silent (Noelle-Neumann 1979). Public opinion polls can connect with those currents of opinion by asking questions which will reveal the dimensions and structure of the debate, but they can also shoot questions off into the void which fail to relate to any real issue of current concern (Starr 1978). The fact that you manage to persuade a sample of a thousand or so respondents to give an answer to a question which you dream up is no evidence that public opinion exists on that topic. This second approach to the concept of public opinion has the great advantage that it allows a critical comparison of public opinion and legislative outcome, and is an important part of the conceptual apparatus of democracy. Yet it is distinct from, and permits criticism of, the populist rhetoric of the pollsters who wish to claim the right to speak on behalf of the public on the basis of the marginal responses to single-item questions.

There is, however, a twist to this second conception of public opinion and public opinion formation. What determines the issues on the agenda for public debate and the terms in which these issues are phrased? The media in general and polls in particular have an important role to play in the dynamic process of opinion formation; the polls themselves generate (often pseudo-) information about issues of public concern and can create the impression of acceptance of particular ways of framing these issues. They are therefore important topics of study in their own right for political scientists who want to understand the dynamics of the politics of Western societies; it is scandalous that the polling industry, its structure and finance, has never been the object of serious academic study.

The pollsters themselves hotly repudiate any suggestion that the publication of their 'findings' itself exercises any influence over people – methinks they protest too much! Their repudiation takes two lines of argument. Their first approach is to set up a hypothesis that this influence would take the form of a 'bandwagon'; people might decide their position on a debate under pressure merely to conform with majority opinion. This thesis is relatively easy to knock down, and the pollsters proceed to demolish it. The experiments that have been conducted to test it, however, have been extremely crude in their manipulation of the subject's perception of majority opinion. The fact that a single poll result, uttered one sentence before the opinion question, fails to alter responses, does not prove that the same polls do not have a glacial effect over time.

The most frequently cited 'refutation' of the bandwagon thesis relates to voting in the USA where late voters in the West can know the results of voting in the East before they cast their vote. No study has ever shown that these late voters are influenced by early returns in the East (the latest is Tuchman and Coffin 1971) but, again, this is hardly surprising; one would not expect one result alone to have a dramatic impact, and especially not on election day, when, as these studies show, the overwhelming majority of people have made up their minds. There is some evidence suggestive of a glacial band-wagon effect in US presidential primaries in fact (Beniger 1976). Ironically it would seem that in Britain there is a good reason to believe that a kind of tactical anti-bandwagon effect exists; people may not be quite so bothered about turning out to vote for the party they perceive to be winning at the polls (Marsh 1982).

The second line of the pollsters' contention consists of pointing to the general failure of media sociology to find discrete media 'effects' in almost any area. Despite evidence of pressure to conform to the perceived majority view in much social psychological research (Asch 1951; Milgram 1961), the evidence of persuasion from mass media sociology has in the past been less clear (see for example Berelson and Janowitz 1966). However, we should note two things. First, as the manual/non-manual divide declines as a basic cleavage in Western politics, and as 'issue politics', nurtured by the mass media, grows, the evidence for media effects is also growing (Blumler 1977; Noelle-Neumann 1973). Secondly, the persuasion paradigm of early media research missed the point that the major effect of these media is to set the very terms of the debate (Curran et al. 1977). The more success-fully they do this, the more completely they have their influence; aspects of social reality that have no variance do not thereby have no cause. It would be foolish to conclude from the rather pedestrian experiments of the early media sociologists that failed to establish effects by looking for changed attitudes after watching particular programmes that the mass media exert no pressure on politics or political discourse.

Research into the effects of the media on public opinion has taken a more productive turn in recent years. Political scientists have begun to test the agenda-setting hypothesis by comparing public concerns as expressed in opinion polls with external measures. During the 1960s in the USA, the public's view of what was important to the nation (in answer to an open-ended question) correlated with newspaper cover-age of topics more strongly than with measures of the 'real world' conditions (Funkhouser 1973). MacKuen (1979) has produced some striking empirical evidence of agenda-setting. He argues that the path of influence from the media to public opinion is corroborated by the fact that there is a clear lag period; changes in issue salience in the media are followed by changes in issue perception, in all but the issues that most directly affect people's lives.

And more sophisticated empirical research into the process of public opinion formation itself has been conducted. Once again

Noelle-Neumann's name stands out. She has advanced a dynamic theory of public opinion formation which rests crucially on an argument about which views get spoken and which views remain silent; her term for this process is a 'spiral of silence' (Noelle-Neumann 1974) because, she hypothesises, once a view is perceived as being a minority position, especially if it is viewed as declining in popularity, then its advocates will remain silent, thus reinforcing the perception of the majority consensus. For example, she looks at some survey data relating to the perceived trend towards socialism in the Federal Republic of Germany, and asks people, not just whether they think it is happening, but also whether they think it constitutes progress or a danger. She obtains a measure of willingness to speak about the subject matter by asking respondents if they would discuss this matter with other passengers on a train; the results are shown in Table 6.2. Those who perceive it as progress can be termed members of a winning faction, and those who perceive it as a danger can be termed members of the losing faction. Table 6.2 shows that the losing faction are the majority (388/229), but that if you went by what people said on trains, the winning faction would appear to be the majority (121/108). (We should want to know the correlation between people's predictions of their behaviour on a train and their actual behaviour.) A word of caution though: the interview is not bound to provide any better an ambience for the voicing of opinions than the railway carriage, of course, so this research does not solve the problem of what public opinion *really* is; it merely indicates the truth of the insight that it is about talking and about silence, and is modified by different speech situations.

Table 6.2   *Willingness of People Who Believe Socialism Will Be Established in the FRG to Talk about It by Perception of It as Progress or a Danger*

	Progress	Danger
Would talk	53	28
Would not talk	41	61
Unsure	6	11
	100%	100%
	(N=229)	(N=388)

Source: Noelle-Neumann 1974.

If, as has been argued, the media set agendas rather than produce discrete media 'effects', and if public opinion is crucially related to which issues receive a public airing, then polling activities require much closer scrutiny than they have received in the past. Bandwagon effects have been something of an Aunt Sally. The role of polls in putting issues on the public agenda by making it appear that they are things about which people are currently concerned is more important, if much less frequently discussed. If we argue further that public opinion is usually concerned with those issues that divide societies and produce debate and dissensus, then it should be clear that agenda-setting goes subtly beyond the selection of the issues, but extends into the presentation of those issues. The vocabulary in which issues are framed often belies a partisan standpoint: do you refer to 'cuts in social services' or 'reduction of public expenditure'? to 'terrorists' or 'freedom fighters'? to 'defence expenditure' or 'arms expenditure'? to 'Rhodesia' or 'Zimbabwe'? By judicious phrasing of a question you can make people appear to endorse a particular rhetoric.

In short, one cannot dismiss polling as an amusing adjunct to journalism, once one accepts that the perception of majority opinion and the adoption of a particular political vocabulary itself plays a crucial role in the very process of opinion formation. We need to look at a different kind of 'bandwagon' hypothesis with regard to polling, in the pressure thus invoked to talk about certain issues in certain ways. The people who frame, commission and report opinion polls have a great deal of influence in this agenda-setting sense. It is not just that pollsters show that 70 per cent 'support the government in the battle against inflation' but that they can demonstrate seeming unanimous endorsement of the existence of such a battle. The democratic claims of the pollsters must be evaluated critically. Those with the money and power to do so can decide when to hold a poll, what to ask questions about, how to frame the questions, which ones to report and whether to report them. The fieldwork company may be bound to certain standards of procedure because it is affiliated to the Association of Market Survey Organisations or because its executives are members of the Market Research Society, but no code of standards yet devised has addressed itself to these important questions of issue selection, question-wording and selective reporting.

The consequences of such activity for democracy are serious when the results of this procedure are adduced as evidence contesting the legitimacy of other voices in society to speak for a constituency, especially when the other 'voices' are the considered end-product of a process of debate and representation. The most powerful alternative voice of public opinion in Britain today is the trade union movement, and the most important areas of ideological conflict are wages, wage restraint, trade union rights and the various provisions of the welfare state. An examination of polling activities will reveal that these are precisely the areas in which the opinion of 'the people' is most often solicited, and set against the opinions voiced by trade union leaders in an attempt to discredit them (see Turner and Martin, forthcoming, Ch. 2; for an interesting debate on this issue from a period when American politics were also heavily concerned with trade union rights and powers, see Kornhauser 1946 and following articles).

Two Examples

As long ago as September 1977 Margaret Thatcher, then leader of the Conservatives in opposition, said that if there was a strike threatened by a major union while she was Prime Minister she would treat it as a confrontation between that union and the people, and 'let the people decide' what should happen through a referendum or poll on the subject (*The Times*, 19 September 1977). (The opinion polling machine soon swung into action and allowed the *Daily Express* to report that two out of three people in the country thought that this was a good idea!) A reasonable person might well question how she intended to achieve this. Such a confrontation seemed to be brewing in the autumn of 1980. The previous government had a long and very acrimonious dispute with the manual workers in the public sector, who put in for a pay rise which exceeded pay policy limits. (The unseemly position of a Labour Party making its political stand against an extremely poorly paid sector which contained some of its most loyal supporters undoubtedly helped bring about Thatcher's success at the ballot box.) Two years later, when inflation was running at around 20 per cent per annum, the same group put in a claim for a 20 per cent increase to the Conservative administration; the symbolic importance of the challenge was very plain. They met with an even brusquer reply that 6 per cent was the ceiling for such increases.

There has, of course, been no referendum on the subject, but you might have been misled by the reports of opinion polls into thinking that there had been one. Opinion Research and Communication conducted a poll in early November 1980 to ask the public what it thought of the 6 per cent limit in the public sector, and showed that two-thirds of people supported the limit, or at least the headline of every newspaper reporting this poll suggested that this is what it showed (reported in daily newspapers on 11 November 1980; fullest report in *The Times.*) However, a closer examination of the questions is necessary. Two questions were asked to elicit views on the government's pay policy for this sector. The first was:

The government believes that in the interests of fighting inflation, Local Authority workers should get no more than a 6% pay rise this time. Do you agree with this view or do you think they should get more?

Notice first that there is a presumed causal link between wages and inflation which would not be accepted by many economists (see Jackson, Turner and Wilkinson 1972); indeed, the government's own policies of high interest rates and increase in VAT were widely thought to be responsible for current inflation. Secondly, the only solution being offered to inflation (a 'bad thing') is reduction in local authority workers' pay. If you present only one solution to a commonly agreed evil, it is well known that people will tend to endorse it. Thirdly, only the government's rationale is presented. How do you suppose people would have responded if the following, structurally identical, question had been asked:

> The public sector unions believe that the Local Authority workers should get a 20% increase in pay so that they will be able to afford to buy the goods being produced by British industry and help stop the recession. Do you agree with this view or do you think the government is right to try to cut their wages?

Finally, if you had to choose, other things being equal, whether other workers should act to help win a national 'battle' or to 'try to get more', what would you recommend that they do?

The responses to the first question are given in Table 6.3. Then respondents were asked:

> The government has said that if Local Authorities do pay more than 6%, rate-payers will have to foot the extra bill. Do you think Local Authorities should go to rate-payers to pay extra or should they stick to the 6% pay limit?

What a choice! The option of central government restoring the level of the rate support grant, for example, is not offered. The responses are shown in Table 6.4.

Table 6.3   *First ORAC Question on Public Sector Workers' Pay*

	TU-ists	*Non-TU-ists*	*All*
Should accept 6%	46	62	56
Should not	49	31	38
Don't know	5	7	6

(Base *N*s for percentages not given)

Table 6.4   *Second ORAC Question on Public Sector Workers' Pay*

	TU-ists	*Non-TU-ists*	*All*
Ratepayers extra	27	18	21
Stick to 6%	55	72	66
Don't know	18	11	13
(Base *N*s for percentages not given)			

There are many ways in which the results of these two questions could be reported. A majority of the trade unionists (the people the government will meet in any confrontation) are against the pay policy. Instead, every newspaper that reported the poll quoted the findings as showing 'Two thirds in support of 6%', without mentioning (except in the *Guardian* and *The Times*) that this second question was posed as an alternative – support 6 per cent or rate increases. Most papers repeated the verdict that these results showed strong backing for the government's 6 per cent policy.

But misreporting is not the major point at issue. These questions utilise the phraseology and the perspectives of only one side of the dispute, and the act of answering either of them commits the respondent seemingly to endorse the theory that wage rises are the cause of inflation, or to agree that the choice is public sector pay rises or increases in the rates. Who decides what questions get asked?

The money for this research was put up by a group of businessmen, known as the 'Committee for Research into Public Attitudes', chaired by Lord Plowden. The press release points out that this body is not aligned in any party political sense, since it commissioned a similar series of polls during the previous Labour administration. However, the issue of wage control has not broken along party political lines; the two basic 'sides' of the dispute are employers (including the government, the largest employer of all) and trade unions. In this sense, this research was paid for by one side in this dispute. The committee itself had no say in the precise wording of these questions; it was a matter for the professional integrity of the ORAC executive responsible. But presumably it did have a say in the choice of topic on which to ask questions of the general public. The borderlines between the broad topic, the selection of issues within a topic, the presentation of those issues and the fine detail of question-wording are very indeterminate, however; one does not accuse ORAC of bias or professional incompetence when one points out that the result of this client–contractor interaction is the presentation of only one side of the case.

The fact of the matter is that different sponsors do pay for rather different questions to be asked. If the TUC had sponsored the poll on pay it would not have agreed to the two questions quoted above. If a co-operative group had wanted to poll on attitudes towards nationalisation of the land, it would probably not have asked, and would certainly not have singled out for the press release, the question cited earlier in the chapter. The problem about these two examples is that the 'other side' has not sponsored any polls which can be compared with them. But there is one issue, abortion, where both 'sides' have been actively involved in polling activities since the agitation to reform the abortion law which led to the permissive legislation of 1967.

In 1980 John Corrie, MP, attempted to introduce a Private Member's Bill to Parliament to amend the 1967 legislation to curtail the situations in which women could obtain abortions, principally by lowering the maximum permitted age of foetal termination from 28 to 20 weeks. Gallup conducted two polls for two different clients, one for *Woman's Own*, under the general advice of Colin Francome, an activist in the Abortion Law Reform Association, and one slightly later for the World Federation of Doctors Who Respect Human Life, an avowedly anti-abortion group. Among the ALRA questions were the following:

Which of the following statements do you agree with:
'The present laws on abortion are satisfactory'
'The present laws on abortion should be altered to make abortion more difficult to obtain'
'The present laws on abortion should be altered to make abortion easier to obtain'

(women) If you had suffered rape and as a result became pregnant, do you think you would:
(men) If your partner had suffered rape and as a result became pregnant, what do you think you would prefer:

continue with the pregnancy and keep the child?
continue with the pregnancy and offer the child for adoption
seek an abortion
doesn't apply to me.

The WFDWRHL questions contained the following:

Do you think that abortions:
should be available on demand
should only be allowed in certain circumstances
should never be allowed

Reducing the upper limit for abortion from 28 weeks to 20 weeks except in the case of the life of the mother and serious foetal abnormality
>   goes too far
>   does not go far enough
>   about right.

I conducted a pilot study with twenty-seven of my students and colleagues to see if they could judge who had sponsored the various questions; I asked if they thought that the questions had been paid for by a group that supported Corrie's amendment of the 1967 Act or a group that opposed it. There was only one question (the first ALRA question cited here) where the majority said that they found it hard to say. With this one exception, the majority identified all the *Woman's Own* questions as sponsored by a group opposed to the amendment, and correctly identified every one of the WFDWRHL questions as sponsored by a group supporting it. (Further details will be supplied on request.)

It is impossible to *prove* that questions lean in a particular way; the fact is, however, that there can be clear consensus about the direction in which they lean (verging on unanimity with some questions), and reliable identification of two different sets of questions, even though their order had been deliberately mixed up.

It would be naïve to round on the agency, and accuse the Gallup executives of acting unethically, of allowing their professional souls to be bought by whichever lobby held the cheque-book. We have noted before in this book that the search for unbiased question-wording is a particularly fruitless and philosophically naïve quest. What must be criticised is the presentation or acceptance of the answers to any one of these single-item, unvalidated questions as *the* reflection of public attitudes towards abortion (see Francome 1980 for a full discussion of why different questions produce different results). The grounds on which it is fair to criticise Gallup are in allowing WFDWRHL to present the results of their first question as advocacy polling in support of the Corrie amendment, when they knew that questions such as the first asked by *Woman's Own* produced such different marginals.

Conclusion

It is because the same instruments of data collection and assembly are used in both surveys and polls that many have become as suspicious of the former as they are of the latter. It should be a matter of professional concern to sociologists and other survey researchers to reveal the flaws in many of these political polls. The more difficult question to answer is what a political response to the growth of these activities should be. Polling is only banned in those countries with very repressive political regimes (although many countries and states forbid it in the run-up to an election). I have discussed it as an instance of 'ideological manipulation' because it is so blatantly artefactual most of the time. One effect of the dramatic increase in the sheer volume of information being generated and communicated in society at the moment could turn out to be not a Big Brother nightmare of central control and manipulation of the means of information, but a very real increase in the potential for local control and decision-making; perhaps, under such conditions, polling will come into its own. Or, perhaps, the British trade union movement, like the Black movement in USA, may decide to join battle and set up its own polling companies asking questions about issues which *they* decide and in ways in which *they* select. This would not imply a genetic fallacy in their theory of knowledge, but rather a grim recognition of the 'information war', and the reality of the interests expressed in polling as it is currently done. Would there be opinion polling in a socialist Britain? It's an open question.

7
Conclusion

The measurement of public opinion brings together some of the most difficult issues faced at the moment in survey research. I do not wish to give the impression that it is impossible; there have been some sophisticated studies of such things as the views of the British electorate towards Europe, which highlight the views of differing sub-groups in the population and investigate the extent to which these views form a coherent and patterned outlook (Jowell and Spence 1975). And there are some issues about which most people have stable and fairly consistent views; capital punishment would be an example of this.

The scholarly study of these political attitudes faces many difficulties, the most severe of which are the problems of measurement. Should one ask open or closed questions (Schuman and Presser 1979a)? Should respondents be asked to record general affect towards people or policies (the Gallup approach) or should they be asked to endorse higher level arguments (the Harris approach)? What models should be used to measure attitude consistency (Judd and Milburn 1980)? Should a 'no option' category be explicitly offered to respondents (Schuman and Presser 1979b)? Which response categories should be used: yes/no; agree/disagree (Bishop et al. 1978)? What causes two identical questions, asked by different research houses, to produce different results and to track differently across time (Turner and Krauss 1978)? Can one avoid socially desirable responses (DeMaio 1980; Bradburn, Sudman et al. 1979)? The list of the current methodological concerns of survey researchers involved in measuring attitudes, opinion and ideologies could be extended indefinitely. Social science is intimately bound up with the subjective reality of social actors; social measurement, if it is to be valid, must have some rather better answers than it currently has to questions like the above.[1]

Surveys have a lot to offer the sociologist. Since experimentation cannot be used to investigate a wide range of macro-social processes, there is often no alternative to considering variation across cases in a systematic fashion. Since the processes of determination in the social world are subjective in important ways, involving actors' meanings and intentions, the survey researcher has to face the task of measuring these subjective aspects. It is not easy. Perhaps the most misguided and damaging of all the criticisms that have been made of survey research was C. W. Mills's contention that their design and implementation involved no sociological imagination, but only the mechanical skills of techniques following time-honoured formulae. Nor are surveys cheap. Because of the ever-present danger of faulty inference from correlational data, measurements of all the possible confounding variables must be made, and the sample size must be large enough to ensure adequate representation of cases the subcells created in analysis.

The survey method is a tool. Like any tool, it is open to misuse. It can be used in providing evidence for sociological arguments or, as in any aspect of sociology, it can be used for ideological constructions. Surveys are expensive, so it tends to be people with power and resources who have used them most heavily. But none of this justifies their neglect by sociologists.

Note: Chapter 7

1   A US National Academy of Sciences panel is reviewing the whole range of errors associated with survey-based measures of subjective phenomena. Two volumes will be forthcoming as a result of these deliberations, a report and a collection of papers addressed to specific problems (Turner and Martin forthcoming).

Bibliography and Author Index

(The numbers following each entry refer to the page numbers in the book where this item is referred to.)

Abel, T. 1948 'The operation called "verstehen",' *American Journal of Sociology*, 54 (3), 1918–49, pp. 211–48. The classic statement relegating Verstehen to role of hypothesis generation. (Criticised by Leat 1972.) It cannot test hypotheses. The characteristic of Verstehen is the postulation of an intervening process in the human organism through which meaning is recognised. 101

Abrams, M. 1951 *Social Surveys and Social Action*, London: Heinemann. This is an interesting historic document now – the passionate advocacy of the use of surveys as a utilitarian instrument to guide the interventionist welfare state in achieving its aims. There is a rather arbitrary selection of surveys to paint the historical background, and some very interesting detail on interwar surveys in Britain, for example, the Birmingham Bournville Village Trust inquiry. There is little sense of these methods being used for explanatory, sociological ends. 16, 18

Abrams, M. 1973 'Subjective social indicators', *Social Trends* 4, pp. 35–50. It explains the basic concepts and methods. 35

Abrams, P. 1968 *The Origins of British Sociology 1834–1914: An Essay with Selected Papers*, Chicago: University of Chicago Press. In a fine piece of intellectual history, Abrams traces the development of British sociology from its origins in political economy, the early statistical societies, and the philosophies of ameliorism and social evolutionism. He concentrates on the contributions of Booth, Comte, Galton, Geddes, Hobhouse, Le Play and Spencer. Essays by Giffen Ingram, Spencer, Rowntree, Hobson, Hobhouse, Galton, Geddes, Bowley and by Hobhouse, Wheeler and Ginsberg are included. 27

Acland, H. 1979 'Are randomized experiments the cadillacs of design?', *Policy Analysis* 5 (2), Spring, pp. 223–50. Traditional criteria for evaluating field experiments are: (1) acceptable definition of treatment: (2) successful administration of treatment; (3) equivalence of experimental and control groups. But we need to add two more criteria, boundary (or total picture of research) and challenge (to accepted findings) to provide a more searching evaluation. 66

Alwin, D. F. 1978 'Making errors in surveys', in Alwin (ed.), *Survey Design and Analysis: Current Issues*, Sage Contemporary Social Science Issues, No. 46, London: Sage, pp. 7–26. Overview of errors in surveys in turgid prose and quaint lexicon. Sampling problems – sampling error and bias; completion rates; sample coverage rates (inc. sample attribution) and response rates, item non-response and weighting. Response errors = ITV-given response; interviewers, question-structure and sequence, method of administration and a variety of 'respondent errors'. Useful as a quick guide to relevant literatures in these area, but not much more. 56

Asch, S. E. 1951 'Effects of group pressure upon the modification and distortion of judgments', in H. Guetzkow (ed.), *Groups, Leadership and Men*, Pittsburgh: Carnegie Press. 138

Atkinson, J. 1971 *A Handbook for Interviewers*, London: HMSO: OPCS, Crown Copyright. 34

Baldamus, W. 1976 *The Structure of Sociological Inference*, London: Martin Robertson. 103

Bartlett, M. S. 1935 'Contingency table interactions', *Journal of the Royal Statistical Society Supplement*, 2, pp. 248–52. 43

Barton, A. H. 1979 'Paul Lazarsfeld and applied social research: invention of the University Applied Social Research Institute', *Social Science History*, 3, October, pp. 4–44. A very clear account of the Bureau's history at Columbia. Barton thinks ultimately it lasted because it was neither methodologically specialised, nor substantively specialised, nor a faculty facility. 45

Bartram, P. and Yelding, D. 1973 'The development of an empirical method of selecting phrases used in verbal rating scales: a report on a recent experiment', *Journal of the Market Research Society*, 15 (3), July, pp. 156–9. 56

Bell, D. 1971 'Post-industrial society: the evolution of an idea', *Journal of East and West Studies*, 17(2), Spring, pp. 102–68. A fairly short and lucid summary of theories of post-industrialism. 128

Bell, F. 1907 *At the Works: A Study of a Manufacturing Town*, London: Edward Arnold. 13

Beloff, H. 1980 'A balance sheet on Burt', *Supplement to the Bulletin of the British Psychological Society*, vol. 33, pp. 1–8. Papers presented to the Annual Conference of BPS in symposium on Burt. The most important one is one by Hearnshaw, eight months after the publication of his meticulous biography of Burt in which the allegations that Burt fabricated his data were given foundation. He sums up and answers the critics of this biography. 44

Belson, W. A. 1968 'Respondent understanding of survey questions', *Polls*, 3 (4), pp. 1–10. Examples from questions in National Readership Survey. Designed study from different sources to test difficulty of different questions. Twenty-nine questions all illustrating only one difficulty. Double interview on these dud questions with 265 respondents. A question heavily laden with information content – only 11 per cent got it right. A vague word like 'usually' caused misunderstanding. Also 'you' – who? Excluding things makes people think of them: 'excluding Westerns'. Difficult words – only 23 per cent understood 'impartial'. Or it may be that the question is difficult to answer, and should therefore be modified. Respondents drive for simplicity, especially when difficult sub-questions lurk. Broad terms will be interpreted less broadly. Respondents avoid pain in what they say and seek reassurance. Closed responses stop respondent giving careful thought. More thought when answer in respondent's terms. 59, 108

Ben-David, J. 1960 'Scientific productivity and academic organisation in nineteenth century medicine', *American Sociological Review*, 25 (6), December, pp. 828–43. On the basis of extremely crude indices of productivity, the performance of US, UK, French and German medical research is examined. The data consist of four time-series of indicators of research productivity, showing steady advance in Germany and decline in UK and France in nineteenth century, and very rapid advance in USA in twentieth. On this basis is erected a very elaborate argument about the necessity of research organisation which can adapt, specialise, train and provide facilities, coupled with the vital ingredient of academic competition for chairs and the recognition of the profession. 15

Beniger, J. R. 1976 'Winning the presidential nomination: national polls and state primary elections, 1936–1972', *Public Opinion Quarterly*, 40 (1), Spring, pp. 22–38. Uses Gallup yearbook data to look for bandwagon effect. Not found in presidential races. Of 183 polls, in 83 leading candidate rose, in 81 he fell and 19 stayed the same. But he suggests an interesting model for primaries: in the short run primaries affect polls, not vice versa; in the long run, glacial effects in opposite direction. 138

Berger, B. 1960 'How long is a generation?', *British Journal of Sociology*, vol. XI, March, pp. 10–23. 55

Berelson, B. and Janowitz, M. (eds) 1966 *Reader in Mass Communication and Society*, 2 edn, Glencoe, Ill.: Free Press. 138

Bishop, G. F., Oldenick, R. W. and Tuchfarber, A. J. 1978 'The effects of question-wording and format on political attitude consistency', *Public Opinion Quarterly*, 42 (1), Spring, pp. 81–92. 142

Bishop, G. F., Oldenick, R. W., Tuchfarber, A. J. and Bennett, S. E. 1980 'Pseudo opinions on public affairs', *Public Opinion Quarterly*, 44 (2), Summer, pp. 198–209. They replicated classic Metallic Metals Act style of split ballot trial on attitude in favour or against repeating the (fictional) Public Affairs Act 1975. They experimented with different ways of eliciting the 'no opinion' response, from recording it only if respondent volunteered it (in which case 33 per cent of respondents voiced an opinion on this Act) to more complex filters (which brought the percentage down to 6 per cent). Respondents who volunteered were more likely to be black, less educated, less interested in politics and less trusting. Interestingly, also asked about a non-existent social service agency, but no significant association between voicing an opinion on this and on the Public Affairs Act. 134

Blackburn, R. (ed.) 1972 *Ideology in Social Science*, London: Fontana. 68

Blackburn, R. M. and Beynon, H. 1972 *Perceptions of Work*, Cambridge: Cambridge University Press. 93

Blackburn, R. M. and Mann, M. 1979 *The Working Class in the Labour Market*, London: Macmillan. 77, 110

Blalock, H. M. 1961 'Evaluating the relative importance of variables', *American Sociological Review*, 26, December, pp. 866–74. Reprinted in Lazarsfeld *et al.* 1972. Straightforward introduction to the logic of simultaneous equation systems, and notion of direct and indirect effects. 76

Blau, P. M. 1957 'Formal organisations: dimensions of analysis', *American Journal of Sociology*, 63, pp. 58–69. 60, 61

Blumer, H. 1954 'What is wrong with social theory?', *American Sociological Review*, 119, pp. 3–10. 55

Blumer, H. 1956 'Sociological analysis and the variable', *American Sociological Review*, 21, pp. 683–90. 55

Blumler, J. G. 1977 'The intervention of television in British politics', Appendix E of the *Annan Report on Broadcasting.* An interesting overview of broadcasting research. Despite the non-findings of the earlier years, the idea that the media of mass communication have an effect on people is open to debate once more. 138

Board of Trade 1888 'Statements of men living in certain selected districts of London in March 1887'. Survey based on 25,451 returns filled in by workmen themselves, therefore exaggerated rents and underestimated wages. Questions printed on large, easy-to-handle cards. Pages and pages of tables. No conclusions from them. 'But in order to avoid possibility of mistake, I may perhaps be permitted to state that, after devoting much time and labour to a careful examination of the returns, and after informing myself fully as to the conditions under which the data were collected, I have come to the conclusion that these returns are of very small statistical value.' William Ogle, Superintendent of Statistics, GRO. 19

Booth, C. (ed.) 1892 *Life and Labour of the People of London, Volume 1: East, Central and South London,* London: Macmillan. 18

Bowley, A. L. 1915 *The Nature and Purpose of the Measurement of Social Phenomena,* 2nd ed, London: P. S. King & Son. Bowley makes the point that you can rank things even when you cannot measure them on an authentic scale. He proposes definitions, classifications and measurement of societies and nations, place of residence, density of population, industrial classification and employment status, degree of dependence of household, lodgers, tenants, people staying, social position, income, family, income distribution, production and consumption, standardising poverty line, economic progress of a nation, GNP, and so on. 25

Bowley, A. L. and Burnett-Hurst, A. 1915 *Livelihood and Poverty,* Ratan Tata Foundation, University of London. This is the famous five towns study. 27

Box, J. F. 1978 *R. A. Fisher: The Life of a Scientist,* New York: Wiley. Joan Fisher Box is RAF's daughter, and this is an excellent biography. She is a statistician herself, and so is capable of combining personal reflections with incisive intellectual history. 41

Box, K. and Thomas, G. 1944 'The Wartime Social Survey', *Journal of the Royal Statistical Society,* May, pp. 151–89. 33

Bradburn, N. M., Sudman, S. and associates 1979 *Improving Interview Method and Questionnaire Design: Response Effects to Threatening Questions in Survey Research,* San Francisco: Jossey-Bass. This book collects together the reports of a series of experiments which grew out of the principal authors' earlier (1974) review of the response effect literature. 56, 142

Branford, V. 1912 'The sociological survey', *Sociological Review,* pp. 105–114. Starts with discussion of the Ordnance Survey and says that most interesting social facts still have to be mapped. 'Socialisation of the Ordnance Survey and emancipation of the scientist for human service'. Already have surveys by mine inspectors, stock-taking of Board of Agriculture, census of production, surveys of slums and tenant areas, of drainage and refuse by sanitary inspectors, of factories and workshops by factory and labour inspectors, of civic hygiene and schoolchildren by medical inspectors, and census. Also unofficial people like Booth, but not sufficient documentation of cultural aspects. Galton's eugenic survey. Some are more historical. Aim of sociological survey to gather fragments of information and fill gaps. Approved of Geddes's approach, and his suggestion of a civic museum. 'The end of the social survey is to make us see Eutopia, and seeing it, to create it.' 27, 30, 31

Brown, G. W. 1981 'Contextual measures of life events', in B. S. Dohrenwend and B. P. Dohrenwend (eds) *Stressful Life Events and their Contexts*, New York: Neale Watson. There is nothing much in this article that is not in Brown and Harris 1978, but it usefully collects together his views on how one sets about measuring contextually and the stages in building up such contextual measures of the threat of life events: (1) record events independently of the subject's opinion of their impact; (2) collect extensive background information about the events; (3) use raters outside the interview situation to use their knowledge of the subject's background context to measure the degree of threat. 117

Brown, G. W. and Harris, T. 1978 *The Social Origins of Depression: A Study of Psychiatric Disorder in Women*, London: Tavistock. A study of the incidence and causation on depression in a sample of women in Camberwell, London. It is discussed fully in Chapter 5 of this book as a modern inheritor of the Durkheimian tradition of empirical analysis. See Tennant and Bebbington 1978 for a critique. 55, 111-25

Bulmer, M. (ed.) 1975 *Working Class Images of Society*, London: Routledge Direct Editions. Reprints Lockwood's 'Sources of variation in working class images of society' of 1966 and a series of articles documenting the empirical research that this has given rise to. 109

Bulmer, M. 1981 'Sociology and political science at Cambridge in the 1920's: an opportunity missed and an opportunity taken', *Cambridge Review*, 27 April, pp. 156-9. He looks at the failure of Cambridge University to set up a chair of sociology in the 1920s, when a grant from the Rockefeller Memorial was made available for that purpose. Such was the poor academic standing of sociology in Britain at the time that the opportunity was passed by, although a chair in political science was established. 1

Burgess, E. W. 1916 'The social survey: a field for constructive service by departments of sociology', *American Journal of Sociology*, 21 January, pp. 492–500. This is a very good source to get the flavour of what early American social surveyors thought they were up to. The 'sociologist' is the football coach for a vast army of local do-gooders who will survey conditions and then propose remedies. A sort of do-it-yourself social Darwinism. 31

Butler, D. and Kitzinger, U. 1976 *The 1975 Referendum*, London: Macmillan Chapter 10 is on the polls about the referendum. 131

Butler, D. and Stokes, D. 1974 *Political Change in Britain: The Evolution of Electoral Choice*, 2nd edn, London: Macmillan (1st edn 1969). A fine example of British survey research, which aims to do more than just describe. It is discussed in Chapter 4 of this volume. 85-97, 111, 134

Campbell, D. T. and Stanley, J. C. 1963 *Experimental and Quasi-Experimental Designs for Research*, Chicago: Rand McNally, pp. 171–246. 66

Carr-Hill, R. A. 1973 *Population and Educational Services: Preliminary Report on a Social Survey*, Geneva: UNESCO (ref. PDEP/Ref. 7). 19

Carr-Saunders, A. M. 1934 'Problems of regional survey', *Public Administration*, XII (1), January, pp. 47–52. Usual definition of a survey as (*a*) factual, (*b*) to assist social reform. He is clearly concerned not to have a mass of community surveys queering his pitch, and suggests they use extant material, leaving the big problems for the professionals. 30

Carr-Saunders, A. M. and Jones, D. C. 1937 *A Survey of the Social Structure of England and Wales,* 2nd edn (1st edn 1927). This is a statistical abstract of contemporary social data from the 'morphological point of view'. It is rather like an early 'Social trends', with chapters on population by age, sex, marriage, housing, region, industry, occupation, on industrial status and class, trade unions, religious organisations, the national income, national wealth, job-seeking and unemployment, state pensions, public services, taxes, friendly societies, charity, poverty, crime, intelligence and fertility. But it is quite 'readable' – giving an 'account' in each chapter. 30

Cicourel, A. V. 1964 *Method and Measurement in Sociology*, Glencoe, Ill.: Free Press. 53-4, 58-62, 117

Clapham Report 1946 *Report of the Committee on the Provision for Social and Economic Research*, London: HMSO, Cmd 6868, July. Complains of under-financing and under-institutionalising of social research in UK.

Cobbett, W. 1975 *Rural Rides* London: Macdonald Facsimile Edition. First published London 1830. 12

Cohen, P. 1980 'Is positivism dead?', *Sociological Review*, 28 (1), pp. 141–76. 3

Cole, S. 1972 'Continuity and institutionalisation in science: a case study of failure', in Oberschall 1972, pp. 73–129. Reprinted in Lazarsfeld *et al.* 1972. There was good research around in the mid-nineteenth century (he cites a monograph by Plint as an example) but, for a variety of reasons, the skills were not institutionalised and were therefore lost. 15

Coleman, J. S. 1959 'Relational analysis: a study of social organisation with survey methods', *Human Organisation*, 17, 1958–9, pp. 28–36. Reprinted in Lazarsfeld 1972. The earliest use by sociologists of survey methods was the study of single-variable distributions, often taken from opinion polls, where the unit was an atomised, independent individual. Slowly the idea of analytical surveys, explaining patterns, developed, and other possibilities began to be revealed. Sampling strategies available are snowball sampling, saturation sampling, dense sampling and multistage sampling. Analytical methods available are contextual analysis, search for the boundaries of homogeneity, pair analysis and partitioning into cliques. 61

Coleman, J. S., Katz, E. and Menzel, H. 1957 'The diffusion of an innovation among physicians', *Sociometry*, 20, pp. 253–70. 61

Committee Investigating the Poorer Classes in St Georges in the East 1848 'Investigations into the state of the poorer classes in St George's-in-the-East', *Journal of the Statistical Society of London*, 11, pp. 193–250. Good because comparable area covered in Board of Trade 1887 inquiry. 19-22

Converse, P. E. 1964 'The nature of belief systems in mass publics, in D. Apter (ed.), *Ideology and Discontent*, New York: Free Press, pp. 206–61. 110, 111

Cullen, M. 1975 The Statistical Movement in early Victorian Britain, The Foundations of Empirical Social Research, Hassocks, Sussex: Harvester Press. The best available source on the early Victorian statistical societies, with an excellent account of the statistical activities of the government. 14, 15

Curran, J., Gurevitch, M. and Wollacott, J. (eds) 1977 *Mass Communication and Society*, London: Edward Arnold in association with the Open University Press. In reaction to the 'who says what, how, to whom and with what effect school', these papers try to ask broader questions of the ideological and cultural role of the media in society. 138

d'Andrade, R. D. 1974 'Memory and the assessment of behaviour', in Blalock 1974, pp. 159–86. Shows how memory distortions may be patterned in such a way that investigators may obtain a totally erroneous picture of the interrelationships among behaviour dimensions, even where memory pertains to very recent events. 82

Davidson, D. 1963 'Actions, reasons and causes', *Journal of Philosophy*, 60, pp. 685–99. 52

Davis, J. A. 1971 *Elementary Survey Analysis*, Englewood Cliffs, NJ: Prentice-Hall. Excellent account of the procedures of survey analysis, but unfortunately in terms of decomposing gamma, which Davis himself subsequently has admitted is not ideal. The appendix criticises the decomposition formula of Lazarsfeld and Kendall of 1950. 45, 73, 77

Davis J. A. 1976 'Analyzing contingency tables with linear flow graphs: D Systems', in D. Heise (ed.), *Sociological Methodology*, San Francisco: Jossey-Bass, pp. 111–45. Expands domain of causal diagrams to cover the analysis of categorical variables, thereby increasing the heuristic, expository and pedagogical flexibility of researchers working with qualitative variates. Lays particular stress on developing diagrams that conform to rules of flow-graph analysis. Concentrates on models for cross-sectional data and gives explicit attention to issues of estimation and statistical significance. 73, 75.

Davis, J. A. 1979 'Background variables and opinions in the 1972–1977 NORC General Social Surveys: ten generalizations about age, education, occupational prestige, race, religion and sex, and forty-nine opinion items, NORC: General Social Survey Technical Report No. 18, August. He empirically establishes which background, 'facesheet' variables are inter-correlated, yielding suggested rules for which of these variables are vital to control when considering the effect of others. Then looks at the relationship between these variables and forty-nine opinions, net of the other independent variables, and comes up with some substantively fascinating general conclusions about the average effects of such things as age, race, religion, education, occupation, and so on. The big question must be whether these results are generalisable beyond General Social Surveys. 102, 103, 111

Dawe, A. 1970 'The two sociologies', *British Journal of Sociology*, 21 (2), June, pp. 207–18. Classic article tracing two problems from the Enlightenment, the orthodox problem of order, and the critical/liberationist problem of control. Sociology is a result of the conflict between the two fundamentally opposed social philosophies which address these problems. 98

DeMaio, T. J. (forthcoming) 'A review of social desirability measures in surveys' in Turner and Martin (eds.) forthcoming vol. 2. 142

Duncan, O. D. 1973 *Introduction to Structural Equation Models*, London: Academic Press. 73

Duncan, O. D. 1979 'Indicators of sex typing: traditional and egalitarian, situational and ideological', *American Journal of Sociology*, 85 (2), pp. 251–60. Analyses responses from 1953 to 1976 of mothers to question about sex-typing of household chores. It is of strong methodological interest, because it proposes model of scale types that have been derived theoretically. One dimension of traditional/egalitarian responses is not enough, but an additional dimension of whether the rationale behind the responses is ideological or situational provides a model that fits well – it pays special attention to the consistently traditional and consistently egalitarian responses. 73

Easthope, G. 1974 *A History of Social Research Methods*, London: Longman. Very disappointing, given the dearth of books on this subject. It is organised by 'method', with a chapter on the origins of sociology which lamely suggests that the motivating forces among sociologists were a drive to be scientific and compassionate. The chapters on the history of individual methods are examples strung together. 16

Editorial 1838 *Journal of the Statistical Society of London*, 1 (1), May. The science of statistics is descriptive, not explanatory. It is connected with geography, geology, agriculture, zoology and botany, and even chemistry, medicine and astronomy. No speculation is permitted. 38

Elesh, D. 1972 'The Manchester Statistical Society: a case study of discontinuity in the history of empirical social research', in Oberschall 1972, pp. 31–72. Historical article on the Manchester Statistical Society, demonstrating early knowledge of precoding, percentages and the need for interviewers. But these gains were not consolidated and often work at a later date is poorer than work at an earlier date. Again, the technically best work is on health. Failed to institutionalise work. Did not establish regular channels of communication, did not mention each other's work, did not do cumulative research (except perhaps in question-asking); did not get to stage of generating their own problems. Why? Because they could not agree on common goals, for example, place of education *vis à vis* religion. They diversified interests, money and manpower to other causes. The government began to develop institutions to gather statistics, the individuals were co-opted by the government. What they were really interested in was social reform. 15

Engels, F. 1969 *The Condition of the Working Class in England from Personal Observations and Authentic Sources*, London: Panther Books. First published 1892. 12

Engels, F. 1976 *Anti-Duhring: Herr Eugen Duhring's Revolution in Science*, Peking: Foreign Languages Press. First published in 1878. 75

Everitt, B. S. and Smith, A. M. R. 1979 'Interactions in contingency tables: a brief discussion of alternative definitions', *Psychological Medicine*, 9, pp. 581–3. 122

Finer, S. E. 1952 *The Life and Times of Sir Edwin Chadwick*, London: Methuen and New York: Barnes & Noble. A good way in to the kinds of moral, political and intellectual concerns of the time. 14

Fischoff, B., Slovic, P. and Lichtenstein, S. 1979 'Knowing what you want: measuring labile values', in T. Wallsten (ed.), *Cognitive Processes in*

Choice and Decision Behaviour, Hillsdale, NJ: Erlbaum, pp. 117–41. People's values are contradictory, incoherent and open to biased elicitation or even creation by questioning. If all we are interested in is how people express themselves, then this may not be so bad. But if we are concerned democratically with what people value and why, we need much finer conceptual elaboration, better questions and a dialectical eliciting procedure which acknowledges the roles of the interviewer. (No data.) 111

Fisher, R. A. 1925 *Statistical Methods for Research Workers*, Edinburgh: Oliver & Boyd. New editions in 1928, 1930, 1932, 1934, 1936, 1938, 1941, 1944, 1946, 1950, 1954, 1958 and 1970. 41, 42

Fisher, R. A. 1935 *The Design of Experiments*, Edinburgh: Oliver & Boyd. New editions in 1937, 1942, 1947, 1949, 1951, 1960 and 1966. 41

Foster, J. 1974 *Class Struggle in the Industrial Revolution*, London: Weidenfeld & Nicolson. 12

Fothergill, J. E. and Willcock, H. D. 1953 'Interviewers and interviewing', Social Survey Papers, Methodological Series, Paper No. M. 69. Historical account of development of interviewing; two mistakes were common: (1) concentration on comprehension of question without adequate reference to how it was comprehended; (2) concentration of formal design of questions. People were more concerned with the adequacy of the question than the adequacy of responses. Move from multidimensional to unidimensional questions, to more structured questions and more factual data. Changes in design have taken place to make sure that similar recorded responses to questions have similar meaning and are additive and that dimensions of responses can be identified. Separation of exploratory pilot from final version. This has meant changes in interviewer's job. Difficulties of getting people to stay long enough in job which requires very diverse attributes – interviewing skills, clerical accuracy and availability – is discussed. Methods proposed for evaluating interviewers. Training is essential. 34

Francome, C. 1980 'Public opinion on abortion: three polls published in February 1980', Department of Sociology, Middlesex Polytechnic, Hendon, for the Abortion Law Reform Association, mimeo. He explains why three rather different questions produced such seemingly discrepant results on opinion towards abortion. 144-5

Funkhouser, G. R. 1973 'The issues of the sixties', *Public Opinion Quarterly*, 37 (1), Spring, pp. 62–75. Compared importance of issues in polls with prominence in quality news magazines. Mostly agreed. Discrepancies came in more personal questions – views on Vietnam or race relations. But looking at Vietnam War, campus unrest and urban riots, did not tally with reality. Coverage of non-newsworthy issues was primarily a function of artificial news. 55, 138

Gallie, D. 1978 *In Search of the New Working Class*, Cambridge: Cambridge University Press. 93

Gallup, G. 1948 *A Guide to Public Opinion Polls*, Princeton, NJ: Princeton University Press. First published 1944. 'Quintamensional' plan of question design. Do not ask 'Do you approve/disapprove $250m. aid to Greece?' Instead: (1) Find out what person knows . . . have you heard? (2) Ask what he thinks – what do you think? (3) Then ask direct yes/no . . . should Congress vote $250m.? (4) Why does person feel this way? (5) How strongly does person hold this opinion? Very persuasive book extolling the virtues of public opinion polling in a democracy. Answers to 100 questions commonly asked about polls. 135

Gallup, G. 1972 'Opinion polling in a democracy', in J. Tanur *et al.* (eds), *Statistics, a guide to the unknown*, San Francisco: Holden Day, pp. 146–52. The common man's quotient of good sense is so high that there is nothing to worry about widespread influence of polls on decision-makers. 135

Galtung, J. 1967 *Theory and Methods of Social Research*, London: Allen & Unwin. 127

Gellner, E. 1974 'The new idealism – cause and meaning in the social sciences', in A. Giddens (ed.), *Positivism and Sociology*, London: Heinemann Educational, pp. 129–56. 52, 98

Giddens, A. 1976 *New Rules of Sociological Method*, London: Hutchinson. 109

Glass, D. V. 1973 *Numbering the People: The Eighteenth Century Population Controversy and the Development of Census and Vital Statistics in Britain*, Farnborough: D. C. Heath. A rather dry but scholarly account of the heated debates between the 'optimists' and the 'pessimists' in eighteenth-century England about population change since the Glorious Revolution, of the introduction of the inadequate census of 1801 and the gradual development towards a more modern census with household schedules in 1841, and of the institution of civil registration of births, marriages and deaths. He still doesn't actually explain why the development was so slow – he uses some comparative material but leaves it as a puzzle. Several source documents for this history are also reprinted. 11

Glass, R. 1955 'Urban sociology in Great Britain: a trend report', *Current Sociology*, 4, pp. 5–76. She explored the popular success of the LePlay-Geddes school, and the subsequent weakness of urban sociology in Britain, by suggesting that LePlay had contrived to appeal to deep-seated theme of British middle class culture – a rooted antipathy to cities. 17, 31

Glenn, N. D. 1967 'Massification versus differentiation: some trend data from national surveys', *Social Forces*, 46, December, pp. 172–80. In response to claims by Hodges, Bell and Boulding that society was increasingly 'massified', first cohort studies tried to examine the thesis. But this trend study provides stronger evidence of the failure of this thesis. Looking only at what are considered to be fairly stable values, only sex and urban–rural differences are declining, and regional, educational and occupational differences are increasing. Ambiguous evidence on social and religious differences. Most of the data gathered in early 1960s when respondents were not socialised in the era of TV. 110

Goldthorpe, J. H., Lockwood, D. *et al.* 1968 *The Affluent Worker*, Vols 1–3, Cambridge: Cambridge University Press (Vol. 2 came out in 1928, Vol. 3 in 1969 and Vol. 1 in 1970). 92, 109-10

Gough, I. 1979 *The Political Economy of the Welfare State*, London: Macmillan. A bold attempt to provide an account of the state's role in various areas of social welfare, and to relate the ideology and reality of its role to the economics of 'advanced' capitalism. 35

Graunt, J. 1939 *Natural and Political Observations Made upon the Bills of Mortality*, Baltimore, Md: Johns Hopkins University Press. First published in 1662. Graunt, spurred on by the information contained in the bills of mortality prepared in connection with the great plague, was the first to reason about demographic material in a modern statistical way. Selvin (1968) considers that he set the pattern of statistical analysis until the nineteenth century with his early work on life tables. 10, 47n1

Gray, P. G. and Corlett, T. 1950 'Sampling for the Social Survey', *Journal of the Royal Statistical Society*, pt II, pp. 150–99 (discussion pp. 200–6). Gives a flavour of survey work done by government. 34

Griffiths, D., Irvine, J. and Miles, I. 1979 'Social statistics: towards a radical science', in Irvine *et al.* 1979, pp. 339–81. An interesting review of the politics of what might loosely be called 'science and society' over the last couple of decades: it argues that one must see scientific knowledge as a social product, claiming that this replaces older versions of how to appraise science. The conclusion discusses the practicalities of what radical statisticians should do. 67

Halsey, H. A. (ed.) 1972 *Education Priority*, HMSO. 66

Hansen, M. H., Hurwitz, W. N. *et al.* 1951 'Response errors in surveys'. *Journal of the American Statistical Association*, 46 (June, pp. 147–90. The classic treatment of error as a deviation from an 'individual true value'. 56

Harrisson, T. 1978 *Living through the Blitz*, Harmondsworth: Penguin. Tom Harrisson had virtually completed this work before his death, but it is in places a bit rough. He based it on the accounts which had lain for years unused in Sussex's Mass-Observation archive. This shows Mass-Observation at its very best, documenting a unique social situation by observation, diary and direct inquiry at a time when other forms of investigations were both politically and practically impossible. 32, 33

Harrop, M. 1980 'Social research and market research: a critique of a critique', *Sociology*, 14 (2), pp. 277–81. Defends the practice of market research companies and complains at the low technical level of most British sociologists. He has an interesting review of sampling strategies in surveys reported in British sociological journals. 5

Hauser, P. 1969 'Comments on Coleman's paper, in R. Bierstedt (ed.), *A Design for Sociology: Scope, Objectives and Methods*, Philadelphia, Pa: American Academy of Political and Social Science, pp. 122–8. 64

Hauser, R. M. 1970 'Context and consex: a cautionary tale', *American Journal of Sociology*, 75, pp. 645–64. 61

Heise, D. 1974 *Causal Analysis*, New York: Wiley. 73

Hennock, E. P. 1976 'Poverty and social theory in England: the experience of the eighteen-eighties', *Social History*, 1, January, pp. 67–91. Re-evaluation of Booth's contribution to late nineteenth-century thought. Hennock debunks many myths about Booth, and argues that his role was as a systematiser of popular concerns at the time to separate the respectable from incompetent working class. There is also a description of the Select Committee of the House of Lord's investigation into the Sweated Trades, and the two case studies are used to argue that the social remedies proposed in the 1880s are not innovatory but have continuity with 1860s. 17

Henry, H. 1971 'We cannot ask "why"', in H. Henry (ed.), *Perspectives in Management and Marketing Research*, London: Crosby Lockwood, pp. 293–311. First given as a paper at a joint ESOMAR/WAPOR conference in 1953. A seminal paper which argues that 'the normal human being in

Western civilisation is usually quite unable to realise, even to himself, what are the motives for many of his actions'. Henry argues this on the basis of evidence of his from product research, showing convincingly that people do not know why they use particular products. 105-7

Hindess, B. 1973 *The Use of Official Statistics in Sociology – A Critique of Positivism and Ethnomethodology*, London: Macmillan. 62

Hindess, B. 1977 *Philosophy and Methodology in the Social Sciences*, Hassocks, Sussex: Harvester Press. 63

Hirschi, T. and Selvin, H. C. 1973 *Principles of Survey Analysis: Delinquency Research*, New York: Free Press. First published as *Delinquency Research* in 1967, and subsequently renamed. Principles of causal analysis are establishing association, and causal order and lack of spuriousness. Very important to establish correctly the intervening process. Introducing test factors may produce internal replication or interaction; they should be introduced for zero relationships. Many false criteria: (1) need for a perfect relationship; (2) argument that if factor is not characteristic of delinquents it cannot be cause of delinquency; (3) argument that if relationship between X and Y, found for single value of contextual Z, then Z is not causal; (4) if X correlates with Y with psychological Z intervening, then X is not causal; (5) if X is measurable, X cannot be causal; only if abstract; (6) if X's correlation with Y is conditional on Z, X is not causal. 39, 45, 85, 103

Hobsbawm, E. 1964 'The Fabians reconsidered', in *Labouring Men: Studies in the History of Labour*, London: Weidenfeld & Nicolson, pp. 250–71. The strength of the Fabians is that they were excellent at singing their own praises. When you actually examine closely any of the claims most are made about their influence – that they destroyed the influence of Marxism in Britain, that they inspired the Labour Party, that they precipitated the welfare state and that they were the instruments of municipal reform, all prove foundless. An analyst of social composition reveals the main support coming from the new brain-worker professionals advocating rational socialism. They were a strange quirk in British left, intellectually a reaction to the collapse of *laissez-faire* ideas more associated with the right, imperialism, big business and government administration elsewhere. 18

Hope, K. 1981 'Vertical mobility in Britain: a structured analysis', *Sociology* 15 (1), February, pp. 19–15. 72

Hopkins, H. 1973 *The Numbers Game: The Bland Totalitarianism*, London: Secker & Warburg. A rather silly book. He has four anti-heroes, Malthus, Booth, Galton and Kinsey, who began the dreaded Numbers Game. He blames Beeching's policies to cut the British railway system on his statistical approach. Thinks public service ideal is disappearing in a Blimpish way. Figures become self-fulfilling prophecies. Wrong to keep harping on that more research is needed. Calls for new Declaration of Independence. Need to educate people better. 128

Horton, J. 1964 'The dehumanisation of alienation and anomie', *British Journal of Sociology*, 15 (4), pp. 283–300. 11

Hyman, H. H. 1955 *Survey Design and Analysis*, Glencoe, Ill.: Free Press. Classic manual of survey research, concentrating on design and analysis, not interviewing, sampling and coding. Good appendix on how to read a table. Designed to train a survey analyst in technical matters as well as theory. Includes questionnaires from major surveys, examples of procedural material and illustrations. Based on practical experiences of author. Argues for a distinction between descriptive and explanatory surveys. 45, 77, 84, 88

Hyman, H. H., Wright, C. R. and Reed, J. S. 1975 *The Enduring Effects of Education*, Chicago: University of Chicago Press. 85

Institute for Workers' Control (IWC) 1977 'Document: A worker's enquiry into the motor industry', *Capital and Class*, No. 2, pp. 102–18. 19

Irvine, J., Miles, I. and Evans, J. (eds) 1979 *Demystifing Social Statistics*, London: Pluto Press. A useful collection of articles written by 'radical statisticians', critical (in a constructive way) of various uses of statistics. 159

Jackson, D., Turner, H. A. and Wilkinson, F. 1972 *Do Trade Unions Cause Inflation?* University of Cambridge, Department of Applied Economics Occasional Paper 36, Cambridge: Cambridge University Press. 142

Jahoda, M., Lazarsfeld, P. F. and Zeisel, H. 1972 *Marienthal: The Sociography of an Unemployed Community*, London: Tavistock. First published in 1933 as *Die Arbeitlosen von Marienthal*. This edition of this poignant study contains an interesting foreword by Lazarsfeld called 'Forty years later' and a historical afterword by Zeisel entitled 'Toward a history of sociography'. 10

Jencks, C. 1973 *Inequality: A Reassessment of the Effect of Family and Schooling in America*, Harmondsworth: Penguin (first published in USA in 1972). 77

Johnson, R. 1970 'Educational policy and social control in early Victorian England', *Past and Present*, 49, November, pp. 96–119. Mainly an examination of Kay's pronouncements on the need for education. Four themes are uncovered in the views of these reformers: the potential benevolence of economic change, an indictment of patterns of working class behaviour, an emphasis on the need to substitute for the abrogated functions of the working class parent, and a demand for close control of that substitute. The early Victorian obsession with education is best viewed as an attempt to exert authority and social control. 14

Jones, D. C. 1931 'The Social Survey of Merseyside', *Journal of the Royal Statistical Society*, 94 (2), pp. 218–50; discussion pp. 250–66. This paper describes conditions on Merseyside. It deals with the extent of over-crowding and poverty and the weak association between the two. Unemployment and casual labour are clearly the conditions most strongly associated with poverty, unlike the five towns study. Policy-oriented discussion ensues on housing policy , and the operation of unemployment relief. 30, 31

Jones, D. C. 1948 *Social Surveys*, London: Hutchinson. Jones, who was in charge of the Social Survey of Merseyside, recounts the origin and present state of play of social surveys. They are to be distinguished from Geddes-type regional surveys, and are rigorously factual, aiming to aid government and reform. His subsequent chapters give succinct delineation of the major surveys up to the end of the Second World War. 30

Jones, E. E. and Nisbett, R. E. 1971 'The actor and the observer: divergent perceptions on the causes of behaviour', in E. E. Jones *et al.* (eds), *Attribution*, Morristown, NJ: General Learning Press. pp. 79–94. Actors are more likely to perceive environmental constraints on their behaviour while observers prefer to put it down to personal dispositions. 71

Jones, G. S. 1971 *Outcast London: A Study of the Relationship between Classes in Victorian Society*, Harmondsworth: Penguin. A penetrating, scholarly, sympathetic study of the urban casual poor, their problems in finding jobs and housing, and their relationship to London's middle class. 40

Jones, R. A. and Kronus, S. 1976 'Professional sociologists and the history of sociology: a survey of recent opinion', *Journal of the History of the Behavioural Sciences*, 12, pp. 3–13. Random sample survey of 792 ASA members (445 responded) on views about and interest in the history of sociology. Least interested are social psychologists and mathematically and methodologically oriented sociologists. Rank ordering of important theorists. History of sociological is seen as separate from sociological theory, but there is still controversy about how to judge the ideas of the past. 9

Jowell, R. and Spence, J. 1975 *The Grudging Europeans*, London: Social and Community Planning Research. 147

Judd, C. M. and Milburn, M. A. 1980 'Structure of attitude systems in the general public', *American Sociological Review*, 45 (4), August, pp. 627–43. Purports to overturn Philip Converse's idea of a marked difference between elite and non-elite samples in terms of ideological thinking by using structural equation models instead of just comparing correlations. 142

Kadushin, C. 1968 'Reason analysis', in D. L. Sills (ed.), *International Encyclopaedia of the Social Sciences*, Vol. 13, New York: Macmillan and Free Press, 338–43. Reason analysis is a set of procedures used in survey research, to construct causal explanations for the actions, decisions, or intentions of individuals. In this article, Kadushin looks at the validity of reason analysis, when it is best to use it, the elaboration of 'accounting schemes' and at ways of designing, conducting and analysing such a study. 108-9

Kalton, G., Collins, M. and Brook, L. 1978 'Experiments in wording opinion questions', *Applied Statistics*, 27 (2), pp. 149–61. 56

Keating, P. (ed.) 1976 *Into Unknown England, 1866–1913; Selections from the Social Explorers*, London: Fontana. Extracts from Greenwood, Sims, Mearns, Charles Booth, William Booth, Sherard, Rowntree, Haggard, London, Masterman, Reynolds, Higgs, Bell and Reeves, with an introduction by the author. 13

Kendall, P. L. and Lazarsfeld, P. F. 1950 'Problems of survey analysis', in Merton and Lazarsfeld 1950, pp. 133–96. A two-part article introducing the logic of survey analysis. Part I covers the analysis of statistical relationships in surveys. It is logically the forerunner of the more familiar works by Hyman and Rosenberg, but is couched in non-familiar language of *m*-type and *p*-type elaboration. Part II tackles the measurement of complex phenomena in the social sciences, response error, index formation and contextual data. 45

King, S. 1979 'Public versus private opinion', paper presented to 1979 ESOMAR conference. There is a genuine difference between people's private opinions and their public opinions, but the requirements of media contests will force research methods to concentrate on the latter; a dangerous trend. 133

Kish, L. 1959 'Some statistical problems in research design', *American Sociological Review*, 24, pp. 328–38. Several statistical problems in the design of research are discussed: (1) The use of statistical tests and the search for causation in survey research are examined; for this, we suggest separating four classes of variables: explanatory, controlled, confounded and randomised. (2) The relative advantages of experiments, surveys and other investigations are shown to derive respectively from better control, representation and measurement. (3) Finally, three common misuses of statistical tests are examined: 'hunting with a shot-gun for significant differences', confusing statistical significance with substantive significance and overemphasis on the primitive level of merely finding differences. 65

Kolakowski, L. 1972 *Positivist Philosophy*, Harmondsworth: Penguin. 49

Kornhauser, A. 1946 'Are public opinion polls fair to organized labor?', *Public Opinion Quarterly*, 10, Winter, pp. 484–500 (reply by Link in 1947). During the war US polling agencies, AIPO in particular, conducted something of a crusade against the unions. The author complains about the cumulative biases in these questions – biased subject matter, varieties of slanted wording and inadequacies of interpretation and report. Calls for more scientific attention to be paid to these polls, and for submission of proposed questions to opposing sides for their comments. 141

Lazarsfeld, P. F. 1949 'The American soldier – an expository review', *Public Opinion Quarterly*, 13, Fall, pp. 377–404. Showed that surveys do not always prove the obvious. Selects some important features of the first two volumes for discussion. 85

Lazarsfeld, P. F. 1955 'The interpretation of statistical relations as a research operation', in P. F. Lazarsfeld and M. Rosenberg (eds), *The Language of Social Research*, New York: Free Press, pp. 115–24. Very straightforward account of what may happen when you bring test factors into a two-variable table. The article is presented in the same style as Kendall and Lazarsfeld 1950, making the distinction between partial and marginal type elaboration. 45

Lazarsfeld, P. F. 1961 'Notes on the history of quantification in sociology – trends, sources and problems', in H. Woolf (ed.), *Quantification: A History of the Meaning of Measurement in the Natural and Social Sciences*, Indianapolis, Ind.: Bobbs-Merrill, pp. 147–203. Rather arbitrary choice of three key figures in the development of quantitative social science: (1) Conring, a German alternative to Graunt and Petty; (2) Quetelet, who developed the ideas of probability; and (3) Le Play, whose influence has been overrated. Lazarsfeld's choice seems to stem from the fact that the contribution of all three has been underestimated by historians. 39

Lazarsfeld, P. F. 1969 'An episode in the history of social research: a memoir', in D. Fleming and B. Bailyn (eds), *The Intellectual Migration: Europe and America 1930–1960*, Cambridge, Mass.: Harvard University Press, pp. 270–337. There is a brief extract in Lazarsfeld 1972; pp. 245–59. Paper first published as 'On becoming an immigrant' in *Perspectives in American History 2*, Harvard, 1968. This is a fine account of the different influences on his work. Social research institutes in USA and style of work done in them have roots in Europe. Europe was philosophical and speculative, but beginning to be empirically oriented. When Hitler put an end to sociology, America broadened. Prewar Vienna dominated by politics, interest is psychology and concern for 'explication'. Lazarsfeld took a degree in maths. Taught at a gymnasium and then studied psychology under the Buhlers in Vienna. Wrote *Marienthal* and then went to USA on a Rockefeller fellowship. At that time, US market research consisted of nose-counting. Joined Psychological Corporation. Got interested in motivation research. Market research in US began to be commercial: psychologists were not interested, so he switched to sociology. Did not aspire to academic job, and social research did not have institutions in which to work. Immigration problems led him to New York to begin work which led to establishment of University of Newark Research Center. 44

Lazarsfeld, P. F. 1972 'The art of asking why', in *Qualitative Analysis: Historical and Critical Essays*, Boston, Mass.: Allyn & Bacon, pp. 183–202. Originally published in 1934 in *The National Marketing Review*. Summary of his Austrian work on the technique. Three rules: (1) Specify: 'why' can mean (*a*) what about product; (*b*) what influences; (*c*) what was wrong with old product. (2) Fit the questions to experience of respondent. Use different questions for different motivation patterns. (3) Bring out the tacit 'as opposed to . . . ' assumptions; these may only be effectively tackled in experiments. Aim to get 'the complete motivational set-up of the first degree'. (Compare this with Henry 1971; for a more up-to-date coverage of the problem, see Kadushin 1968). 109

Lazarsfeld, P. F. and Menzel, H. 1961 'On the relationship between individual and collective properties', in A. Etzioni (ed.), *Complex Organisations*, New York: Holt, Rinehart & Winston, pp. 422–40. 61

Le Roy Ladurie, E. 1980 *Montailloux*, Harmondsworth: Penguin. Translated by Barbara Bray. First published in France in 1978. 50

Leat, D. 1972 'Misunderstanding Verstehen', *Sociological Review*, 20 (1), pp. 29–38. Discusses meaning underlying a correlation. Criticises view that Verstehen is only important in generating hypotheses (Abel 1948). Abel restricts his comments to erklarendes Verstehen, and ignores aktuelles Verstehen. When interpreting a correlation between crop failure and low marriage rate, we use aktuelles Verstehen, and need to know what both these things mean. Unless we know what these are, and mean, all we have established is a sociologically uninteresting correlation between X and Y. We do not accept correlations we do not understand as evidence of causal theories. So Verstehen plays an integral part in proof. It is not one research method among many. 104

Lessnoff, M. 1977 'Technique, critique and social science', paper presented to a British Philosophical Society conference at University of East Anglia, Easter. 125

Lever, J. W. C. 1839 'On the sickness and mortality among the troops in the United Kingdom. Abstract of the Report of Major Tulloch', *Journal of the Statistical Society of London*, II, July, pp. 250–60. 38

Lukes, S. 1977 'Relativism: moral and conceptual', in *Essays in Social Theory*, London: Macmillan, pp. 154–76. 52

MacIntyre, A. 1967 'The idea of a social science', *Aristotelian Society Supplement*, 41. pp. 95–114. Reprinted in Ryan 1973. MacIntyre questions Winch's equivalence between rule-governed and meaningful. 52

MacKenzie, D. 1979 'Eugenics and the rise of mathematical statistics in

Britain', in Irvine *et al.* 1979, pp. 39–50. Mainly covers the dispute between Yule and Pearson over whether Q or tetrachoric *r* was the better measure for a 2 × 2 table. He traces Pearson's position, and dominance, to his research programme on heredity and eugenics, although the author is careful to avoid the genetic fallacy. 40, 42

Mackie, J. L. 1974 *The Cement of the Universe: A Study of Causation*, Oxford: Clarendon. 69

MacKuen, M. B. 1979 'Social communication and the mass policy agenda', Ph.D. dissertation, University of Michigan. 138

Maclean, M. and Genn, H. 1979 *Methodological Issues in Social Surveys*, London: Macmillan. An account of how the design of a major screening survey into personal misfortunes was conceptualised and evolved. Discusses alternative sources of data for a sampling frame, the development of a screening instrument, the use of proxy respondents, deciding between postal and personal inquiries and sample design. Probably more interesting to subject specialists than to general methodologists, despite authors' claims and the title. 80

McNemar, Q. 1946 'Opinion-attitude methodology', *Psychological Bulletin*, 43, pp. 289–374. A solicited review by a critical outsider with no vested interests into opinion-attitude methodologies. A classic on methodological problems of attitude research, stipulating three basic requirements of validity, reliability and unidimensionality. Replace single questions by scales. Get off campus. Do more experiments. Try more factor analysis. But the author is struck by how little basic methodological work on attitudes being done in the big research institutes. 77, 133

Madge, J. 1953 *The Tools of Social Science*, London: Longman. Still an influential textbook, though inevitably very dated. It is mainly about methods of data collection – documents, observation, interviews and experiments, with an introduction on the logic of the procedure of drawing inferences and the problems of definition. Passionately pro-experiment. 64

Malthus, T. 1970 *An Essay on the Principle of Population*, edited with an introduction by A. Flew, Harmondsworth: Pelican. First published in 1798. This first essay attracted such publicity that Malthus devoted the next years to travelling doing further research, and a more mature edition appeared in 1803. It passed through six editions, the last one in 1816. The work is mainly derivative of Hume, Wallace, Smith and Price, and where it is original it is, in the main, wrong. (See a useful entry on Malthus in 11th edition of Encyclopaedia Britannica.) 11

Marsh, C. 1976 *Guidelines for Commissioning an Interview Survey from a Research Company*, London: Social Science Research Council Survey Unit. Mainly a guide to putting a specification out to tender. 48

Marsh, C. 1979 'Social sciences methods bibliography: British Universities 1978', Cambridge: Social and Political Sciences Committee, University of Cambridge, mimeo. An analysis of the bibliographies included in John Wakeford (compiler and editor), 'Research methods syllabuses in sociology departments in the UK' for the BSA Methodology Conference in Lancaster, 1979. The number of times each item is cited is given. Compiled for the SSRC Conference on Postgraduate Methods Training, 1979 (see Sociology 1981). 54, 62

Marsh, C. 1982 'Do polls affect what people think?', in Turner and Martin (eds) 1982. A review of the bandwagon literature. 138

Mass-Observation 1945 *Britain and her Birth Rate: A Report Prepared by Mass-Observation for the Advertising Service Guild, the Sixth of the 'Change' Wartime Surveys*, London: Murray. There was a great fear, before and during the war, (1) that Britain was becoming depopulated and (2) that the eugenically best were breeding least. This Mass-Observation study is based on such a flimsy sample and arbitrary methodology that the fears of the authors (alas unnamed) can closely reflect through the data. They conclude that neither financial circumstances nor contraception are at the root of the problem. Women are going to have to be positively induced to breed. 32

Mass-Observation, edited by Charles Madge and Tom Harrisson 1938 *First Year's Work: 1937–38*, with an essay on A Nationwide Intelligence Service by Bronislaw Malinowski, London: Lindsay Drummond. This book gives a good flavour of Mass-Observation. There is a brief portrayal of how M-O has illuminated smoking as a social habit. The pub as a social centre and the motivation behind betting. Two chapters, one on the press criticism Mass-Observation received and one on a detailed analysis of the characteristics and motivations of its observers, will be of especial interest to the historian. Malinowski's postscript criticises them mainly methodologically, but he is very sympathetic to the idea that 'anthropology begins at home'. 32

Mayhew, H. 1861 *London Labour and the London Poor*, 3 vols, London: Griffin, Bohn. This brings together the weekly and monthly editions that streamed out during 1851 and 1852. Thompson (1973) considers that the third volume has been padded out in a sloppy fashion. In 1862 a fourth volume was added. 12, 13, 18

Medawar, Sir P. B. 1968 *The Art of the Soluble: Creativity and Originality in Science*, Harmondsworth: Penguin. 36

Merton, R. K. 1968 *Social Theory and Social Structure*, New York: Free Press. 96

Merton, R. K. and Lazarsfeld, P. F. (eds) 1950 *Continuities in Social Research: Studies in the Scope and Method of 'The American Soldier'*, Glencoe, Ill.: Free Press. 34, 64

Milgram, S. 1961 'Nationality and conformity', *Scientific American*, 205 (6), December, pp. 45–51. 138

Mills, C. W. 1959 *The Sociological Imagination*, New York: Oxford University Press. Social science is the practice of a craft and this book is a review of the qualities needed to perfect that craft – from 'understanding the larger historical scene in terms of its meaning for the inner life and external career of a variety of individuals' to the considerations of whether social scientists are (*a*) morally autonomous, (*b*) subject to the morality of other men, or (*c*) morally adrift'. 45, 60, 148

Moser, C. A. and Kalton, G. 1971 *Survey Methods in Social Investigation*, 2nd edn, London: Heinemann Educational. First edition by Moser in 1958. There is an historical sketch of surveys in the first chapter. It starts, as so many of these histories do, with the chocolate sociologists, but its coverage thereafter is quite good. The emphasis in sampling in this book is typical of the British view of surveys. 25

Moss, L. 1953 'Sample surveys and the administrative process', *International Social Science Bulletin*, 5, pp. 482–94. 34

Moss, L. and Goldstein, H. 1979 *The Recall Method in Social Surveys*, University of London Institute of Education: Studies in Education, 9. A mixed collection of papers on this important topic. 82

Mosteller, F. and Tukey, J. W. 1977 *Data Analysis and Regression: A Second Course in Statistics*, Reading, Mass.: Addison-Wesley. 47, 84

Murdock, G. P. 1967 *Social Structure*, New York: Free Press. 55

Nagel, T. 1979 'Subjective and objective', in *Mortal Questions*, Cambridge: Cambridge University Press, pp. 196–213. A very clear, reasoned defence of the irreducibility of the subjective and the objective to one another, and the attendant problems this brings in many areas of philosophy, for example, in agency/causality debate. 103

Newby, H. 1977 *The Deferential Worker*, London: Allen Lane. 93

Ni Bhrolchain, M. 1979 'Psychotic and neurotic depression: some points of method', *British Journal of Psychiatry*, 134, pp. 87–93. This paper is a more extended discussion than that in Brown and Harris 1978 on the danger of aetiological classification systems in the study of depression. She argues that only symptoms should be used in the first instance if one is to avoid confused interpretation. She then discusses the practical difficulties of how one designs a discriminant analysis to answer the question, are there two distinct types of depression or not? 114

Nisbet, R. 1975 'Public opinion versus popular opinion', *Public Interest*, 41, Fall, pp. 166–92. This is a good source for the Burkeian heritage in public opinion theory, a tradition which tends towards anti-democratic positions. He traces a distinction between popular opinion (capricious, mob psychology, and so on) and public opinion (rooted in institutions, furthering the interests of the people if not what they say they want) back to Burke, de Tocqueville, the Federalist, Bryce, Lowsell, Lindsay Rogers and Walter Lippman. 136

Nisbett, R. E. and Wilson, T. D. 1977 'Telling more than we can know: verbal reports on mental processes', *Psychological Review*, 84 (3), pp. 231–59. People are often unable to report the existence of evaluative and motivational responses produced by a stimulus, to report that a cognitive process has occurred, to identify the existence of the critical stimulus, or to report the effect of the stimulus on the response. When respondents give erroneous explanations for their behaviour, they seem to resort to a pool of culturally supplied explanations of behaviour. 106-7

Noelle-Neumann, E. 1973 *Return to the Concept of Powerful Mass Media*, Radio and TV Culture Research Institute, Nippon Hosda Kyokai, Studies of Broadcasting 9. The reason media 'effects' have not been discovered in the traditional lab experiment is the failure adequately to operationalise and vary (1) cumulative effect, (2) ubiquity and (3) consonance in reporting events. The results of several survey studies into the effect of the media are reported which suggest that the mass media occupies an important function in providing information to individuals on the dominance of certain opinions in the environment. 138

Noelle-Neumann, E. 1974 'The spiral of silence: a theory of public opinion', *Journal of Communication*, 24, pp. 43–51. This is a highly original piece about the construction of public opinion. Individuals discern the distribution and strength of opinion around them; their willingness to expose themselves depends on that, and on the future trend they perceive in that; this becomes circular, because the less they voice a minority opinion, the more people are cowed. Shows some very interesting examples which corroborate this from current German issues and two (out of twelve) which show the minority more prepared to speak. The media must be the main agents for creating perceptions of public opinion. 139

Noelle-Neumann, E. 1979 'Public opinion and the classic tradition: a re-evaluation', *Public Opinion Quarterly*, 43 (2), Summer, pp. 143–56. As early as the seventeenth and eighteenth centuries, classical writers like Locke, Hume and Rousseau introduced the concepts of climate of opinion, law of opinion and reputation, and public opinion. In their analyses their emphasis was on the social controls, social pressure dimension of the phenomenon – 'all governments rest on opinions'. The concept of public opinion permits us to draw conclusions: public opinion can be used for social control because of the individual's fear of isolating himself; moreover, public opinion facilitates social integration and social stability, establishes priorities and confers legitimation. 137

Oberschall, A. (ed.) 1972 *The Establishment of Empirical Sociology*, New York: Harper & Row. 156

Oldman, D. 1973 'Sociologists, survey analysis and statistical tests', *International Journal of Mathematical Education in Science and Technology*, 4, pp. 51–60. 45

Orr, J. B. 1937 *Food, Health and Income*, London: Macmillan. Orr, Director of the Rowett Research Institute, performed a survey on 1,152 (mainly working class) families in Great Britain to see how many had the optimum requirements for good nutrition. The fieldwork took place during the depression, and showed that over half had an insufficient diet to promote good health. This was one impetus (the other was the need for rationing) which pushed the new Ministry of Food into doing its own food surveys. 30

Packard, V. 1957 *The Hidden Persuaders*, London: Longmans. 128

Parsons, T. 1949 *The Structure of Social Action*, Glencoe, Ill.: Free Press, pp. 27–41 contain a discussion of the distinction between a unit and its qualities. 115

Parsons, T. and Shils, E. 1951 *Toward a General Theory of Action*, Cambridge, Mass.: Harvard University Press. 109

Pawson, R. 1978 'Empiricist explanatory strategies: the case of causal modelling', *Sociological Review*, 26 (3), pp. 613–45. Worried by the large residuals in most causal models, Pawson asserts that these can be put down to (1) unrecognised 'structural' effects, (2) the fact that there are few 'shared first order meanings', (3) the fact that significantly heterogeneous sub-populations exist. These empiricists are then driven to 'interpretive empiricism' which is *ad hoc*. Not clear what he is advocating instead. This is a classic example of someone criticising surveys without knowing the relevant survey literature on how to tackle the problems he is referring to. 68

Payne, S. 1951 *The Art of Asking Questions*, Princeton, NJ: Princeton University Press. The best book on question-wording that there is, even if some of the results reported have not been replicated. 56, 134

Pearson, K. 1892 *The Grammar of Science* London: Contemporary Science

Series. 2nd edition 1900, 3rd edition quite substantially revised and enlarged in 1911. 62

Perry, N. H. 1975 *The Organization of Social Science Research in the United Kingdom*, Occasional Papers in Survey Research No. 6, London: SSRC Survey Unit. 3-4

Petty, W. 1851 *The History of the Survey of Ireland*, Commonly Called the Down Survey. Published in Dublin for the Irish Archaeological Society. First published 1656. Survey dates 1655-6. Purpose, according to O'Donovan, was to facilitate the distribution of forfeited land from rebels to Cromwell's army and supporters. 10, 47n1

Petty, W. 1970 *The Political Anatomy of Ireland, with the Establishment for that Kingdom and Verbum Sapienti*, introduction by John O'Donovan, Shannon: Irish University Press. First edition London 1691. Believed written 1672, not published until 1691. Valuable author's preface on why anatomy is so vital, why Ireland is a good place to begin and an apology that the instruments are not sharper. Documents details of the land, people and their work, churches, rebellion and political union, government, militia, air, soil and product, valuation, money and inflation, trade, religion, language and manners, and so on. 10, 47n1

Phillips, D. L. 1971 *Knowledge from What? Theories and Methods in Social Research*, Chicago: Rand McNally Sociology Series. Sociologists use self-reported behaviour which is highly reactive and does not explain much variance. Reviews literature on sources of bias, lack of validation, effects of interviewer, respondent's attributes, physical settings and modelling effects. Social research is conducted in a social setting and the same efforts at self-preservation can be found, through physical, non-verbal cues. In an interview, a respondent will respond especially to the social class of interviewer, and to the degree of rapport established; he or she will probably engage in 'expression games' (Goffman). Interviews are sometimes the most appropriate form of data collection, and could be improved by validation studies, experimental variations and better interviewer training. But other forms of data collection, participant observation, non-reactive measures and, importantly, introspection should also be used. 57

Phillips, D. L. 1973 *Abandoning Method: Sociological Studies in Methodology*, London: Jossey-Bass. Techniques of social research are full of error and explain very small amounts of variance. Quotes three studies of his own into (1) response bias (acquiescence and social desirability); (2) the interrelation between need for approval and trait desirability with such background factors as sex, invalidating previous correlations; and (3) modelling effects, (where his results are weak). Therefore we need a radically new approach, accept objectivity is impossible and see sociology as a discipline bound by consensus. There is no formal way to warrant knowledge; do it by introspection and common sense. Stop trying to prove things; argue them. In fact, abandon method and accept the fact that anything goes, from play to novels to sociology. 57

Pilgrim Trust 1938 *Men without Work: A Report Made to the Pilgrim Trust*, with an introduction by the Archbishop of York and a preface by Lord Macmillan, Cambridge: Cambridge University Press. 28

Platt, J. 1971 *Social Research in Bethnal Green: an Evaluation of the Work of the Institute of Community Studies,* London: New Perspectives in Sociology. The Institute is in a tradition of commitment to social improvement and policy, from Booth, Rowntree and Titmuss (who influenced it directly). Anthropological methods are used, and the reports often smack of sentimentality, where behaviour is considered quaint. Platt argues that the Institute made an important contribution in stimulating interest in social research, but she is critical of their methods. They split qualitative research on 50–100 cases off from the larger numbers of more superficial interviews done by a market research company. The level of theorisation on an operational level was poor, the data collection often not very rigorous and the analysis rather superficial. 32

Platt, J. 1972 'Survey data and social policy', *British Journal of Sociology*, 23 (1), March, pp. 77–92. 127

Platt, J. 1976 *Realities of Social Research: An Empiricist Study of British sociologists*, Falmer: Sussex University Press. This is the result of personal interviews which the author conducted with a sample of British Sociologists to investigate some of the conditions of research not commonly discussed in methods texts. 5

Platt, J. 1981 'The social construction of "positivism" and its significance in British sociology 1950–1980', in P. Abrams, J. Finch and P. Rock (eds), *Practice and Progress: British Sociology 1950–1980*, London: Allen & Unwin, pp. 73–88. Analysis of *British Journal of Sociology, Sociology Review* and *Sociology* 1950–79 of articles that reported British research to look for trends. Despite the growing tendency in teaching texts to mention an earlier 'positivistic' phase of sociology, no empirical evidence for this can be found in the journals. 3

Reeves, T. K. 1979 'Ballotting in trade union recognition disputes', paper read at the 'Surveys and the Law' session of the British Sociological Association Annual Conference, April. Under British employment law, in union recognition disputes, the Advisory, Conciliation and Arbitration Service is required to test employee opinion. This has led to several high court cases over methodological issues in such polls, which are documented very fairly and comprehensively in this paper. In one of these polls, the judge was extremely critical of Market and Opinion Research International (see the *Guardian*, 20 April 1979) and the case was referred to MRS professional standards committee. 130

Reeves, T. K. and Harper, D. 1981 *Surveys at Work: A Practitioner's Guide* Maidenhead, Berks: McGraw-Hill. 130

Reiss, A. J. 1968 'Stuff and nonsense about social surveys and observation', in eds. H. S. Becker *et al.*, *Institutions and the Person*, Chicago: Aldine, pp. 351–67. Partly as a result of taste, partly as a result of training, sociologists end up choosing either to do a structured interview survey or to do unstructured observation in the field. But the history of surveys shows they have not always involved sampling and structured questionnaires. Discusses problems of systematic observation, and calls for broadening our conception of appropriate research methods. 33

Reiss, A. J. Jr 1971 'Systematic observation of natural social phenomena', in H. Costner (ed.), *Sociological Methodology*, San Francisco: Jossey-Bass, pp. 1–33. Stresses similarities between survey or demographic data collection and unsystematic, impressionistic first-hand observation. 38, 55

Rex, J. 1961 'Sociology as science', ch. 2 of J. Rex, *Key Problems in Sociological Theory*, London: Routledge & Kegan Paul. Facts on their own rarely yield sociologically significant truths. They may imply them. Much empirical research is done outside a social and dynamic context which might discover social determinants. Too much emphasis on administrative problems and reform. If sociologists want to move beyond descriptive fact-gathering they must consider causes. 109

Roberts, K., Cook, F. G., Clark, S. C. and Semeonoff, E. 1977 *The Fragmentary Class Structure*, London: Heinemann. 93, 111

Roll, C. W. and Cantril, A. H. 1972 *Polls: Their Use and Misuse in Politics*, New York: Basic Books. Seven Locks edition in 1980, with a new preface. This book is written for a non-academic audience, and so spends some time on sampling and so on. There are many illustrations of uses, and fewer of abuses. The discussion of the political implications of polling as an enterprise is not very adequate. 136

Rosenberg, M. 1968 *The Logic of Survey Analysis*, New York and London: Basic Books. This book, along with Hirschi and Selvin 1973, represents a style of survey textbook which has never been widely known in Britain. It is not a statistics text, nor is it a 'how to do it' guide, but discusses precisely what its title says, the logic of the procedures underlying the analysis of survey data, using nothing more complex than a percentage table. I refer to the steps it advocates using in analysis in Chapter 4. 45, 85-97, 103

Runciman, W. G. 1966 *Relative Deprivation and Social Justice*, London: Routledge & Kegan Paul. 92

Runciman, W. G. (ed.) 1978 *Weber*, Cambridge: Cambridge University Press. 101

Rutter, M., Maughan, B., Mortimore, P. and Ouston, J. 1979 *Fifteen Thousand Hours*, Shepton Mallet: Open Books. Financed by ILEA and directed from the Institute of Psychiatry, this study picked twelve ILEA secondary schools to represent different school types. Data consisted of classroom observation, teacher interviews and school records. It is a good example of how contextual analysis can be used imaginatively. Disagrees with the Jencks conclusions about schooling, and shows that the school 'ethos' also has independent impact. 62

Ryan, A. 1973 *The Philosophy of Social Explanation*, London: Oxford University Press. This issue is raised differently in the philosophy of science traditions so this good collection is not central for this course (York). 165

Schuman, H. 1979 'Polls, surveys and the English language', unpublished manuscript. There is no objective basis to the distinction between polls and surveys other than the snob value of Latin-root words as opposed to Anglo-Saxon ones. Poll is to survey as cow is to beef. (I would prefer poll is to survey as beef is to cow – partial as opposed to whole and frequently cooked!) 126

Schuman, H. and Presser, S. 1977 'Question-wording as an independent variable in survey analysis', *Sociological Methods and Research*, 6 (2), November, pp. 151–70. Reports results of an investigation into effects of form of question-wording on response:(1) agree-disagree *v.* forced choice; (2) formal *v.* substantive balance; (3) inclusion of a middle alternative; (4) screening filters; (5) open *v.* closed questions. 134

Schuman, H. and Presser, S. 1978 'Attitude measurement and the gun control paradox', *Public Opinion Quarterly*, 41, Winter 1977/8. Public opinion on gun control is in favour, whereas legislation is much more permissive. One explanation for this discrepancy between the two is that those who argue against gun control feel more intensely about it. This article tests this hypothesis. 134

Schuman, H. and Presser, S. 1979a 'The open and closed question', *American Sociological Review*, 44 (5), pp. 692–712. Suggests that if closed questions are constructed on the basis of detailed open questions then the difference between question types are due mainly to coding problems and interviewing effects in open questions, rather than bias in closed questions. 142

Schuman, H. and Presser, S. 1979b 'The assessment of "no opinion" in attitude surveys', in K. Schuessler (ed.), *Sociological Methodology*, San Francisco: Jossey-Bass. Although 'don't know' is a possible answer to many questions, it is not always provided as an option. Authors compare responses for filtered and unfiltered forms, and trace some of the effects of observed differences. 142

Schuman, H. and Presser, S. 1981 *Questions and Answers*, New York: Academic Press. This book is the classic text on question-wording. Each chapter is an overview of an important problem area and cites new research into the topic: for example, ch. 7 – effects of balance and imbalance; ch. 9 – measurement of attitude strength, centrality, crystallisation, and so on. 56

Searle, G. R. 1979 'Eugenics and politics in Britain in the 1930's', *Annals of Science*, 36, pp. 159–69. One might think that the 3 million unemployed in the 1930s would have exploded the eugenic theory that people became unemployed because they were congenitally inferior. In fact eugenics had something of a comeback. This article documents eugenicists' views of the census and of the depression. There were totalitarians among them who wanted Britain run by experts, but they were a fringe. Mosley's overtures were ignored, and they were so anti-Hitler (many being Jews) they passed a motion deprecating the use of eugenics to stir up racial animosities. 40

Seeman, M. 1959 'On the meaning of alienation', *American Sociological Review*, 24 (6), pp. 783–91. 111

Selvin, H. C. 1965 'Durkheim's "suicide": further thoughts on a methodological classic', in R. A. Nisbet (ed.), *Emile Durkheim*, Englewood Cliffs, NJ: Prentice-Hall, pp. 113–36. 39

Selvin, H. C. 1968 'Methods of survey analysis', in D. Sills (ed.), *International Encyclopedia of the Social Sciences*, New York: Macmillan/Free Press, Vol. 15, pp.411–18. Specifically differentiates the style of reasoning of survey analysis from the statistical account of urban life in the British survey tradition. 159

Selvin, H. C. 1976 'Durkheim, Booth and Yule: the non-diffusion of an intellectual innovation', *European Journal of Sociology*, 17, pp. 39–57. Yule's work could have reached Booth and Durkheim; they probably would have been able to understand it if they had tried. It was important for both of them, yet neither showed signs of having read it. Selvin concludes that Booth was underintegrated into the scientific community, while Durkheim was overintegrated into a closed intellectual community. 17, 43

Selvin, H. C. and Stuart, A. 1966 'Data-dredging procedures in survey analysis', *American Statistician*, 20, pp. 20–3. 65

Sennett, R. and Cobb, J. 1977 *The Hidden Injuries of Class*, Cambridge: Cambridge University Press. 105

Shapley, D. 1974 'Jury selection: social scientists gamble in an already loaded game', *Science*, 185, 20 September, pp. 1033–4, 1071. A good account of the growing use of jury selection surveys in USA. 130

Sharpe, S. A. 1978 'Much ado about nothing: an evaluation of the Thomson-Spearman debate', Godfrey Thomson Unit, University of Edinburgh, mimeo. Debate between Thomson and Spearman was ostensibly about intelligence, but in fact several extrinsic considerations entered in. Spearman was defending his position as the central one in current psychology, and Thomson continued the debate because (1) horrified at Spearman's refusal to accept rational argument immediately; (2) spurred by his evolutionary views of psychology and education. 41

Sheatsley, P. B. 1978 'History of NORC', paper presented to NORC Operations Seminar II, November. A brief history of one of the most successful social research institutes, from its establishment in 1941 by Harry Field, through private funding in the 1950s, to government contracts in 1960s, to the more competitive 1970s. Sheatsley's verdict is that NORC has the best field force, best sampling division, very wide experience and a high reputation, but is always more expensive than its competitors. 2

Simmons, M. and Gordon, L. 1980 'Pattern of market research in the 1980's', paper read to the MRS Conference. General assessment of how market research fits into the economy. In 1970s, the demand for market research increased three times as fast as the economy. They estimate growth of 66 per cent 1969–79, from £14–17 million to £85 million. They then extrapolate into the 1980s and anticipate problems with economic growth, but expect that social research will advance in the latter half of the decade. 4

Simon, H. A. 1954 'Spurious correlation: a causal interpretation', *Journal of the American Statistical Association*, 49 pp. 467–79. Reprinted in Blalock 1972. Simon shows how the assumptions about the behaviour of the error terms are used to provide the rationale behind our more intuitive ideas about spurious correlations. If you are not satisfied, having time-ordered the variables under consideration, that the error terms are uncorrelated, you must specify the system and bring in new variables. 88

Sinha, C. 1978 'Children, logic and learning', *New Society*, 12 January, pp. 62–4. A brief report of some rather startling disconfirmations of Piaget's experiments. The discrepancy is put down to the child's perception of the test situation. This has important ramifications for people who design questionnaires, for it suggests that response effects may exist from the very fact that one is being asked a question in a test-like situation. 108

Sociology 1981 'Special issues on "The teaching of research methodology" ', *Sociology*, 15 (4) November. 166

Sonquist, J. A. and Dunkelberg, W. C. 1977 *Survey and Opinion Research: Procedures for Processing and Analysis*. Englewood Cliffs, NJ: Prentice-Hall. 61

St Phillips Settlement 1919 *The Equipment of the Workers, An Enquiry by the St Phillips Settlement Education and Economics Research Society*

(Sheffield) into the Adequacy of the Adult Manual Workers for the Discharge of their Responsibilities as Heads of Households, Producers and Citizens, London. Using depth interviews on a small random sample (selected on Bowley's advice), the investigators sought to measure the 'physical and moral equipment' of the workers of Sheffield, including such things as their love of goodness. 19, 23-4, 43

Starr, J. M. 1978 'Mass or public? The American people as revealed through polls', paper read at 1978 ASA meeting at San Francisco. Analysing opinion polls, the author concludes the respondents have the characteristics of an unstructured mass, rather than a coherent public. Very important public policy issues have low centrality in people's minds and so their 'opinions' lack coherence. This leads to popular susceptibility to suggestion over such issues. 137

Stephan, F. 1948 'History of the use of modern sampling procedures', *Journal of the American Statistical Association*, 43 (241), March, pp. 12–39. 26

Stevenson, J. 1977 *Social Conditions in Britain between the Wars*, Harmondsworth: Penguin. Contains very useful background essay on the conditions of life, and four detailed chapters including lengthy quotations from current investigators of poverty, health, housing and unemployment. However, his assessment of that research, that 'The intense period in Britain was one of great achievement in the field of social enquiry and investigation', is questionable, and his insistence that unemployment (rather than housing) was the focus of most of the investigatory activity is wrong. 28

Stinchcombe, A. L. 1968 *Constructing Social Theories*, New York: Harcourt, Brace & World. 73

Stouffer, S. A. 1949 'How these volumes came to be produced', in S. A. Stouffer *et al.*, *The American Soldier: Adjustment during Army Life*, Vol. 1, Princeton, NJ: Princeton University Press, pp. 3–53. 34, 64

Struik, D. 1956 *A Concise History of Mathematics*, London: Bell. 53

Sutherland, G. and Sharp, S. 1980 'The first official psychologist in the wurrld': aspects of the professionalization of psychology in early 20th century Britain', *History of Science*, vol. xviii, September, pp. 181–208. 'The immediate education needs and problems of LCC thus brought about the first formal and institutional separation of the psychology of individual differences from medicine in the UK ... Until the Second World War at least, the role models offered by the medical profession continued to exert a powerful attraction for psychologists.' Mainly an account and comparison of Burt and Winch. 44

Teer, F. and Spence, J. D. 1973 *Political Opinion Polls*, London: Hutchinson University Library. An excellent, comprehensive, lucid guide to the theory and practice of polling in Britain. 135

Tennant, C. and Bebbington, P. 1978 'The social causation of depression: a critique of the work of Brown and his colleagues', *Psychological Medicine*, 8, pp. 565–75. The authors claim that loglinear analysis fails to substantiate their differentiation of risk variables into vulnerability factors and provoking agents. 122

Thompson, E. P. 1973 'Mayhew and the Morning Chronicle', in E. P. Thompson and E. Yeo, *The Unknown Mayhew*, Harmondsworth

Penguin, pp. 9–55. Portrays Mayhew as a prodigious but undisciplined bohemian critic, and tries to unravel his political beliefs, which change throughout his works. 18

Thompson, E. P. 1979 'The poverty of theory: or an orrery of errors', in *The Poverty of Theory and Other Essays*, London: Merlin Press, pp. 193–398. 62

Thompson, E. P. 1980 'The State versus its "enemies" ' in *Writings by Candlelight* London: Merlin.

Tropp, A. 1980 'Current issues in social research', Social Research Association Opening Address, *Social Research Association News*, January. In 1956 at a conference on research needs, Tropp identified three groups, broad evolutions, younger people keen to do empirical research and Marxists who repudiated 'cow sociology'. 1979 similar meeting, the same three schools, but the younger element carrying out a mock battle with positivism. 3

Tuchman, S. and Coffin, T. E. 1971 'The influence of election night television broadcasts in a close election', *Public Opinion Quarterly*, 35, pp. 315–26. Repeat of earlier studies of bandwagon effect using East–West time difference. 138

Tukey, J. W. 1977 *Exploratory Data Analysis*, Reading, Mass.: Addison-Wesley. 47, 72

Turner, C. F. and Krauss, E. 1978 'Fallible indicators of the subjective state of the nation', *American Psychologist*, 33, May, pp. 455–70. Compares NORC's and Harris's series measuring the public's confidence in the leadership of cultural, political and commercial institutions. In forty-five instances, twenty-seven estimates differ by 5 per cent and in ten more than 10 per cent. The article then explores various explanations for the discrepancies, and concludes that context effects are the most likely. 142

Turner, C. F. and Martin, E. (eds) forthcoming *Survey measurement of Subjective Phenomena*, Report of the Panel on Survey Measurement of Subjective Phenomena, Committee on National Statistics, Assembly of Behavioral and Social Sciences, National Research Council–National Academy of Sciences. 141, 148

Webb, B. 1971 *My Apprenticeship*, Harmondsworth: Penguin. First published in 1926. The bits of this autobiography that are of particular interest are the appendices on note-taking and interviewing; ch. V, pp. 216–56 (where she describes Booth's method), 'Cross verification of whole-sale statistics by personal observation of individual cases'. 17, 18

Webb, N. 1980 'The democracy of opinion polls', paper presented to 63rd ESOMAR Seminar on Opinion Polls at Bonn, 23–6 January. Polls are linked with freedom to publish historically. The polling profession is now mature and responsible, so there is no need to control it more than intra-professionally. Polling between elections monitors a government's standing, corrects views of public opinion on issues and public perception of political priorities. 135-6

Webb, S. and Webb, B. 1975 *Methods of Social Study*, Cambridge: Cambridge University Press. First published by the London School of Economics in 1932. Early textbook of empirical research in Britain. Abrams calls them 'slaves to empirical purism. Much of that work reads like a parody of the worst features of the statistical tradition'. None the less, an important historical document. 24-5

Weiss, H. 1936 'Die "Enquête Ouvrière" von Karl Marx', *Zeitschrift fur Sozialforschung*, V (1), pp. 76–98. 19

Wells, A. F. 1935 *The Local Social Survey in Great Britain*, London: Allen & Unwin. 28, 102

White, J. 1977 'When every room was measured', *History Workshop Journal* 4, Autumn. 29

Willer, D. 1967 *Scientific Sociology: Theory and Method*, Englewood Cliffs, NJ: Prentice-Hall. The adequacy of certain conventional research methods and sociological 'theory' for developing cumulative knowledge is examined in ch. 1. Chapter 2 presents the basic ideas of the 'theory-model method' in which it is suggested that sociological theory may be developed through models. Chapter 3 is concerned with the means of constructing concept models, leading to the development of scientifically useful viewpoints towards social phenomena with which simple and effective theoretical relationships may be developed. Chapter 4 concentrates on formal systems of hypotheses or theories, their statement and their relationship to the model. Chapter 5 is concerned with related problems of measurement. A particular form of validation which can result in conditional universals (laws or theories) is the subject of chs. 6 and 7. 62-4

Willer, D. and Willer, J. 1974 *Systematic Empiricism: A Critique of Pseudoscience*, Englewood Cliffs, NJ: Prentice-Hall. 62-4

Williams, R. 1976 *Communications*, Harmondsworth: Penguin. 128

Winch, P. 1958 *The Idea of a Social Science*, London: Routledge & Kegan Paul. Argues that an internal understanding of groups of people of the rules and conventions in terms of which they carry on their lives is of special importance in the explanation of human behaviour. 52

Wonnacott, R. J. and Wonnacott, T. H. 1970 *Econometrics*, New York and London: Wiley. The econometric bible. 81

Worcester, R. M. (editor in chief) 1972 *Consumer Market Research Handbook*, London: McGraw-Hill. Chapter 20 by Worcester describes the aims and practice of corporate image research. 128, 129

Yeo, E. 1973 'Mayhew as a social investigator', in E. P. Thompson and E. Yeo *The Unknown Mayhew*, London: Penguin, pp. 56–109. Presents Mayhew, rather too uncritically, as an early social scientist. 13

Young, P. V. 1939 *Scientific Social Surveys and Research*, Englewood Cliffs, NJ: Prentice-Hall. New editions in 1949, 1956 and 1966. The changes of the various editions across the years tell an interesting story of differing views of survey research. The chapters (by Schmid) on graphical techniques are still among the best contributions on the subject. 31

Yule, G. U. 1911 *An Introduction to the Theory of Statistics*, London: Griffin. Shows that the analysis of tabular data was not clearly understood and clear layout was not available in the early years of this century. By the 11th edition (the first one with M. G. Kendall as a joint author in 1937), there are three chapters on separating correlation and causation. 14th edn 1950 was a substantial rework, but even here there is no idea of interactions in tables. No advance in analysis of tables; introduction of Tschuprow's T; recognition of counter-sorters. 42

Subject Index